NEW

OXFORDSHIRE COLONY

Turners Court Farm School, Wallingford,
1911-1991

Christopher Sladen

authorHOUSE®

AuthorHouse™ UK Ltd.
500 Avebury Boulevard
Central Milton Keynes, MK9 2BE
www.authorhouse.co.uk
Phone: 08001974150

©2011. Christopher Sladen. All rights reserved.

No part of this book may be reproduced, stored in a retrieval system, or transmitted by any means without the written permission of the author.

First published by AuthorHouse   2/18/2011

ISBN: 978-1-4520-7729-1 (sc)

Front cover: Turners Court clock tower (author's photo)

This book is printed on acid-free paper.

Remembering,

my parents, Mary and Edward Sladen, and all those who served at Turners Court, 1911-1991

CONTENTS

Acknowledgements		ix
Prologue		xiii
Chapter # 1.	Antecedents: charities and colonies	1
Chapter # 2.	Founding the 'Colonies'	33
Chapter # 3.	Colony Life, 1912-1933: the 'Hunt Era'	65
Chapter # 4.	Colony Life, 1935-1954: Interregnum	121
Chapter # 5.	Colony life, 1955-1967: the 'Menday era'	167
Chapter # 6.	The End of Turners Court: 1968-1991	203
Chapter # 7.	Reflections, conclusions	233
Select Bibliography		279
Appendix 1 Turners Court Wardens, Superintendents, Principals, Instructors, etc.		283
Appendix II Other 'Christian' and/or 'Social' organisations		287
Index		299

ACKNOWLEDGEMENTS

A great many people have helped with the writing and production of this book; my apologies to any whom I have, regrettably, missed from the following list.

My thanks, first, to the Trustees of the Turners Court Youth Trust and their Administrator, Sallie Pickering, for giving me access to the records of Turners Court and its originator, the National Union for Christian Social Service; the Trust also kindly agreed that I could use photographs from their archive to illustrate the book. Personal thanks to Brian Basden, a former Turners Court director and member of one of the founding families of the 'Colony', who has taken a particular interest in, and provided helpful comments on, my research. The use I have made of this material, any errors that may have crept in, and the conclusions I draw from it are, of course, my responsibility.

As readers will see, Turners Court's records are now in the safe hands of the Oxfordshire County Record Office, where thanks are due to Chris Gilliam and his fellow archivists in Cowley Road (the OCRO also refreshes researchers with the best value cup of coffee in Oxford). At the other end of Oxford, in Bonn Square, Dr. Carl Boardman and his staff at the Centre for Oxfordshire Studies (CFOS) have provided invaluable help. Dare we hope that OCRO and CFOS will one day share the same post-code?

The final chapters in the book contain references to film and video material in the Turners Court archive; I was greatly helped by David Lee and his colleagues at Wessex Film and Sound Archive (Hampshire Record Office) who made this material available in digital form to me and future researchers. Other county record offices, including those in Cumbria and Hertfordshire have contributed information on 'colonies' in their counties.

Thanks are also due to librarians and archivists at: the Bodleian Library, Oxford; British Library, London; the Congregational Library and Dr. Williams Library - together they make up a delightful corner of Bloomsbury which deserves to be better known; Friends House Library in London; London Metropolitan Archives; National Archives (formerly Public Record Office) at Kew; William Booth College and the Hadleigh Training Centre, both of the Salvation Army.

Archivists and others who have contributed are from: National Centre for Young People with Epilepsy (the Lingfield heirs of the NUCSS); RAINER Foundation (ex-Royal Philanthropic Society); International Brigade Memorial Trust (see Chapter 4); Peace Pledge Union (see Prologue).

Mrs Jenny Busby, John Glavey and Peter Honeybone contributed personal memories from the point of view of former instructional staff at Turners Court. As becomes apparent in the book, I also received contributions from former residents (it seems anachronistic to term them 'lads'); they were promised anonymity and, although many said they were happy for their names to be used, I thought it best to conceal them all. Thanks, too, to the courteous residents of what is now 'Clock House', Oakley Court – the former Ogilvie

Hall, Boys Club and 'Pop's Shop' of Turners Court – who were forbearing and hospitable when author and collaborator appeared in their front garden.

Finally, a word of thanks to my wife and family, who have so patiently supported the lengthy research and writing of this book, and to the equally patient staff at AuthorHouse who have helped it emerge in print.

Woodstock, Oxfordshire, 2010

PROLOGUE

May, 1916

'Now's the time for country labour!' – Social Service, 1916

On Tuesday 30 May 1916, the day after the Whitsun Bank Holiday, while war raged in Flanders and elsewhere in Europe, two young men wearing somewhat shabby civilian clothes arrived by train in the small market town of Wallingford then in the county of Berkshire.[1] They had travelled from the north of England by a circuitous route, making a final change of train at Cholsey & Moulsford, from where they took the Great Western Railway's shuttle service, known not too affectionately as 'The Bunk,' for the final three miles to Wallingford.

Leaving the station, carrying small suitcases and miscellaneous bags (four years later one of them would be among a party from London which contrived to mislay its luggage on Wallingford's single short platform) the men walked, through the town, over the medieval stone bridge across the Thames, continuing through the village of Crowmarsh and up the hill towards Henley. After what an earlier traveller had noted as 'half an hour's steep walk',[2]

---

1. Wallingford was re-assigned to Oxfordshire in the local government reorganisation of the 1970s.
2. The significance of the distance between Crowmarsh and their destination will appear later.

and feeling considerably warmer (ten miles away in Oxford, the few undergraduates still in residence enjoyed excellent weather for college cricket matches that week), they reached their destination, the 500 acre estate known, since the 14th century as 'Turners Land' and later 'Turners Court' but now re-named Wallingford Farm Training Colony. This 'Colony' was the latest enterprise, officially opened by the Lord Mayor of London just three years earlier, of the National Union for Christian Social Service (NUCSS).

The two men, Frank Horsfall and Edward Sladen, were conscientious objectors, (COs) pacifists who had refused to be conscripted into the British army. They came from the same small Lancashire cotton manufacturing town of Bacup. Both were in their mid-20s, Wesleyan Methodists and with a taste for light opera (Horsfall a tenor, Sladen a bass-baritone); they had worked together as clerks for the Manchester & County Bank in Bacup before Sladen, having taken a part time Commerce degree at Manchester University, became a teacher of commercial subjects. His first teaching position was in the technical school at Newry, Northern Ireland from where he moved, just before the outbreak of war, to Halifax as head of the technical college's commerce department. His opposition to conscription cost him his job and then his liberty, and eventually saw him assigned to work at the 'Colony'.

Conscription had been introduced, for the first time in British history, by the Military Service Act which came into operation on 3 February 1916. It had been made necessary by the substantial losses incurred during the first two years of the war against the central European powers by Britain's peacetime volunteer army: a 'contemptible little army' Hindenburg may or may not have called it; it was certainly little. The 1916 Act provided for exemption on conscientious grounds. Local authorities set up tribunals to deal with applications for exemption; three degrees of conscientious objection were recognised: exemption without conditions; exemption conditional upon performing alternative civilian work; or non-combatant service in the army. Long established religious organisations like the Peace Society (1816) and the Fellowship of Reconciliation, were supplemented, after 1914, by the Union of Democratic Control (UDC) formed by the former government minister, Charles Trevelyan, Ramsay MacDonald and others with the aim of effecting a negotiated peace and asserting the right of 'the people' to 'control policy and create a different kind of post-war world.'[3] Even more directly relevant was the formation, in December 1914, of the No Conscription Fellowship (NCF) by Fenner Brockway and Clifford Allen; by the end of 1915 the NCF had more than 60 local branches (in November 1919 the one in Oxford would be trashed by an exuberant Armistice Day crowd).

An article in *Social Service*, a journal published since 1911 by the NUCSS and a substantial source for this book, dealt with the problem of COs and anti-COs – the not inconsiderable number of people who took vociferous and sometimes violent exception to young men who refused to take up arms; the comment of a *Times* editorial,[4] 'Conscientious Objectors are intractable folk' was, in the circumstances, a restrained rebuke. Under the legislation, COs were to be allowed to take alternative non-combatant service in organisations such as the Friends Ambulance Unit (FAU).

---

3. I F W Beckett, *Home Front*, 2006 (Kew: National Archives) p. 153.
4. Reprinted in *Social Service (SS)*, April 1917.

When the FAU and its like could take no more, the Government agreed that up to ten thousand COs would be set to work in agriculture, replacing labourers in the armed forces: 'An excellent idea,' commented the editor of *Social Service*, not, as we shall see, without self-interest, adding ' . . . Now's the time for country labour!' In the event, of 16,000 men who came forward as conscientious objectors during the war, 400 were granted absolute exemption, 5,000 were enlisted in the Non-Combatant Corps of the army, and 6,500 were given conditional exemption and told to perform 'alternative service' of national importance.[5] Most who fell into that last category did work on the land; by April 1917, a year after the Act came into force, 655 were doing so. Smaller numbers were engaged on road making, municipal or other waterworks, or other manufacturing, construction or extraction industries. One CO later wrote about his time doing 'alternative service' on the land in another part of England:

> 'The great compensation of farm-work is that it is in the open air. Thinking of it now makes me long for the sunshine, wind and rain of my brief spell on the land . . . It is far from a holiday, and it would be foolish to neglect the seamy side . . . I found my fellow COs on the farm very pleasant mates.'[6]

Horsfall and Sladen were not the first COs to be taken on at the 'Colony'; half a dozen had already arrived, and another handful joined them later in 1916; coincidentally or not, many

---

5. The remainder were either forcibly enlisted into combatant units, or spent the war in prison. Much detail in this section comes from the Peace Pledge Union (PPU) publication *Refusing to Kill*, 2006 (London).
6. PPU, *Refusing to Kill*, 2006, p.42.

of them also originated in the north of England. Altogether, more than two dozen conscientious objectors spent some time at Turners Court before conscription was suspended in 1919, some of them for only relatively short periods of time (several appear to have been judged unsuitable for the work and moved to other jobs, presumably with the consent of the authorities).

How to get young men like this to their allocated places of work sometimes taxed the brains of the local authorities; a September 1916 local press report concerned an undisclosed number of COs being taken to work on the roads of Suffolk from temporary lodgings in the Haverhill workhouse, under the direction of the Risbridge Board of Guardians. The clerk asked if the parish should provide a motor bus to take the men to work each day: would the time saved offset the expense of the hire? Eventually the Guardians agreed that they should walk, the chairman 'humorously' adding that he wondered if they might be met by a band on their arrival.

At the end of *their* warm walk from Wallingford station on 30 May, the two young men destined for the Colony were met by the Superintendent, William H. Hunt. Then aged 40, Hunt had worked as editor of several local newspapers before becoming part of the group known as The Forward Movement (of which more in Chapter 2). Having spent 10 years as manager of the NUCSS' first 'colony', at Lingfield in Surrey, he had been put in charge of Turners Court when it opened in 1912. He also edited – and probably wrote most of - the NUCSS's monthly journal *Social Service*. Hunt also wrote brief but often revealing comments on individual members of his staff, some of which survive among the institution's papers.

Both Horsfall and Sladen feature again later in this narrative. Frank Horsfall, indeed, spent the rest of his working life (he never married) at the 'Colony', first as a clerk, then general administrator, bursar and, effectively, second in command to the Warden (as the Superintendent became known in the 1930s). Frequently mentioned in the institution's minutes and other papers, Horsfall briefly took a more public role in an odd episode involving the Colony, Oxford undergraduates and local 'communists' in the late 1930s (see Chapter 4). Edward Sladen (Hunt's comment on him in the staff ledger reads, 'Book keeper for a period. Ought to have continued in this work') left the Colony in 1919 and resumed his teaching career, this time at George Williams College, then attached to London's Central YMCA.[7] In the early 1920s he was appointed Head of the Commerce Department at the technical college in Swindon. In 1923 he married a Wallingford girl, who was (surprisingly, it may be thought, in the light of Sladen's pacifism) the daughter of a warrant officer in the Volunteer Reserve Battalion ('the Territorials') of the Royal Berkshire Regiment, who had served in France during the First World War.[8] Edward Sladen maintained contact with Horsfall, Hunt and others and paid periodic social visits to the Colony over the next 30 years: a couple of such visits feature in later chapters.

The institution into which Frank Horsfall and Edward Sladen walked on that summer day was what today would

---

7. The College is now located at Canning Town and linked to Canterbury Christ Church University.
8. The present author is the younger son of that marriage.

be considered a decidedly odd mixture of farm, school, penitentiary, seminary and orphanage. They and their fellow conscientious objectors were being taken on in the role of 'Brothers', laymen with a religious tinge, whose job it would be to train, look after and control a constantly shifting population of 'colonists' – young men and boys who had arrived at Wallingford through a variety of routes, mostly referred by parish Boards of Guardians or local authorities. The NUCSS had added to Turners Court's original farm buildings two substantial residential blocks for 'colonists' and Brothers, plus communal dining rooms, kitchen, offices and so on. But to understand how the 'Colony' came to be founded and what 'colonists' and 'Brothers' actually did, it is necessary to work through, in the next Chapter, some of the social, religious, economic and political history of the late 19th century, not only of England but other European states, notably Germany.

CHAPTER 1
Antecedents: charities and colonies

All Institutions for reception of Foundlings and Beggers are established within Towns. Why are they not removed from Towns, which they infect and which infect them, to the Country? - Mirabeau, 'Mémoires', 1834

What, then, must be done with [the unemployed]? The answer . . . seems to me obvious. They must go upon the land!
- William Booth, 'In Darkest England', 1890

The events immediately leading to the formation of the National Union for Christian Social Service (NUCSS) and its Colonies, including Wallingford, are quite well documented, as are details of many of the main actors. Although a history of the NUCSS privately published in 1963 (when, abbreviated to 'Christian Service Union', it ceased to exist) claims that the Wallingford Colony was a 'pioneer example of . . . co-operation between . . . statutory and . . . voluntary services' it was in fact preceded by a number of similar efforts at social reform promoted by philanthropists in the 19th and early 20th centuries. After covering the NUCSS's own immediate origins, this chapter will sketch the economic and political background to this and other inland 'colonies.'

The birth of the NUCSS followed a meeting held at Christ Church, Westminster Bridge Road, on 27 February 1894. It had been convened by the Rev. J.F.B. Tinling, a Congregationalist minister and prolific author of sermons and pamphlets on such hot topics among late Victorian dissenters as Conditional Immortality. Together with his friend Dr. F.B. Meyer, Tinling wrote to all Free Church ministers in London; Congregationalist and other non-conformist clergy and lay supporters would remain prominent in the CSU, although it also attracted support from the Anglican clergy and laity, and some Roman Catholic participation; its 'colonies', unlike those of the Salvation Army, were never single-sect institutions.

What spurred Tinling and Meyer into action was a book published a few months earlier, originally in German, then English, by Julie Sutter entitled *A Colony of Mercy*: 'With this book in his hand,' wrote the biographer of another founding father, 'Tinling determined to attempt similar work in this country.'[1] Sutter, born in India, was the daughter of a British missionary, later redeployed to the Church of Scotland Jewish Mission in Germany. She trained as a teacher, earning extra money by translation and while living in Germany agitated against the slave trade. A life-long Teutonophile, she greatly admired the efficiency of German municipal government, the role of the Burgomaster and the 'Elberfeld' system of poor relief (of which more later).[2] As the principal and, according to press reports, inspirational, speaker at the 27 February meeting, Sutter reiterated the message in her book extolling 'Bethel', the 'labour colony' directed by Pastor Friedrich von Bodelschwingh at Bielefeld in the Teutonberger forest (scene of the Roman legions' defeat at the hands of the German tribes led by Arminius).

---

1. J. Marchant, *J.B. Paton, educational & social pioneer*, 1909 (London: James Clarke) p.159.
2. When she died in 1924, at the age of 78, her obituary also recalled her scorn for English cuisine, with its over-cooking of vegetables.

The von Bodelschwinghs were wealthy and politically important landowners in Westphalia. Friedrich's father, Ernst, trained as a lawyer then served in the Prussian army against Napoleon before becoming first an official, then successively Finance and Interior Minister in the Prussian government. Resigning in 1848 (the 'year of revolutions') he became leader of the *Zentrumspartei* in the Prussian legislature. Friedrich was born in 1831[3]; his school-age friends included the future Kaiser, Friedrich Willhelm III. Initially marked down for a career in estate management or politics, in his mid-20s he switched courses, studying theology at Basel, Berlin and Erlangen before taking up posts as Protestant minister, first to the German community in Paris, then in the Ruhr. He served as an army padre in the wars of 1866 and 1870, the latter culminating in the siege of Paris and the turmoil of the Commune.

In 1872 Friedrich von Bodelschwingh was invited to take over the running of an institution for epileptics which had been founded in Bielefeld in 1867, together with the adjoining training centre for deaconesses. Although von Bodelschwingh may not strictly speaking have been the founder of what was soon renamed the 'Bethel' colony, it appears that it was his energy, aristocratic connections and bureaucratic efficiency which ensured its expansion and success. His technique, a fellow member of the Bethel board is alleged to have said, was to 'listen patiently to all that was said without contradicting, and then to go off and do what he thought was right,'[4] a

---
3. www.bethel.de, website of the 21st century v.Bodelschwingsche Anstalten Bethel.
4. Ibid.

management style not unknown among British companies – and charities.

By the time Julie Sutter visited it, the foundation provided homes for over 1,000 epileptics, 'the central object round which other needs have gathered.'[5] Capital outlay to date was said to have been about £15,000 (perhaps coincidentally, the CSU would come up with the same figure in due course). On the same site were the deaconesses' training home, a further house for the training of 'Brothers' or lay workers, a 'Workman's Home', providing affordable housing for the labouring classes and, most importantly as a model for the CSU, the 'labour colony' for men to be 'saved' from unemployment and, eventually, shown the way to redemption through work. Sutter seems to have disapproved of the pressure for instant Damascene conversion in the Salvation Army (although she acknowledged a debt to 'General' William Booth's 1890 book *In Darkest England*').

By the late 1880s, there were some 225 'colonists' (the term adopted in turn by the NUCSS) in residence; in its first 14 months, 1,200 men had passed through Bethel, of whom 966 were said to have been placed in employment. Most of the men worked on the colony's farm, 'cheerfully,' said Sutter, 'though it was pouring with rain', under the supervision of a 'Housefather' and 'brothers' (both terms later adopted by the NUCSS); starting at 5.30 in the morning, Sutter claimed, the brothers kept up the 'cheerful tone' of the colonists' labours not by talking religion, but *'just working with them'* and showing them 'the beauty of work'. From this example, the men might 'get religion . . . but unconsciously.'[6]

5 Julie Sutter, *A Colony of Mercy* (London: Hodder & Stoughton) 1893, p. 1-2.
6. Sutter, 1893, p.145, 159; original emphasis.

Von Bodelschwingh thought the labour colony could be self-supporting with about 100 colonists, although at the time of Sutter's visit the number was over 200; Sutter wrote that, 'Anyone presenting himself is admitted', given new clothes and asked to sign a contract, effectively exchanging his labour for food and lodging and a daily 'wage' of around five pence (2p) which was paid to him on leaving the colony. She noted, with apparent approval, that the men chose their own clothes, usually according to previous occupation so 'there is a sort of class distinction in the colony.'[7]

Although it was certainly Bethel's example that spurred the CSU into action, it was by then far from unique in Germany. In 1895, the Rev. J. B Paton[8], by then judged to be the driving force behind the NUCSS, wrote that von Bodelschwingh's efforts, which had 'truly startled' Germany, had resulted in 27 other – Protestant - colonies being founded (there was at least one Roman Catholic colony, in the Rhineland). In 1885 a monthly journal, *The Labour Colony*, appeared to serve the movement, another feature that would be copied in due course in England. Paton believed that Bielefeld proved that ' . . . little expenditure is needed at the outset' after which colonies should be self-supporting, adding 'We should do better than Germany [because] we have better land and better marketing [sic] in England.'[9] Another enthusiastic visitor to Bielefeld was the diplomat turned philanthropist the Earl of Meath, (who will appear later as the aristocratic figure-head of the NUCSS).

7. Sutter, 1893, p.151, 155, 153.
8. 1830-1911. Born into Congregationalist (and former Covenanting) family in Ayrshire. Worked briefly in printing office before training for the Ministry.
9. London Metropolitan Archives A/FWA/C/D254/, MS letter, addressee unknown.

The pioneering system of social legislation introduced by Bismarck in the 1880s, while it included medical, accident, old age and invalidity insurance, provided no protection against unemployment. One recent history suggests that, although eye-catching and well in advance of any such legislation in Britain, Bismarck's provisions were meagre, far from comprehensive: the medical insurance, for example, did not cover rural workers; from the Chancellor's point of view, however, the innovations were successful in that they deflected support from the growing Social Democratic party.[10]

As in Britain, therefore, the problem of the unemployed was left to local authorities and private institutions; Sutter and Paton's claim that 'Bethel' offered a self-supporting model has to be modified by the fact that it received an annual subsidy of £1,500 - £2,000 from the provincial government. Sutter believed the German local authorities were happy to subsidise the privately-run colonies because of a then prevailing rule that two years residence in one town entitled unemployed men to public support (Bethel and other German colonies therefore limited men to less than two years' stay); it was, she claimed, more efficient to subsidise the colonies than to provide training and jobs in the public sector. The state also benefited, she thought, because the colonies were able to reclaim land not otherwise in economic use (Booth's *In Darkest England* envisages the same thing happening in Britain).

Although the network of colonies for unemployed men in Germany was certainly the main model followed by the NUCSS, Sutter and Paton also noted in passing examples from other parts of Europe, although most of these were more

---

10. C Clark, *Iron Kingdom*, 2007 (London: Allen Lane) *passim*.

overtly inland penal establishments (use of *overseas* penal colonies, of course, was common to British and other colonial administrations) to which convicted men and boys were sent direct by the courts. Descriptions of many of these appeared later in the CSU journal *Social Service*.

Continental European practice had, indeed, been cited as one that Britain might follow some decades earlier. In 1851, Joseph Fletcher, a London barrister, gave a paper entitled 'The Farm School System of the Continent and its applicability to the preventive and reformatory education of pauper and criminal children in England and Wales' to the Royal Statistical Society. In this paper, Fletcher covered both institutions for the repression of adult mendicancy and vagabondage, like Merxplas in Belgium, free colonies or farm workhouses aimed at 'indigent adults' and 'agricultural reform schools'. It was those last which link more directly to NUCSS and other farm colonies in England. Here, Fletcher emphasised the need for 'proper education' of the pauper child to take precedence over 'proper reformation of the *criminal* child'. He particularly approved the part played in such education by men working alongside the children to impart the 'simplest practical labours of husbandry.'

Fletcher regretted that such examples had not yet been much copied in England: 'Between the workhouse school on the one hand, and the public indifference, on the other, the efforts even of *private* charity . . . by means of the farm-school have been very limited.' Among roughly comparable institutions then struggling to exist he cites the Royal Victoria Asylum at Hackney Wick (its female department at Chiswick recently notorious because of claims of child abuse) and schools or colonies of industry at Lindfield in Sussex, and Ealing, both of which were on the point of being abandoned.[11]

Of the more overtly penal establishments, Merxplas had been re-founded by the Belgian government in 1891 after the collapse of an original colony started by the Dutch Benevolent Society in 1818. In due course *Social Service* would describe it as a 'huge, highly organised agricultural and industrial Colony, whose fame among social reformers is world-wide'. 'Thousands' of colonists, most of them 'professional vagrants' who must be 'kept under control' were housed in military conditions. NUCSS commentators sound somewhat lukewarm about the example this regime offered: 'The best thing to be said for Merxplas. It sweeps the tramp off the road and keeps more or less under permanent control a horde of undesirables.'[12]

In Switzerland, the Rev Lord William Gascoyne-Cecil reported in glowing terms on the Swiss penal colony at Witzwil where selected convicts worked on the land to offset part of the cost of their confinement. Cattle were grazed, free, on the mountains in summer but even so the colony made a small annual loss. Gascoyne-Cecil, however, noted that although otherwise resembling an ordinary prison, with white-washed cells and barred windows, the colony was exemplary in the way in which the warders,

---

11   J Fletcher, *The Farm School System of the Continent*, 1852 (London:James Ridgway) p.45; original emphasis. The Ealing school was funded by Lady Noel Byron, who is commemorated in local street names.
12   *Social Service (SS)*, 1913, p. 220 (Oct), p.251 (Dec).

'have to work with the men . . . example is better than precept . . . a skilled man working with the others teaches them both how to work and also how to love it.'[13]

In France, an Agricultural Colony had been set up in 1839 at Mettray to employ boys on the land; they were accommodated in houses under masters who shared their life and work – another model that would be echoed by the NUCSS and others in England. Not all Frenchmen were in favour; a threat to close the popular Parisian 'national workshops' and send able-bodied unemployed men either into the army or to land reclamation labour camps in the provinces was, according to a recent biography of the 19th century French historian and politician de Tocqueville, a major cause of the violent unrest of 1848.[14]

From yet further afield, *Social Service* carried a report on 'Boysville', 20 miles outside Cleveland in the USA, which was said to house about 300 boys 'mostly under the authority of the Juvenile Court . . . taken from the streets or from unhappy circumstances.' The boys were given schooling, and worked on the land, at carpentry and painting; unlike Merxplas, there was no militaristic drill and the boys were, wrote the anonymous correspondent, 'as happy as the day is long . . . it is a very rare thing for a boy to bolt.'[15]

Although Bodelschwingh's Bethel was publicly lauded as their avowed model, the begetters of the National Union for Christian Social Service did not need to look outside England for authors who wrote about the problem of the

---

13. *SS*, 1913 p. 264, (Dec), 1910 (Jan).
14. H. Brogan, *Alexis de Tocqueville*, 2006 (London: Profile Books)p. 460-462.
15. *SS*, 1913 p.239-240 (Oct)

urban poor and put forward solutions, some of them, at least, incorporating that ideal combination of hard work, vocational training, Christian thought and simple living which Tinling and his colleagues felt stood the best chance of 'redeeming' the boys and men whom other systems failed.

In the early 1880s Congregationalists had been stirred into action (in some cases involvement with the Christian Socialist revival – see Appendix II) by a book entitled *The Bitter Cry of Outcast London, an inquiry into the condition of the abject poor*, based on a survey of East London poverty and recommending the setting up of non-denominational inner city mission halls where 'An attempt must be made to relieve in some wise . . . the abounding misery.'[16] In 1885 the Congregational Union itself published a report, *Light and Shade: Pictures of London Life*, recording the flow of aid to the unfortunate London poor and viewing the results of Congregationalists' work in this field 'with some complacency'.[17] Neither these reports, however, nor a roughly contemporaneous series of articles by the housing reformer Octavia Hill, featured shifting unemployed men and youths to the country to be taught agricultural skills.[18]

Other Victorian authors, including Henry Mayhew (*London Labour and the London Poor*, 1851) and Charles

---

16. A. Mearns, *The Bitter Cry of Outcast London*, 1970 ed. (London: Frank Cass) p. 21. Originally published anonymously in 1875, Mearns was identified as author in the 2nd, 1883, edition. Prefatory notes to the 1970 edition suggest that the principal author was William Camall Preston, a Congregational minister in Wigan, together with Mearns, secretary of the Congregational Union, and Rev. James Munro.
17. P. d'A Jones, *Christian Socialist Revival*, 1968 (Princeton: Princeton Univ. Press) pp. 414, 417.
18. Octavia Hill, *Houses of the London Poor*, 1970 (London: Frank Cass). Hill's main theme was the need to improve housing conditions, provide open space and fresh air (she lobbied for the Artizans Dwelling Act, 1875), a cause later taken up by the NUCSS' President, Lord Meath.

Antecedents: charities and colonies

Booth (*Life and Labour of the People in London*, 1889) produced graphic pictures of the poverty of the unemployed, the casual labourer and those in low-paid industry in London and elsewhere. Again, the use of the agricultural training colony as a remedy for society's ills was not prominent in these works. Charles Booth, apart from proposing national non-contributory old age and health insurance, contributed rather vague prescriptions - 'Socialism in the arms of Individualism': the poor should be encouraged to live and work as families in 'industrial groups', the Government supplying materials and capital equipment in exchange for the work done.[19] Mayhew, too, was an observer rather than a prescriber (he and the Bohemian friends who worked with him might at a pinch be viewed as precursors of mid-20th century Mass-Observation reporters and diarists). In correspondence with readers of his book, he explained that he wanted capitalists and workers to be complementary: 'every worker investing in a bank loan would become a small capitalist helping another working class person', blithely ignoring the fact that the great majority of workers had no cash to invest.[20]

'In Darkest England – and the Way Out'

Apart from Julie Sutter's passionate advocacy of von Bodelschwingh and Bethel, the published work which did most to promote the practical development of the farm colony in Great Britain, and probably the one best remembered today (it has already been mentioned in the present work)

---

19. H.W. Pfautz ed., *Charles Booth on the City*, 1967 (Chicago: Univ. of Chicago Press) p.30-31.
20. B. Taithe ed, *The Essential Mayhew*, 1996 (London: Rivers Oram) p.41.

was William Booth's *In Darkest England and the Way Out*. First published in 1890, its title deliberately mimicked that of H.M. Stanley's *In Darkest Africa*, equating pygmies, fighting their way through the equatorial jungle, with those city dwellers who had lost all hope in the face of disease, squalor, dirt, unemployment, crime and immorality. 'The lot of a negress in the Equatorial Forest is not, perhaps, a very happy one, but is it so very much worse than that of many a pretty orphan girl in our Christian capital?'[21] Booth asks rhetorically, adducing plentiful evidence to support his contention that the 'submerged tenth' of Britain's population was indeed living in conditions as bad as, if not worse than, those of the most primitive tribe anywhere in the world.

Booth, born in 1829, was well acquainted with poverty, the uncertainties of life and the vagaries of mid-Victorian charity from his own childhood, the early death of his father and his apprenticeship as a young teenager to a Nottingham pawnbroker. Originally a member of the Church of England, he came under the influence of the American Methodist and revivalist James Caughey and became a Methodist lay preacher in London, where he married the formidable – and better educated – Catherine Mumford. Booth's entry in the DNB describes him as largely ignorant both of religious doctrine, science and philosophy: 'In everything intellectual he was an obscurantist of the most pronounced type.' A perpetual Millenarian, his one clear and unchanging idea was to convert the masses, while doing what he could to alleviate their poverty.[22]

---

21. W. Booth, *In Darkest England,* 1970 edition. (London: Charles Knight) p.13.
22. Frank Prochaska, *William Booth*, 2004-5, Oxford Dictionary of National Biography.

Booth brusquely dismissed all previous attempts to solve the problem of the 'submerged tenth' – socialism, the Poor Law, mass emigration: 'It is simply criminal to take a multitude of untrained men and women and land them, penniless and helpless, on a new continent'.[23] Contemptuously saying that he left 'the limitless infinity of the future to the Utopians' Booth proceeded to construct his own Utopia, based, as he saw it, upon real experience. *In Darkest England* set out the three elements of his vision:

- *City Colonies* ('Moral and social casualty clearing stations', said Booth, his phraseology perhaps influenced by newspaper reports of the Franco-Prussian and other European wars) would give men and women employment in workshops and public services such as salvage collection, in return for shelter, regular meals and a minimum wage. After a year, a review found ten such shelters in London, providing nightly accommodation for 2,000 men; the workshops employed 14,000 men and 1,500 women. 'The Salvation Army, on the evidence of a less than laudatory report, was the biggest and most comprehensive welfare organisation in Britain'.[24] From these City Colonies, the most able-bodied men would transfer to . . .
- *Farm Colonies,* which would teach basic agricultural skills on previously un-used strips of land and fit some of the men for onward migration to . . .
- *Overseas Colonies*, 'simply pieces of Britain distributed about the world', said Booth, trying to

23. Quoted R Hattersley, *Blood and Fire,* 1999 (London: Little Brown) p. 364.
24. Hattersley, 1999, p.395.

distance himself from accusations of sponsoring mass transportation. The Salvation Army already claimed adherents in 'almost every country in the world' who would not only be on hand to help the able-bodied emigrants to set up ('laying the foundations, perchance, of another Empire'), but would keep their eyes open for 'every useful notion and every conceivable contrivance for increasing the yield of the soil' in their own colonies and in those back home in England.[25]

Of this three-pronged plan of attack (the military analogy is irresistible: both within the Salvation Army and outside, William Booth was known as 'The General', to his evident pleasure), the third element would leave the least permanent impression. 'Nobody,' writes a recent biographer 'took wholly seriously [Booth's] plans to establish Overseas Colonies'. Of the few that materialised, one, for discharged prisoners, was set up at Rondesbosch, South Africa; the Salvation Army also ran colonies, at different times, in Switzerland, Indonesia and the Netherlands (that last still in existence after the World War II, although all its cattle had been slaughtered during the German occupation).[26]

When in 1898 Cecil Rhodes visited the Salvation Army colony, by then established at Hadleigh, Essex, he is said to have encouraged the idea that Rhodesia would be the natural end product of Booth's ambitious world plan, but Overseas Colonies needed capital, and Rhodes was apparently unable to provide

---

25. Booth, *In Darkest England,* 1970 ed., p. 133.
26. R Sandall, *The History of the Salvation Army Vol. III*, 1955 (London: Nelson) p. 142.

that.[27] Booth's heart was clearly more fixed upon the inland farm colonies each of which he envisaged as a self-sustaining community, 'part co-operative and part benevolent autocracy': in the event, the latter would emerge as the dominant management style, as those acquainted with Booth's dirigiste manner might have guessed. Other aspects of Booth's plans veered from the grandiloquent to the quirky: all over England, he alleged, were vacant farms which,

'. . only need the application of an industrious population working with due incentive to produce twice, thrice and four times as much as they yield today. While other people talk of reclaiming Salisbury Plain and cultivating the bleak moorlands of the North, I think of the hundreds of square miles that lie in long ribbons on the sides of our railways.' [28]

Booth's generally sympathetic biographer points out that this last idea must also have occurred to 'thousands of travelling schoolboys' who, like the General, never paused to consider the practicality of cultivating these line-side strips, or the cost of collecting 'fruit enough to supply all the jam that Crosse & Blackwell ever boiled.'[29] Some details of the proposed agricultural regime were left hazy:' I am not an agriculturalist; I do not dogmatize', Booth wrote loftily. Others were more clearly spelled out; *In Darkest England* recommended a farm of 500 to 1000 acres (202 to 404 hectares), of land suitable for

27. Hattersley, 1999, p. 428. Rhodes' enthusiasm may have cooled when Booth suddenly insisted they both kneel in prayer in the first class compartment of the train back to London.
28. Sandall, 1955, p. 136. Never shy of the grand gesture, Booth wrote in 1890 of his 'ultimate vision' being that of roofing over Hyde Park to become 'The World's Great Grand Central Temple' (G K Horridge, *The Salvation Army*, 1993, Godalming, p.226).
29. Hattersley, 1999, p. 369.

market gardening, within 'a reasonable distance' of London while having some clay on it for brick-making and for crops demanding a heavier soil. The site should also be served by a railway line 'managed by intelligent and progressive directors' and should also have access to sea and river. Above all, the colony should lie 'at some considerable distance' from any town or village, well away from any public house, 'that upas tree of civilisation.' Such a colony, Booth thought, could be sustainable with a shifting population of around 200 'colonists' – unemployed men and lads. Many of these same conditions would be laid down by the founders of the NUCSS, notably the caveat about access to public houses.

In March 1891, Booth's vigorous fund-raising activity (around £100,000 in total was contributed, thanks largely to the publicity generated by *In Darkest England*) enabled the Army to buy 1,236 acres (c. 500 hectares) of farm land at Hadleigh in Essex; the purchase price was £12,000. The site met many of Booth's stipulations in *In Darkest England*, although not the one about distance from existing settlements: unlike Wallingford, the Salvationists' colony was cheek by jowl with a pre-existing village, to the consternation of many residents. Some of the land purchased was already under cultivation; the rest was said to be poor quality and had earned the local name 'the Bad Lands.' By good chance – or perhaps thanks to the Army's surveyors - the site did, however, contain an area of clay which unskilled labour could turn into bricks for delivery by barge to the booming London house building market.[30]

---

30 M Hancock & S Harvey, *Hadleigh, an Essex Village*, 1986 (Chichester: Phillimore) p. 18-19.

In May 1891 the first batch of 30 unemployed men moved into temporary buildings on the Hadleigh site. Permanent structures – dormitories, dining room, hospital, offices and so on – were not completed until 1912, when the Hadleigh Colony celebrated its coming of age and the CSU Farm Training Colony at Turners Court opened its gates. Unlike the Wallingford Colony, much of the land at Hadleigh remains in the ownership of the Salvation Army into the 21st century, although it is now commercially farmed; vocational training also continues on the site but of a different character from that envisaged by the General.

Later in this narrative some comparisons may be attempted between Wallingford and Hadleigh. Meanwhile, in the 1890s, the Rev. Tinling and his Congregationalist associates might also have learned from the experience of other more or less flourishing English colonies. In 1891 the newly painted sign on the gate of the Salvation Army colony at Hadleigh stated confidently, 'The Castle and Park Farms have been purchased by General Booth for the establishment of the first Farm Colony and elimination of the submerged tenth.' This was literally true (William Booth would surely not have countenanced prevarication, even on a gate post) if it were meant to refer only to *Salvation Army* institutions.

But the NUCSS journal *Social Service* and other sources reveal a number of similar 'colonies', funded in the 19th and early 20th centuries by a variety of national and local institutions.

Encouragement of the rural labour colony as an economic proposition can be found in reports and journal articles of the 1880s which would have been available to Tinling and his contemporaries. Some such colonies appear only fleetingly; some were never more than pious or politically naive hopes, like the one proposed by the Eccleshall (Sheffield) Board of Guardians for lands in Derbyshire 'which at the present time are of no use except for rearing grouse', and which it was argued could be reclaimed for cultivation by the unemployed on small holdings; 'The task of gathering stones and preparing the land', wrote the *Social Service* journalist hopefully, 'will find work for any unemployed.'

Few Victorian Boards of Guardians thought so boldly – or foolhardily: two Kentish parishes which ran, apparently with some success, 'Poor Law Farms' for those capable of work but temporarily unemployed, sound exceptional: 'They found no imitators', their work catching the attention only of scattered local historians, according to one recent account. Regular boarding schools, without the farming element, for orphans and others put into the care of the parish were more common; among the best of them was one built in Surrey by the Kensington and Chelsea Unions which gave one late Victorian (anonymous) visitor 'the impression of a well-designed model village, delightfully placed amid country surroundings of woodland and down.'[31]

Of the more substantial and long-lived colony sites already in existence when Tinling called his meeting the following exemplify the variety of size and parentage:

- *Duxhurst, Surrey*: an industrial farm colony for inebriate women financially backed by Lady Henry Somerset, survivor of a famous late Victorian marital

---

31. G. Slater, *Poverty & the State*, 1930, London, p.65-66, quoted W Court, *Concise Economic History of Britain*, 1967 (Cambridge: CUP) p. 138-139; N. Longmate, *The Workhouse*, 2003 (London: Pimlico) p.180.

dispute, who pooled her own considerable resources with those of the American philanthropist Frances Willard and the British Womens Temperance Association;

- *Hollesley Bay, Suffolk*: a 'Colonial College', opened in 1887, specialising in preparing 'gentlemen emigrants' for the colonial frontiers, to help maintain Anglo-Saxon superiority in the matters of empire. In the years 1887-1900, more than 700 boys graduated from the College. A French visitor sang its praises. In 1905 it switched to retraining destitute London working men for rural work and by the late 20th century was a young offenders' institution, its inmates conspicuous in their luminous orange jackets.[32]
- *Laindon, Essex*: a colony run by the left-leaning Poplar Board of Guardians, frequently accused of squandering public money on high-living for the unemployed colonists;
- *Marple Dale, Cheshire*: founded by the philanthropic 'Back to the Land Committee' in Manchester to train 15-30 unemployed Mancunians in basic agricultural methods, it suffered from internal strife: the Committee accused the paid manager of profligacy, feeding the unemployed men on beefsteak at 10d or 1s. 2d (4p or 6p) per lb; as we shall see, it was taken over by the CSU in 1909, but closed 11 years later;

---

[32] E. Richards, *Britannia's Children*, 2004 (London: Hambledon & London) p.216-217; W.G. Sebald, trans M Hulse, *The Rings of Saturn*, 2002 (London: Vintage) p. 223.

- *Ruthwell, Dumfriesshire* '8 miles from Dumfries, 4 miles from Ruthwell station and 5 from a public house...the only institution of its kind in Scotland', supported by churches in Glasgow and elsewhere. Early in the 20th century it housed a variety of unfortunates, including 'a minister's brother . . . formerly a commercial traveller, but being exposed to the severest temptation on the road, gave way to intemperance and fell from his respectable position to vagrancy, until . . . brought to the Colony' where he worked 'splendidly' and was expected to take up permanent work and 'rejoin his motherless children';

Libury Hall, Ware, Hertfordshire: a colony founded by the German banker Sir John Henry Schroder, where his fellow countrymen and other 'Continentals' who had become stranded in this country could seek help to re-establish themselves 'in morale and physique' and enabled to return home. *Social Service* (October, 1902) reported that enough capital had been raised from among philanthropic Europeans to buy a farm, put up permanent buildings, stock the farm with horses and cattle 'among the best that money can buy' and maintain them 'in a condition which leaves nothing to be desired.' Any NUCSS colony, it was implied, should not skimp on land, buildings and stock.

One of the longest lived farm colonies for boys, which would have been familiar to Tinling and his friends, was the *Royal Philanthropic Society's Farm School for boys at Redhill*, Surrey, modelled on the colony at Mettray in France. The Society, formed in 1788, with 'reformation of children engaged in criminal practices' as an objective, was incorporated by statute in 1806. The 150 acre (60 hectare) Redhill farm was purchased in 1848 and a number of 'houses' (in the public school sense) built, each accommodating about 50 boys; the Prince Consort attended the opening in 1849. As well as agriculture, boys were taught carpentry, tailoring, shoemaking and smith's work. As would be the case at Hadleigh, Wallingford and other colonies, a high proportion emigrated to the Dominions. Anticipating changes that will be covered in later chapter, in 1933, Redhill became an Approved School and in 1973 control of the school (but not the land and buildings) passed to the London Borough of Wandsworth. By then called the Philanthropic Community, the school closed in 1988 but the Society now funds projects aimed at filling gaps in provision for young people.[33]

---

33. Anon, *A History of The Royal Philanthropic Society 1788-1988*, 1988. From the outset the Society championed emigration as a solution to social distress at home, and 'the suitability of . . . training for colonial life' apparently proved at Redhill, agents were appointed in North America, Australia and S. Africa (*vide* A. G Scholes, *Education for Empire Settlement*, 1932, London: Longman, p.16).

Sturdy beggars and impotent poor

As Tinling and his fellow philanthropists left that meeting in 1894, what was passing through their collective mind may be thought of in terms of a crowded stage picture, one crammed with characters, colourful, dramatic, like something from a Beerbohm Tree extravaganza at Her Majesty's Theatre. Centre stage stand Sutter, Pastor von Bodelschwingh and his 'Bethel' colony. Pressing close behind them are the mid-Victorian journalists and agitators – the Booths, Mayhew and the rest – the various nostrums they propose, the colonies and other institutions they have started. And filling in the vast spaces around the principals is the army of unemployed, or unemployables, the 'submerged tenth' or the 'residuum'. Who were they, what did the comfortable middle classes think of them, and why at this particular juncture should Tinling and company have come to believe that they, and they alone, had the key to solving their problems?

Today, thanks to the printed word, the cinema and television, the picture of 19th century deprivation that we conjure up is likely to be one of *urban* squalor, overcrowded and insanitary slums, out of work dockers, juvenile crossing-sweepers and pickpockets, the Ragged School of the East End of London, the child labourers and cellar-dwelling families of Manchester and the Lancashire cotton towns. But such public provision as existed to help those who could not earn enough to support themselves and their families harked back to a time when the economy of England and Wales was primarily agricultural.

In medieval times 'the poor' – whatever the reason for their poverty – could only look to their own families or to the church to provide food, shelter, health care, alms. The 16th century dissolution of monastic houses disrupted this already fragile system (some religious foundations had always preferred to spend money on their own comfort rather than on relieving the poor); in London and other towns the emergent trading classes became worried about the perceived army of 'sturdy beggars'. This threat, although nebulous, its precise composition uncertain, was nevertheless firmly believed to exist over subsequent centuries. It was the product of many economic and political forces: periodic agricultural and industrial failures; improvements in agricultural efficiency; enclosure (in the 17th century Archbishop Laud would come unstuck, partly at least, because he tried to reverse the process of transforming English agriculture from tillage to grazing, causing the gentry to flex their muscles against him). Foreign protectionism could also, from time to time, throw into poverty numbers of workers in the textile and other trades. Soldiers discharged from Tudor, Stuart, Hanoverian and later wars, often disabled, certainly untrained for civilian life, added periodically to the numbers of the unemployed: Mrs. Gaskell's Captain Brown, in *Cranford*, soon found he could not survive on his half-pay alone; those of lesser rank would have been markedly worse off.[34]

As to remedies, 'simple whipping of sturdy beggars', as Trevelyan puts it, 'was found to be by itself no solution.'[35]

34. The popular historian Arthur Bryant fatuously wrote (in *The Age of Elegance*, 1950) about 'merry old soldiers' adding to the colour and gaiety of the early 19th century village scene.
35. G M Trevelyan, *English Social History*, 1944 (London: Longman Green) p.113.

The royal government therefore intervened; a Statute of 1556 enjoined the clergy to provide Poor Relief, always discriminating between the various classes of the indigent: the 'impotent poor' (the sick, mad, crippled etc) and the 'able bodied poor', who simply lacked work and wages. Elizabethan and Stuart legislation enforced the duty of poor relief on local magistrates, paid for by a compulsory Poor Rate, which became levied with increasing regularity. The Overseers not only gave out relief in cash or kind, but could also spend the product of the Rate on materials to provide work for the unemployed. At the same time, the Privy Council was controlling the price of grain. The system was certainly not foolproof, although Trevelyan, perhaps the Whiggest of historians, believes that provision for the poor, ' . . . was better than anything there had been in an older England, and better than anything there was to be for many generations to come in France or other European countries.' [36]

Charles II's Act of Settlement, at the time of the Stuart Restoration, included provision for parishes to turn away, without relief, those paupers they believed not to be native to the parish: 'The panic fear of some parish authorities, lest newcomers should some day fall on the rates, caused them to exercise this unjust power in quite unnecessary cases' comments Trevelyan, writing about 18th century practice, whereas in other parishes 'outdoor relief' – paying off the pauper in cash or kind – was said to be given 'with mischievous profusion.'[37]

By the 19th century, Trevelyan struggles to portray the development of poor relief as anything other than an unsavoury

36. Ibid, p.171, 230-231.
37. Ibid, p. 230, 278.

and uneconomic mess. The famous meeting of Berkshire magistrates at Speenhamland, near Newbury, in 1795 was originally intended to fix and enforce a minimum wage for the county, in relation to the price of bread. This policy, if it had ever been adopted country-wide, would indeed have been both radical and, arguably, economically sound: when the idea of a national minimum wage was eventually accepted in the late 20th century, it was put into place without undue fuss. But in the early 1800s the idea was doomed to failure in the face of the farmers, who naturally preferred to have the burden of low wages – insufficient to support life for the farm labourer and his family – remain with the rate payer, rather than the employer.

Continued disquiet about the efficiency of the system and complaints from ratepayers at its cost, together with the nightmare scenario of the 'army' of unemployed roaming the country initiating rebellion on the scale of 1789, led to the Poor Law Amendment Act, 1834, which established supposed national oversight of poor relief and parish workhouses through three Poor Law Commissioners, their Secretary (Edwin Chadwick) and nine clerks. The Poor Law Commission was not directly represented in Parliament, had no official spokesman, and its ability to inspect the 600-odd English and Welsh Poor Law Unions (earlier legislation had permitted parishes to join together to share the burden of poor relief) was questionable. Trevelyan, clutching at straws, thought that, however ineffective, the Commission at least 'contained the seeds of its own reform.'[38] A more recent historian summarises the system less kindly,

---
38. *Ibid*, p.538.

'There were 650 or so Poor Law Unions, and each board of guardians could do more or less as it liked. As a result, conditions varied greatly. Although the Poor Law Commissioners and their successors in Whitehall could make a lot of noise, they had surprisingly few direct powers over the guardians. Most guardians were happy to follow the Commissioners' lead, as there were many benefits in doing so, but even then they often did not do things properly or misinterpreted the regulations.'[39]

Reformers were not unaware of the failings of the system. Poorly educated, eccentric, venal, Boards of Guardians often saw their main priority as providing cheap labour to local employers: '. . . long serving members of a Board, however conscientious, were rarely the stuff of which reformers were made,'[40] and there was little competition to be elected as a guardian. The general principle was that receipt of public money, whether through 'outdoor relief' or the workhouse, must be made less attractive than any employment in field or factory; rather than impose a minimum wage, the New Poor Law effectively lowered the standard of workhouse provision: 'Some workhouses were awful, particularly in the 1830s and 1840s, and even in the 1890s conditions in a few . . . were dreadful.'[41] Only a small minority offered young inmates the apparently idyllic conditions of Kensington and Chelsea's school in Surrey.

The creation of the Local Government Board, in 1871, was intended to impose firmer central guidance on these ramshackle boards of guardians but resulted in little immediate improvement. The 1880s began to show signs of

---
39. S. Fowler, *Workhouse*, 2007 (Kew: National Archives) p. 225.
40. N. Longmate, 2003, p.266.
41. *Ibid,* p.226.

reform: higher class clerkships brought in better educated officials; working class candidates and some women started to be elected as Guardians and in the 1890s Will Crooks and George Lansbury embarked on their course of what came to be termed 'Poplarism' – 'I determined to fight for . . . decent treatment for the poor people, and hang the rates!' But the Poplar-based farm colony at Laindon, in Essex, as we have seen, attracted a poor reputation; the press printed the 'worst stories of extravagance and indiscipline' with the colonists, 'to the great indignation of all Poor Law vigorists, actually being given pocket money.'[42]

By then, the transformation of British society from rural to urban was virtually complete, making the poor relief machinery plainly unsuited to the times, and adding to the fears of the bourgeoisie. By the 1870s, the rural-agricultural base of the economy had been effectively destroyed by industrial-commercial growth and 'commercial profit-making.'[43] The first-ever national Census of 1801 found that 35% of the total working population of 4.8 million was employed on the land; by 1901 total employment had grown threefold to 16.7 million, but the agricultural sector represented only 9% (and had fallen in real terms). Where, in 1851, around half the population lived in the towns, by 1891 the figure approached three quarters.[44]

By the time William Booth was writing *In Darkest England* and Julie Sutter was being captivated by Pastor Bodelschwingh's farm colony, therefore, it was evidence of mass poverty, crime,

---

42. Longmate, 2003, p.272.
43. H.W. Pfautz ed, 1967, p. 13.
44. *Vide* e.g. F.M.L. Thompson ed., *Cambridge Social History of Britain*, 1999 (Cambridge: CUP) p.133.

disease and destitution in London and other great cities, on their own doorsteps, that concerned politicians, journalists and philanthropists. A combination of economic, social and political factors enhanced their fears: the final decades of the 19th century saw prolonged agricultural depression; the violent upheavals in mainland Europe of 1848 and 1870, could, it was feared, be replicated in Britain;[45] British manufacturers laid off hands when faced with contracting markets and increasing competition from the USA and Germany, the latter growing in confidence after victories in the wars of 1866 and 1870; better communications, especially the cheap newspaper, quickened the spread of bad news; successive epidemics of cholera and pervading evidence of poor sanitation, including the 'Big Stink' of 1858 in London, also focussed attention on the unspecified but fearful miasmic dangers of the unwashed 'underclass.'

In the 1880s, working class areas of London saw what one left-wing commentator calls a 'dramatic transformation', with many traditional trades facing cyclical depression and secular decline in industries such as tanning, sugar processing and marine engineering, all leading to 'endemic conditions of under-employment'. Supplementing the colourful portrayals of Mayhew, Booth and other commentators, the report of the Royal Commission on Housing revealed that the 'chronically poor' composed 'a substantial proportion of working-class

---

45. The Westminster cleric Thomas Beames was ' . . much impressed with the French Revolution of 1848: the social condition of the poor had a great deal to do with it [though] I doubt if even St. Antoine could exhibit a Rookery like that of Church Lane, St. Giles' (Beames, *Rookeries of London*, 1850; Beames' book is today chiefly remembered as a source for Virginia Woolf's 'biography' of Elizabeth Barrett's dog, Flush, who was dognapped by villains from an East London 'rookery').

London' adding that the 'improvidence and thriftlessness' which so obsessed charity workers, 'were relatively venial sins.'[46]

Dramatic press reports of damage to property in London's West End during riots of 1886 and 1887 sharpened middle class concern, the mid-1880s seeing 'a major reorientation of middle-class attitudes towards the casual poor.' While the many existing charitable organisations, marshalled by the Charity Organisation Society (COS) remained 'obsessed by the demoralizing effects of indiscriminate charity [i.e. giving money to the undeserving poor] . . . the middle-class public was primarily concerned to avert what they conceived to be the imminent threat of an insurrection of the poor.' The time seemed ripe, therefore, for the adoption of new, interventionist, remedies, replacing the prevailing laissez faire attitude of mid-Victorian society, and coming as much from the right as from the left of the political spectrum: 'society should take active steps to disperse this [unemployable] class which would otherwise continue to increase and degenerate.'[47]

But if cash hand-outs could not solve the problem, few politicians wanted to go down the road of state-funded collectivism in the provision of farm colonies, despite the string of articles by heavy-weight commentators which appeared in the 1880s advocating public funding for such institutions.[48] One of these authors, Charles Booth, concluded

---

46. G Stedman Jones, *Outcast London*, 1971 (Oxford: Clarendon Press) p.282-283.
47. *Ibid*, p.296, 300, 303.
48. E.g. S. Barnett, 'A Scheme for the Unemployed' in *The Nineteenth Century Vol. 24*, 1888; A Marshall, 'The Housing of the London Poor', in *Contemporary Review*, Feb. 1884; C. Booth 'The Inhabitants of the Tower Hamlets School Board Division etc', in *Journal of Royal Statistical Society Vol. I*, 1887

unequivocally that the state must move the 'casual poor' out of London into labour colonies, where they would exchange their 'half-fed and half-idle and wholly unregulated life for a disciplined existence, with regular meals and fixed hours of work (which would not be short).'[49]

Leading politicians, including Chamberlain and Salisbury, expressed polite interest in the idea of 'public works' funded by local or central government. Apart from the small but vocal minority of Christian Socialists (see Appendix II), however, few national politicians spoke up in favor of farm colonies: 'Apart from the practical difficulties attending them . . . it is to be feared that they would lead to a widespread belief that it is the business of the government to provide work at suitable wages for all who apply to it for employment', concluded the Parliamentary Commission on Poor Relief in 1888.[50]

William Booth and the Salvation Army, the Rev. Tinling and the National Union for Christian Social Service, had the answer. Pastor Bodelschwingh's example showed clearly that the problem of the unemployed could be solved charitably, efficiently and economically by philanthropic institutions driven by common purpose and utilising military-style organisation and attention to detail:

---

49. quoted Stedman Jones, 1971, p.306-307.
50. *Some* money was spent, for example on road-building although at most 8% of the unemployed benefitted. A 1930s historian enthused that 'No less than 133 miles of streets were improved during . . 1863 and 1864 and one all-but-immortal monument to the relief works still remains in the granite setts or cobble stones with which so many of the cotton towns are [still] paved'. (G. Slater, *Poverty & the State*, 1930, Cambridge: CUP, p.363. Presumably the danger that cobbles might serve as missiles was discounted in favour of their cheapness.

'The problem that we have to face is the *regimentation, the organisation, of those who have not got work*, or who have only irregular work, and who from sheer pressure of absolute starvation are driven irresistibly into cut-throat competition with .. better employed brothers and sisters.'[51]

One final piece of the picture that might have filled the minds of those attending Tinling's inaugural meeting is the emergence of what is now conveniently called the 'social imperialist' position, which linked concern about poverty, unemployment, squalor and crime with the late Victorian push to imperial expansion and national security. Here, as always, economic and political strands intertwined: Germany's military successes and her growing political self-confidence cast a shadow over British world ambitions, as German manufactures threatened British factories and jobs. As memories of 1870, 1848 and 1789 gradually faded, fears that the mass of the unemployed – 'the residuum' – represented a revolutionary threat, were being overlaid by their portrayal as a dangerous source of weakness to the imperial race. By the 1890s 'The freedom of the casual labourer to live out his degenerate existence and reproduce his kind in filthy overcrowded slums was .. seen as a lethal menace to national efficiency'.[52]

Could *In Darkest England*'s third level, the overseas colony, perhaps kill two birds with one stone – getting the unemployed and the unemployable off the streets, and bolstering Britain's potential economic and military allies in the far-off Dominions? The role to be played by planned emigration, and its advocates within the NUCSS and elsewhere, will be more conveniently covered in the next chapter.

---

51. Booth, *In Darkest England*, 1970 ed, p.35, emphasis added.
52. Stedman Jones, 1971 p.330-331.

CHAPTER 2
Founding the 'Colonies'

> . . . *we bespeak practical interest first and chiefly on behalf of the unemployed. The land, our ultimate source of wealth, is largely uncultivated, and tens of thousands of decent men are sinking into degradation and despair for want of the opportunity and guidance needed to enable them to win a modest living from the land*
> - NUCSS fund-raising pamphlet, c.1895

It comes as no surprise to find that the first outcome of the meeting of 27 February 1894 was the formation of a sizeable Committee, composed of those who signed up to the concept of voluntary social service and labour colonies. A small governing Council was formed, of which Tinling was the first Secretary, Dr Meyer (another Congregationalist) initially the Chairman and W.R Galbraith the Treasurer; a high profile President was to be found later.

The name first proposed, 'Christian Union for Social Service', was then at various times lengthened ('National Union for Christian Social Service'), reversed ('Christian Social Service Union') and finally shortened ('Christian

Service Union'). In 1909 it was incorporated under the Companies Acts (primarily to make it easier to borrow on the security of its properties) with the formal title 'Incorporated National Union for Christian Social Service.' The handier form 'Christian Service Union' (CSU) came to enjoy the greatest usage over the years and when the organisation was re-incorporated as an Association not for profit under new legislation in 1948, this was the name registered. *A Brief History of the Christian Service Union* is the title of the only previous (privately published) history of the organisation to have been located; from now on, 'CSU' will generally be used to identify the institution in this book. Appendix II lists late 19th and early 20th century organisations with similar sounding names, some of which had parallel aims, some quite different ones; confusion between these bodies could be worse confounded by the habit of the press using 'Christian social service' as a generic term for any ecumenical attempt to influence social legislation or practice.

The enthusiasm shown by the audience at the inaugural meeting seems not to have struck an immediate chord with the wider non-conformist community: 'there was despondency,' writes the previous CSU historian.[1] After some months, an injection of fresh personnel at the top helped galvanise the movement. The first major recruit was the Rev. J.B. Paton, a Scot, principal of the Congregational [training] Institute in Nottingham, one of the originators of Nottingham University College, a pillar of the Free Church Union and active in the co-operative movement and other philanthropic fields.

---

1. D McClellan, *Brief History of the Christian Service Union*, typescript, undated, p.1.

'The idea of a *training* colony, as distinct from a mere *labour* colony' was Paton's, according to one of his biographers.[2] He certainly had ideas about the different categories of colony on the Continent which might be transplanted to Britain; some years later, in a pamphlet 'Unemployable and Unemployed', which he sent, in 1912, to John Burns, President of the Local Government Board, Paton listed what he saw as distinct classes of colony and 'colonist':

1. Colonies for epileptic and defective children and adults.
2. Colonies for .. youths who now potter away an idle and sordid existence in our workhouses.
3. .. the class of lads in our big cities .. *for whom I am more concerned than any other* .. who are .. engaged in many kinds of casual and irregular employment and are not trained to the habit and love of regular work.
4. The able-bodied men in our workhouses might be received in such colonies as . . . Poplar, and Hollesley [see Chapter 1, above].
5. Free Labour Colonies for men .. who are seeking work but cannot find it .. to have a place where they can find labour until an opportunity be given them.
6. .. *by far the most important kind of colony for England at the present time* [where] families are established on the land, and single men are also received either

---

2. J Marchant, *J B Paton, educational & social pioneer*, 1909 (London: James Clarke) p.162.

in a special home, or as lodgers with small holders in their cottages.[3]

But which of these did Paton really believe was the 'most important' category – the casually employed lads, or the unemployed men with an aptitude for agriculture?[4] In the end, it probably mattered little; the CSU's first major colony was to take in a mixture of idle lads from the big cities, older men - both 'unemployed' and 'unemployable', according to Paton's taxonomy - and also, as we shall see, epileptics. There is, however, plenty of evidence for Paton's keenness to focus the CSU's resources on agricultural *training*, and his ability to get things done. He successfully solicited support not only from the free churches, but among prominent Anglicans: Dr Percival, Bishop of Hereford was an early recruit to the revived CSU committee.

In later years Tinling seems to have felt that *his* role in getting the organisation on its way had been sidelined. In 1931, at the age of 90, he wrote to the editor of the CSU journal, emphasising that he and Meyer were the real founders. The editor replied, perhaps not as tactfully as he might, saying

---

3. L Paton, *John Brown Paton, a biography*, 1914 (London: Hodder & Stoughton) p.264, added emphasis.
4. Paton's final category was exemplified, not by Bielefeld but another German colony at Fredericksoord, where unemployed men who showed some aptitude for agricultural work were encouraged – and subsidised – to settle for a probationary period followed by more or less permanent tenure as small holders. This kind of scheme would be promoted by a retired army officer, Col. Henry Pilkington, and led to a few such 'colonies' for ex-servicemen during and immediately after WWI, during which legislation was passed in their favour, but did not in practice influence the development of the CSU or most other English colonies (see e.g. H Pilkington, *Land Settlement for Soldiers,* 1911, London: William Clowes; an introduction to the book emphasises the prospects for emigration among the ex-soldiers).

that while he always recognised Tinling's inaugural part, he thought that Paton had, 'at a critical moment, become the driving power.' And it was Paton's name, rather than Tinling's, which was to be perpetuated in bricks and mortar at the Wallingford colony

Paton, like many before him, preached and wrote against rural depopulation: 'One thing, more than any other, I believe, has driven the people from the land. It is the intolerable bovine dullness of the country – the lack of those interests and pleasures that are needed to refresh and inspire human life.'[5] Refreshingly unsentimental though it may be, Paton's belief had little basis in economic fact: rather than boredom, enclosure, the agricultural depression of the last quarter of the 19th century and employment opportunities in manufacturing industry were the causes of the drift away from the land (they had also lowered land prices for the Salvation Army and others setting up colonies). Nor, by then, was it true (as the CSU pamphlet quoted at the head of this chapter claimed) that land was the true source of Britain's wealth. But the idea that something more active was needed than just planting unemployables on pieces of land and hoping for the best, did make sense and continued to inform the operations of the CSU.

Touring the country, Paton's real job was to raise money. He asked Julie Sutter to join him in this work because, he wrote flatteringly, although in terms that might now be considered ambiguous if not politically incorrect, 'the power is given you to rouse men'. Her reply was a polite rebuff: she felt that she had played her part - 'You are roused; Mr Tinling

---

5. J Marchant, *Paton,* 1909, p.178.

Oxfordshire Colony

is roused; quite a number are roused; let me see a Colony of Mercy growing up here! I have given you a book showing the way; go and do likewise!'[6] Three years later, Tinling and Paton appear to have written again to Sutter asking if she would transfer the copyright in *Colonies of Mercy* to the CSU for the benefit of its work.

She replied (30 May 1898) declining, but suggesting that a separate edition might be produced, with the CSU under-writing production costs and taking any profit; she also suggested that the CSU might like to contribute towards bringing out a second book, presently 'shipwrecked' (i.e. unpublished); these suggestions do not seem to have been taken up.[7]

Paton and Tinling produced and distributed the pamphlet seeking financial support for the proposed training colony. Their covering letter dated February 1895, a year after the inaugural meeting, extols the 'Wonderful results that have followed Pastor Bodelschwingh's efforts [which] have truly startled Germany,' before explaining that 'We cannot expect the State [to help] until a Colony has been successfully founded' and concluding, optimistically, '. . . little expenditure is needed at the outset' and the colony would soon become self-supporting.

Reaction, however, was mixed. The writer of a letter, dated only 26 April (probably 1895) to the national council of the Charity Organisation Society (COS – see Appendix II) from one of its local branches, thought 'a small and well-managed Farm Colony might be distinctly useful for [some men] if they <u>could be induced</u> to stay long enough.' Less encouragingly, a

6   ibid, p. 160; L Paton, *John Brown Paton*, 1914, p.248.
7. OCRO, TCYT Archive Box. H02. Tinling & Paton's original letter is missing.

pencilled note (presumably written by the unknown addressee) on a typewritten letter signed by Tinling, Carlile and other CSU supporters, scoffs: 'Miss Julie Sutter has not a critical mind . . We have already got Genl. Booth's farms [etc] . . . Colonies only a way of treating vagrancy & unemployment anyway'; in other words, they treated only the symptoms, and were not an efficient way of getting men back into permanent work. An even blunter comment is found in a letter from Sir Charles Loch, Secretary of the St. Marylebone committee of the COS and author of a number of influential works on charitable donations: 'I have no hesitation in prophesying it will be as ridiculous a failure as all its predecessors.' Other responses noted that the German colonies were run with a degree of compulsion, implicit if not overt, which the CSU never sought.[8]

Lingfield: 'unemployables' and epileptics

To reach the founding of the Wallingford Colony it is necessary to take a substantial detour into Surrey, and briefer ones to Cumbria and Derbyshire, with at least a glance at events in Bradford and the small German town of Elberfeld (now part of Wuppertal).

The fund-raising letter of February 1895 claimed that a farm somewhere in Kent had been offered to the CSU. Nothing more is known of that site. Landowners might have had mixed feelings about a sale of this kind. British agriculture suffered sharply between 1870 and 1914 from overseas competition, land prices had fallen and many

---

8. London Metropolitan Archives (LMA) A/FWA/A/C/D254/1.

landlords would have been delighted to find a buyer. On the other hand, local sentiment was often fiercely antagonistic to the idea of unemployables camping on their doorsteps; back in the 1840s, the Royal Philanthropic Society, seeking a site for its Farm School, claimed to have been offered £1,000 by 'one lady' to keep away from the neighbourhood.[9] When 'General' Booth was known to be buying up over 1,200 acres (480 hectares) of farmland at Hadleigh in Essex, there was local outrage:

> 'Hadleigh village cried aloud that cut-throats and pickpockets would be let loose upon it, and all the villages and hamlets of the district echoed the cry and made indignant protests.'[10]

Bearing in mind the depressed state of agriculture at the time, this view is not necessarily contradicted by a Salvation Army historian's claim that 'no disinclination to sell was shown by the various landowners.'[11] At all events, there is no record of local opposition when, eventually, the CSU hit upon the 250 acre (c.100 hectare) St Piers Farm on the outskirts of Lingfield, Surrey, for its first colony. Despite Paton and Tinling's fund-raising activity, the purchase price of £3,300 was beyond the reach of the CSU; Paton persuaded three (unnamed) colleagues to join him in guaranteeing the money and the initial purchase, in March 1896, was made in Paton's name on the understanding that the property would

---

9. Anon, *A History of the Royal Philanthropic Society*, 1988, London.
10. M. Hancock, S. Harvey, *Hadleigh, an Essex Village*, 1986 (Chichester: Phillimore) p. 19.
11. Anon, *Hadleigh, the story of a great endeavour*, c.1902 (London: Salvation Army) p.11.

be transferred in trust to the CSU.[12] The Rev J.L. Brooks, one of Paton's former students at the Nottingham Institute, became the first Director of the Lingfield Colony, and an ex-journalist, William H. Hunt (who was to play a substantial role in the Wallingford colony's development) was 'House Father', with a number of 'House Brothers' to help him.

The CSU's original aim, to concentrate on training 'within a Christian framework' to help temporarily unemployed or poverty stricken men switch to agricultural employment and so regain their previous self-sufficiency and self-esteem, had quickly to be modified; 'the prevailing social conditions resulted in a change of emphasis', says Lingfield's official history.[13] Consultation with the (parish) Boards of Guardians – it might, perhaps, have been wiser if this had occurred earlier – revealed that what the Guardians wanted was somewhere, other than their own workhouses, where they could send so-called 'unemployables', men (no women at this stage) who had never received training of any kind, either because they were considered lacking in intelligence, or because they had some form of mental or physical defect. Since the CSU's financial planning was based on receiving per capita payments from the Boards of Guardians, it was agreed that Lingfield should focus on these 'unemployables' – 'the most deserving in society'.

The initial provision was for 50 'unemployables', of whom half had arrived by September 1897. The existing St

---

12. S Turner, *One Hundred Years of St Piers*, 1997, Lingfield, p.8. This guarantee may equate to the '£1,000 donation' which one biographer says Paton made at this time. (Marchant, *J B Paton*, 1909, p.160). This would have been a considerable sum for a non-conformist clergyman to find (at his death, Paton's estate was valued at around £9,000). The Paton family were also principals in a Liverpool cotton-broking firm.

13. Turner, *St Piers*, 1997, p.9.

Piers farmhouse was not large enough, and some temporary buildings had to be put up. Finance was a problem from the outset and would continue to dog the CSU throughout its lifetime. There were continual appeals for extra funds; in 1904, Julie Sutter handed over donations from her 'Britain's Next Campaign' (see below) to pay off a debt on Lingfield's water supply.[14] St Piers had been chosen because it was thought capable of self-sufficiency; the land could support a variety of crops, produce could easily reach the London markets, and there was some timber. The Boards of Guardians paid five shillings (25p) per week, later increased to 7s 6d (37p) for each man Unfortunately, Boards of Guardians lacked faith in Lingfield's training methods and did not send enough men for the farm to break even. Brooks and others had to tour the country to promote their work, drum up support, and identify men suitable for agricultural training.

It was during these tours that Brooks noted the substantial number of young people in workhouse infirmaries and asylum wards who appeared to be suffering from epileptic fits, co-existing with the old and insane and provided with no education or normal social life. At the same time a wealthy supporter, widow of the East Anglian agricultural machinery manufacturer and philanthropist Joseph Ruston, offered to provide money for a new building which would be used to house epileptic boys. On 18 July, 1898 *The Times* reported the laying of the foundation stone for the new sanatorium, together with the fact that the Lingfield farm had made a profit of £36 in the previous year; a year later the first epileptic <u>colonists arrived</u>. Three years later the Education Act 1902

14. The sum was variously described as £600 or £1,000: Turner, *St Piers*, 1997 p.15; L Paton, *John Brown Paton*, 1914, p.261..

placed a duty on local authorities to provide some degree of education for 'defective' children – including epileptics; Lingfield was certified as an educational establishment in 1905, meaning that children would be placed there by Local Education Authorities as well as the unreliable Boards of Guardians.

Whereas, in the early days, numbers of 'colonists' (that is, unemployed men) and epileptics were roughly equal, by 1905, when Princess Louise visited Lingfield, there were 110 epileptic children, only 60 farm trainees and the colony was generally perceived as a special educational establishment. The London County Council, from whose territory many of the epileptic children now came, asked the CSU if they would extend this side of the work by setting up a new facility to deal with cases of infantile phthisis, and although this was not followed up, the concentration on epileptics accelerated; by 1911 Lingfield was caring for 200 epileptics and 100 'unemployables' and the opening of a new building for children over school age was the highlight of that year's summer festival.[15]

The work of the 'Brothers' with unemployed 'colonists' became quite distinct from caring for the epileptic children, and the latter continued to dominate in terms both of numbers and of the building programme. W.H. Hunt was given responsibility for the now minor role of farm training with the colonists; although overall numbers were always small, the reported success rate sounds reasonable: between

---

15. *The Times*, 11 May 1911.

1903 – 1909, of just over 400 men leaving Lingfield, rather more than 50% immediately found employment.[16]

The Farm Colonies Forward Movement

By the end of the decade it was clear that so far as boards of guardians were concerned, Lingfield's role as an educational and care establishment for epileptic children completely overshadowed its potential for helping the unemployed back into work. To redress the balance, the CSU entered a second phase with the launch of the *Farm Colonies Forward Movement*. A Farm Colonies Committee with W.H. Hunt as Secretary was charged with identifying a site and raising funds so that the work of agricultural training could be moved from Lingfield. An existing 'brand name' seems to have been appropriated: since the 1880s there had been a 'Forward Movement', a largely Methodist body of 'social progressivism',[17] inspired by Andrew Mearns' pamphlet *The Bitter Cry of Outcast London* (1883). However, where the Victorian 'Movement' had political ambitions, the 20th century CSU committee was in the business of fund-raising rather than political agitation.

Apart from the speaking and letter writing activities of Paton and others a key component of the new Forward Movement was repetitive advertising and editorial in the institution's journal, *Social Service*. Originally launched as *Christian Social Service* in January 1902, it shortened its title and appeared

16. Turner, *St Piers*, 1997, p.20, quoting from *Social Service* various dates. Of those who did not get jobs, the largest proportion were shown as 'dismissed', i.e. the Colony had given up on them.
17. see e.g. E Norman, *Victorian Christian Socialists*, 1987 (Cambridge: CUP) p.146.

regularly until the 1950s. Surviving issues provide a useful source of information about the development of the CSU's Colonies. The first editorial, signed 'J.F.B.T[inling]' envisages a wider constituency than the CSU itself: 'We derive our impulse to this undertaking [the journal] from The Christian Union for Social Service. But we desire also to serve older and newer causes which have proved, however obscurely, their divine significance and energy.'

By 1910, W.H. Hunt had taken over as editor and the journal carried a running tag line – 'To act as a means of communication between all those engaged in Social Service and to interest a growing number of people in Social Work.' An early issue contained, as well as CSU's own news, an article (by Hunt) on 'Co-operation, its weaknesses and its strengths' and others on model villages such as 'Bourneville' [sic] and Port Sunlight, London 'settlements', housing problems and the continuing curse of urban drunkenness, to counter which the anonymous author suggested that 'Teetotal Public Houses' with names like 'The Blue Woman' or 'The Green Man' might be set up. Over the years the journal regularly reprinted articles on social issues from the national press and other media.

Apart from Lingfield, the Wallingford Colony was preceded by other CSU-run colonies at Marple Dale, already briefly mentioned (see Chapter 1, above) and Starnthwaite near Kendal in Westmorland. The early history of Starnthwaite is obscure[18] but its prehistory may have included a 'co-operative agricultural village' set up by Herbert V. Mills around 1892. When, around 1901, Mills fell out with other members of

---

18. Its foundation does not figure in the McClellan history of the CSU. I am indebted to Kendal Record Office for further information.

the co-op, A.W. Simpson, a Quaker from Kendal, took over with the aim of running a training colony for workhouse men (ex-servicemen from the South African war one sizeable constituency) and epileptics. By 1905 the CSU was listed in local directories as the controlling body of the training colony (aim: 'to save youths and men from the listless apathy produced by workhouse life') but five years later it had become, as was the case at Lingfield, purely a home for epileptic boys. In the 1930s, the Board of Education decided that it was too small to be educationally effective and it took on the role of Approved School under Home Office supervision.

Marple Dale was always purely a training establishment for the unemployed, and with similar numbers to Starnthwaite - around 25 men each. It had, however, attracted 'colonists' from Boards of Guardians as far away as London and the CSU thought its design could be scaled up to a much larger colony to complement Lingfield. A series of articles in *Social Service*, between December 1908 and October 1911, unsigned but almost certainly the work of Hunt, described, not always quite consistently, the ideal facilities for this new venture. An early article considered that good agricultural land was not necessary: better to go for 'derelict land for the derelict man.' The model here may well be Hadleigh where, in 1891, only part of the 1,236 acres (494 hectares) acquired by Booth, was under cultivation. Much of the rest was the poor terrain nicknamed by the locals (see Chapter 1) 'the Bad Lands'; a Salvation Army publication would later boast that 'Had it achieved nothing else, The Army deserves credit for keeping in cultivation land which otherwise would have become valueless.'[19]

On the other hand, an article in the first issue of *Social Service* (January 1902) had commended the 'fertile and well cultivated' land bought for the German colony at Ware (also featured in Chapter 1), where no expense seemed to be spared:

> '. . the criticism launched against the German Colony is that the capital invested is so considerable that to pay interest on it would be to do away with any prospect of making [it] a paying concern. . . [but] such an institution cannot be expected to be a money-making concern . . if the philanthropic public is willing to give money so that land, buildings and stock may be of the best, it is wise to make them such.'

The small numbers at Lingfield, Starnthwaite and Marple Dale were now seen to be uneconomic; the new colony was initially planned to house 100 men, living in two residential blocks of 50 and divided into 'classes' - 'willing and able', 'willing but unable', 'able but unwilling'. Alternatively, new arrivals might be sorted by physical strength and/or degree of 'blamelessness' (for the lack of employment): the obsessive fear of using scarce resources only on the 'deserving' poor, which had informed Victorian philanthropy, continued to inform the CSU's planning.

Simplistic or patronising as these taxonomies may now sound, Hunt's basic assumption, that different men needed different treatment, was not unreasonable, and certainly less hide-bound than the rigid and unimaginative regime of the

19. Anon, *Hadleigh great endeavour*, 1902, p.12.

workhouse. Further, the CSU now accepted that farm colonies were essentially for men who had never had a proper job, for whatever reason, rather than for seasonally or cyclically unemployed labourers. It was admitted that originally (that is, in 1894/5) 'the main idea' had been to find remunerative work for the temporarily unemployed, whereas it was now realised that 'a developed farm is no place for [them] in winter, when all agricultural work is slack'; a CSU Colony should be 'a training ground for the unemployable.'

By 1911 the ideal number of colonists had crept forward to 150 men. The Forward Movement drew up its plans up on the assumption that, once established, the colony should be self-sustaining (with the receipt of fees from Boards of Guardians). A visit to Bielefeld by members of the Forward Movement in Autumn 1909 found von Bodelschwingh terminally ill ('the end is not far distant', the committee was told: he died on 9 April, 1910) but the committee were somewhat cheered not only by the cleanliness and efficiency of the colony's workshops, but the assurance they were given that it was financially self-sufficient.

Acreage was now seen as the key factor: the new farm had to be large enough for men to be taught marketable skills - milking, stable work, ploughing and the care of live stock – for which Lingfield had no room. Market gardening might have some value 'because there are times when men can be so employed in large numbers when otherwise they would be idle', but in general fruit-culture and 'fancy farming' were judged to have no practical value to the men who had neither the time nor the ability to get the best out of such occupations. A farm of 500 to 600 acres (200 to 240 hectares) would give scope for a herd of 20 to 30 cows, a flock of sheep and ten or a dozen horses.

Hunt and his committee generally (but not invariably) ruled out the Home Counties because of high land prices: CSU finances were already stretched, and another bargain like Lingfield seemed unlikely. The CSU did not think it could match the generous resources seemingly commanded by the German management at Ware. Many of the farms inspected were felt to be too small – 150 to 250 acres (50-100 hectares) – with few buildings to house the incoming 'colonists'. Some cheap farms 'which look all right on paper' proved only to have grazing land, with no arable. Large cheap farms in counties such as Wiltshire or Shropshire were available, but too remote from London whence many of the 'colonists' were expected to come, and which would be the main market for agricultural and horticultural products.

The final, apparently crucial, factor considered by the Committee in selecting a site was distance from existing settlements, *Social Service* (1911) commenting that, 'Where size, price and locality are fairly right, position is an absolute bar. It is impossible to establish a Colony on a farm which is in close proximity to a village.' In writing thus, the writer – yet again, almost certainly Hunt – was thinking not only of local opposition to Hadleigh and other colonies, but at least as important, distance from public houses which were thought to offer irresistible temptation to the colonists.

The continued enthusiasm in the pages of *Social Service* and other CSU papers makes it sound as though the idea of a dedicated farm training colony, larger than Lingfield, better run than Laindon or Hollesley Bay, enjoyed wide public support. In fact there was still widespread opposition to the whole idea. Hunt's optimism that colonies might enjoy goodwill within Government seems modestly supported from other sources: the *Daily Telegraph*, for example, (18 July 1899) wrote that Lingfield had the support of the Local Government Board (LGB), and indeed a letter from LGB officials to Lingfield in December that year recognised that the Colony 'provides men with wholesome work.'[20]

Later reforms, including the establishment of Labour Exchanges and provision for funding of 'Farm Institutes' for educational work, via the new Development Commission, seemed hopeful examples of a radical change which might indeed include government money for the CSU's new colony. But there is no evidence that John Burns, President of the LGB, had changed his mind since *Social Service* (April 1907) reported his strong opposition to colonies, which he regarded as costly and ineffective; their trained 'colonists', he thought, merely diluted the existing pool of agricultural labour: 'The agricultural labourer, deprived of his livelihood, was demoralised by knowing that men were receiving the equivalent of more than double his old pay for doing work that was practically valueless.' Taking a sombre view of the electorate, Burns thought that the two principal causes of poverty were drunkenness and betting, and that 'All attempts at social reform were hopeless unless the workers co-operated with the authorities.'

In 1899, a round robin from COS central office to local committees, asking for their opinion of the NUCSS, revealed mixed reports from the Boards of Guardians who had sent

20. LMA, A/FWA/C/D254/1.

unemployed men to Lingfield: some had emigrated, some merely absconded. 'The accommodation and arrangements for epileptic children appear to be excellent..' but 'rough wooden huts' for the men were considered inferior to workhouse accommodation. A longer (manuscript) COS report that same year doubted if the Lingfield farm could ever be a financial success. More anecdotally, a private letter, seemingly from a privately financed 'colonist' whose family may have been paying for him to stay at Lingfield, complains bitterly at the harshness of the farm training regime which, among other things, was ruining his handwriting: 'This is another Scheme [sic] under the philanthropic guise of making money.'

By 1903, the COS view was that 'Some of the ideas of the founders of the [Lingfield] Colony may perhaps appear to be visionary . . [but] . . the unsatisfactory part is that we can get no clear statement of results . . [although] in some cases the system may be very good' and the next year another MS draft concludes that Lingfield provided generally good conditions for its colonists, but with poor financial results because, although it was good agricultural land, the men sent there were '. . . morally and physically deficient and generally incapable of any hard continuous labour. They represent a class that has proved a constant difficulty in all systems of employment relief,' without suggesting anything much by way of remedy for this state of affairs.[21]

Contemporary press reports suggest continued strong political opposition to colonies on the grounds that the taxpayer or ratepayer should not subsidise the unemployed trainee to compete unfairly with the resident agricultural

---

21. ibid

labourer who had saved enough to buy or rent his own smallholding. In 1909, as the Forward Movement committee was sifting through possible sites, the CSU's own enquiry of those already running farm colonies seems to indicate that, contrary to what they had been told at Bielefeld, organisers never expected to be able to run them without subsidy of some sort because of the cost of training staff (the CSU hoped to cut costs by the use of volunteer 'Brothers'), the low physical and educational level of most new recruits and the frequent turnover of inmates. Most existing colonies, however, were optimistic enough to think that the typical colony trainee, when he left, would be able to support himself on his own small holding: how the capital was to be raised to buy that small holding was not clear.

Even Julie Sutter, who has thus far appeared only as the prophet of the farm colony, had other priorities. Her first book, *Colony of Mercy*, which had high-lighted the German colonies, also praised the efficiency of other social policies in that country, notably the system of 'local work stations' for unemployed vagrants, where they could stay for just one night, do some work, usually wood chopping (providing much of the fuel for German homes) in return for meals and a bed. Each vagrant carried a pass-book which had to be stamped at each station in the precise order laid down in an itinerary for that man.[22] Small wonder that the apparent orderliness of this system compared with the randomness of the English poor law, with its casual wards of distinctly variable quality, had caught Sutter's eye.

---

22. J. Sutter, *Colony of Mercy*, 1893, (London: Hodder & Stoughton) p.178.

Sutter's later books,[23] published in the first decade of the 20th century, much of whose content originally appeared in the (Liberal) *Daily News*, particularly commended the German 'Elberfeld' system, where provision of relief to those in need was based on close and continuous personal supervision of each applicant by a local unpaid worker, who was legally bound to offer these services, under the supervision of the local authority. With hindsight, the successful transfer of such a private/public partnership to Britain at that time sounds far-fetched: one recent commentator, indeed, thinks it would have been impossible 'until British voluntary workers were better trained . . . given the well developed nature of British local administration compared to Germany.'[24]

Sutter was not the first to be taken with the neatness of the Elberfeld system, combining voluntary enthusiasm with municipal organisation, and it inspired at least some temporary imitators in Britain. *The Elberfeld System and German Workman's Colonies* by Charles Loch (who has already been quoted as a sceptical commentator on the CSU's plans) was published in 1888, but the first major move towards adapting such a system to English conditions seems to have come from a meeting chaired by the Mayor of Bradford in September 1904 which gathered together 'all the community who have a desire and more or less capacity for social services'. The meeting led directly to the launch of a Bradford *Guild of Help*, designed to coordinate charitable provision in that town.

---

23. *Britain's Next Campaign*, 1901; *Britain's Hope*, 1907.
24. J.Lewis, *The Voluntary Sector, the State & Social Work in Britain*, 1995 (Aldershot: Elgar) p.51,73.

Over the next decade Guilds sprang up, predominantly but not exclusively in the North of England (there were also several in London), with over 80 in existence by 1916, some operating under other names such as Guild of Social Services, Civic Aid Society. A Guild would organise a rota of 'Helpers' to visit and keep a logbook on each poverty-stricken family, assess its needs and provide a link to an appropriate charity. The Guilds also acted as clearing houses to avoid or reduce overlapping charitable work and root out 'scroungers and beggars.' The National Association of Guilds of Help held annual conferences and lobbied central Government on a range of social issues and published a journal, confusingly also entitled 'Social Service' (some individual Guilds had journals of their own).

The Guilds are said to have come into their own during the First World War, when they were described as 'handmaiden of the War Pensions Committee', although their German origins, along with the Teutonic efficiency so admired by Sutter, had to be played down.[25] They were dominated by the middle class, never commanding any significant working-class support. Sutter, while admiring voluntary effort, believed that, as in Germany, the movement would eventually have to be operated from the town hall: Liberals and Conservatives naturally suspected any such tinge of municipal socialism, while actual socialists – such as the SDF – attacked the

---

25. In 1915, a speaker at a meeting of the Croydon Guild admitted that the Guilds 'owed much to the Elberfeld system, which had at the back of its mind some of the impersonal cast-iron ideas that had made the Prussian army. But the effects of Guild thoroughness in the light of the present knowledge made him suspect the system of mechanical tidiness . . . and exclaim "Liberty with all thy faults I love thee still.' (K Laybourn, *The Guild of Help & the Changing Face of Edwardian Philanthropy*, 1994 (Lampeter: Edwin Mellen) p. 146)

'Gilded Help' basis of charity. Overall, while 'making a modest impact on public health and environment conditions', the Guilds are now judged to have played no significant role in combating unemployment,[26] and the Guild movement is perhaps better remembered as a precursor of the post-WWI National Council of Social Service (NCSS) now National Council for Voluntary Organisations, NCVO).

Turners Court

Fund-raising continued to be a struggle, but despite public doubts about the likely efficacy of colonies, by 1910 around £3,000 had been donated in response to appeals in *Social Service* and elsewhere for a capital sum of £5,000 (later increased to £15,000, then £20,000) with Paton's two sons, the Quaker chocolatiers the Cadbury brothers and the Earl of Meath (since the early 20th century President of the CSU) among cited donors. The next year a suitable farm was found. This was the estate known as Turners Court, in Oxfordshire, about three miles from the village of Benson, and rather less, across the Thames, from the town of Wallingford from which the new Colony would take its name. The property of *Tourneureslondes* has been identified as early as 1316. Thomas Chaucer, Constable of Wallingford and Steward of the royal manor of Benson (or Bensington) held it from Henry IV; it passed to Chaucer's heiress, Alice Duchess of Suffolk but was later forfeited to the Crown and leased to tenant farmers. Charles I, perennially short of cash, sold the manor to City of London speculators and over the next three centuries

---

26. Laybourn, *The Guild of Help etc*, 1994 p. 6, 65.

landlords and tenants changed frequently. The last private owner, who died in 1907, was a William Purves.[27]

The estate had been on the market since 1910; a map produced by the Wallingford agents Franklin and Gode, shows its boundaries as measuring nearly two miles long, by three-quarters of a mile wide, either side of the road from Wallingford to Nettlebed, with the main farm buildings in the NW corner of the site. At 515 acres (208 hectares) Turners Court was twice the size of Lingfield – large enough to support training for 200 or 300 men, was an initial CSU estimate, later reduced to 120. It offered 100 acres of pasture, around 90 acres of woodland, with the remainder mainly arable. The price of the land, £5,925, represented around £11.50 per acre, compared with the £13/acre paid for the smaller Lingfield property, and rather more than the £9.7/acre which the Salvation Army had given in 1891 for the 1,200 acres of Hadleigh, including the supposedly worthless 'Bad Lands'. The total cost of the purchase, however, including stock, equipment and, crucially, a number of existing buildings – seven cottages, three sets of farm buildings and a substantial farm house – amounted to £8,675, much of which had to be borrowed; in October 1911 *Social Service* envisaged the need to raise upwards of £20,000, to cover not only the purchase but an estimated £9,000 towards new buildings.

A CSU publicity leaflet, published a year or so after the purchase, describes the site as having light fertile soil, suitable for the sort of varied farm training the CSU planned – 'hay, corn, roots, potatoes, cattle and sheep farming, with a fair amount of horse labour.' The site was described as 'a breezy

---

27. E.M.R. Ditmas, *A History of Benson*, 1983 (Wallingford: private) p.147.

Founding the "Colonies"

down ... offering a bracing atmosphere to men who greatly need to be invigorated', free of fog when the Thames Valley was fog-bound, 'the soil porous and workable in all seasons.' It is indeed a steep pull – 'half an hour's sharp walk' - from the riverside villages of Newnham Murren and Crowmarsh, the nearest small settlements, and the upward sweep of the land from the Thames certainly ensures plentiful fresh air from the prevailing south-westerly winds. There is, however, some suspicion that not everyone rated the area so highly in terms of agricultural value: the adjacent Mays Farm, which was later added to the original 'Colony', had already been on the market in 1906 when it was advertised in the local press as 'a most beautiful site for a Garden City.'[28]

Although further from London than Lingfield, Turners Court offered reasonable access to the capital, and to the less important but sizeable market of Reading. A description in *Social Service* commends Turners Court for being two miles from the nearest inn (at that time there were at least four at roughly that distance, in Crowmarsh, one of which, 'The Bell', was flourishing enough to have been bought by the brewers, Morlands, in 1910); the same writer then oddly gives Wallingford town and station as being also 'only' two miles away: in actuality the railway was the best part of a mile beyond Crowmarsh, as the 1916 COs and many other visitors would in due course discover. Just as oddly, the 1998 history of Turners Court, while getting the distance from Wallingford station about right, at 2.5 miles, thought that in 1911 there was no public house within 6 miles of the Colony, managing to ignore not only those in Crowmarsh, North Stoke and (in

28. K. Tiller ed, *Benson, a village through its history*, 1999 (Cholsey: Pie Powder Press)

57

the opposite direction) Nuffield, but the considerable number of inns and hotels in Wallingford itself.[29]

By contrast with the Salvation Army's experience at Hadleigh, neither CSU records nor the local press reveal local opposition to the charity's purchase of Turners Court. The choice of a site some miles from other settlements may have paid off. Perhaps, too, the CSU benefited from the fact that at least two people closely associated with the Wallingford Colony were themselves journalists, able to deal with the media. First of these was William H. Hunt, who, as we have seen, was manager of the non-epileptic programme at Lingfield when he was chosen to be Wallingford's first Superintendent. Born in Stratford on Avon and educated at that town's British Elementary School (not the Grammar School which produced William Shakespeare) he started work in a printing office at Stamford, becoming editor of, first, the *Stamford and Rutland News* and then local newspapers in, successively, the Isle of Wight and Brighton. Developing an interest in social policy, he worked at a Bermondsey 'settlement' before joining the CSU at Lingfield. He brought with him to Wallingford his role as editor of *Social Service* in whose pages his sermonic style prevails up to the time of his death in 1934.

The incorporation of the CSU in 1909 retained the large (and largely quiescent) Council including churchmen, politicians and donors, but the management of the organisation and its colonies now fell to a London (or 'Executive') committee of around 20 members which met about once a month, plus separate management committees for Lingfield, Starnthwaite

---

29. R.P. Menday, *History of Turners Court*, 1998 (Privately published) p. 9. In its heyday Wallingford is said to have boasted 13 churches, with 2 pubs for each church.

and Wallingford (replacing short-lived 'Northern' and 'Southern' committees). Duncan Basden[30] who had trained first as a farmer, then estate agent and finally a City accountant, and had joined the CSU in its early days, served at varying times as chairman of the London and Lingfield committees and – between 1911-1936 – that for Wallingford/Turners Court. Other long-serving committee members included Congregationalists like Tinling, and Quakers like George Cadbury and Edward Sturge.

After the purchase, farming continued at Turners Court under CSU management. At the end of 1911, eight labourers were looking after the animal stock, including 89 breeding ewes, together with a substantial market garden. The first 25 'colonists' – adult unemployed – with two Brothers, arrived from Lingfield in April 1912, travelling by train to Wallingford and then taking the invigorating walk up the hill from Crowmarsh, and were housed initially in a barn. That summer the Lingfield Boy Scout troop, 24 strong, also visited Turners Court for their annual camp, walking not only the 13 miles from Lingfield to Redhill station, but also the 14 miles from Reading to the Colony.[31]

Temporary wooden buildings were brought in during 1912, and plans drawn up for permanent buildings to house up to 140 colonists, which would provide 'all the necessities for a village' – water supply, sewage plant, shop and so on – and form 'a group of dwellings that could be the envy of social reformers.' The £20,000 fund was intended to cover

30. 1855-1944: three generations of Basdens would serve the CSU, Duncan's grandson, B.E.Basden, helping facilitate the writing of this book. The CSU's 1909 Articles of Association also list Mr. J.M. Sladen and Colonel Sydney St.B. Sladen as members of the Council but sadly neither has yet been traced.
31. Menday, *Turners Court*, 1998, p.8.

the first two accommodation blocks and an administrative building; as donations never approached that sum it was fortunate that the costs were in the event around £11,000. The architect chosen was T. Phillips Figgis[32], a Dublin-born London practitioner who had already worked for the CSU at Lingfield (Duncan Basden's wife, Hope, was Figgis's sister). The builders were Brasher and Sons of Wallingford. Subsequent accommodation blocks followed much the same rectangular floor plan, with three storeys, a pitched roof, brick walls with pale cement rendering over the upper storeys. Each block contained day rooms, dormitories, wash rooms and some staff accommodation. A central administrative block followed, with a dining hall, kitchen, boiler house, and laundry. An electricity generation plant was operating by December 1912 – at a time when few Wallingford houses enjoyed such a novelty. Initially, the dining hall also served as place of worship, and was the only space available for any major social activity.

R.P.Menday, Turners Court's 1998 historian, wrote that the architect had been 'most imaginative in his choice of site . . . with magnificent views of . . . the farmland, the beech hills and in summer rolling golden acres,' while the buildings

---

32. 1858-1948. Born Dublin, trained there and London. Practising in Lincoln's Inn 1886 onwards, often working with others, although not in formal partnership. Apart from CSU colonies his work included London churches, houses in the home counties, Radium Institute (Riding House Street), Coopers Company School at Bow, 13 stations on the London Underground and a 'Highly original' design for the Free Public Library, Ladbroke Grove: 'Economies in the execution and the subsequent depredation of air bombardment on materials of poor quality have left a building in which the published . . . design is scarcely recognisable.' (A.S. Gray, *Edwardian Architecture*, 1985, London: Duckworth, p. 180). Figgis was also said to have possessed 'a delightful baritone voice' and to have been 'a grand old man with all the warm-hearted characteristic of his race' (obituary, *RIBA Journal* May 1948).

themselves were 'architecturally far ahead of their time.' One sympathetic visitor wrote that the two accommodation blocks were 'far from barrack like in appearance'; to a lay observer, however, pictures of the Turners Court blocks (now all demolished) call to mind many university and municipal administrative buildings built in that era around Oxford, not least the remnant of the former Military College in Cowley (now private residences). The approach to Turners Court, however, certainly never had the distinctly 'guard room' look shown in photographs of the main gate to the Salvation Army colony at Hadleigh.[33]

The CSU's financial situation would remain a perennial concern. Hunt's ability to raise the capital sums needed to establish the Wallingford colony and keep it growing looks to have been less developed than his way with words (an obituarist paid tribute to Hunt's persuasive powers when speaking up in the magistrates' courts for colonists who had run into trouble with the police).[34] 'Overall the cash flow situation was not easy', writes Menday; after the initial construction work in 1912 the CSU's debts amounted to around £11,000, including £500 borrowed to build a granary for the first harvest at Turners Court.[35] By September 1912, all the remaining eligible (i.e. non-epileptic) colonists had been transferred from Lingfield and in October there were 80 men and youths in training, towards the projected total of 140. A Harvest Home Supper

---

33. Menday 1998, p. 9; *Social Service*, Dec. 1912; 60 years on, the Colony went unremarked by Pevsner, who did devote 5 lines to the 'Tudor irregular' house at Huntercombe Place – 'now a Borstal' – just up the road (Sherwood & Pevsner, *Buildings of Oxfordshire*, 1974).
34. *Oxford Times*, 2 March 1934.
35. Menday, *Turners Court*, 1998, p10-13.

was held on 30 October; the local press, no doubt briefed by Hunt, 'were generous in their notices about it.'[36]

Nine months later, on 14 July 1913, a grand opening ceremony was attended by the Lord Mayor of London (Sir David Burnett) supported by his sheriffs and the mayors of Abingdon, Oxford, Reading and Wallingford plus CSU Council members and other supporters. After the singing of the hymn 'All people that on earth do dwell' there was an address by Duncan Basden before the architect, Figgis, presented a gold key to the Lord Mayor; the latter then unveiled a tablet at the entrance to the first accommodation block, recording the contribution of £2,100 by the family of J.B. Paton, who had died in 1911 and whose name the block now carried, and declared the Wallingford Farm Training Colony officially open. The second block, also virtually complete, was left unnamed (it was sometimes referred to as 'Z Home') in the stated hope that a wealthy benefactor would come forward to match Paton's legacy, in return for having his – or her - name perpetuated on the building. The programme helpfully noted that after the dedicatory prayer, the Lord Mayor would accept 'gifts and promises' towards clearing the Colony's debts, and during the singing of another hymn, Brothers would be making a collection. Around 400 people were served tea ('entirely catered for by the ladies on the Colony') on the lawn, and the train back to London left Wallingford station at 7 p.m.

Again, local press dealt kindly, not to say fulsomely, with the day. The *Oxford Journal Illustrated* published a whole page of photographs. *The Oxford Times* and *The Oxford Chronicle*

---

36. ibid.

(18 July) both described in some detail not only the day's events but the history of the CSU and the Colony's new buildings. There was briefer coverage further afield, including, bizarrely, a note apparently spotted in the *Budapest Birlap*. Hunt, writing in *Social Service* (August 1913) did report one (unidentified) journal which unkindly described the colonists as 'a company of abandoned wastrels', an even less kind description than 'unemployables.'

Among the information which it seems Hunt had fed to the press beforehand, were some statistics about the colonists. Out of 107 colonists in residence at the beginning of 1913, 48 had been 'put up for emigration', following a visit by the Canadian Emigration Commissioner, Malcolm Jones, and a Mr Surties of the Self-help Emigration Society. On 24 May 1911, just over two years before the Colony's official opening, *The Times* had printed a special report on the benefits of emigration to the Empire, mentioning the recent migration of 80 men from the Salvation Army colony at Hadleigh and smaller numbers sponsored by the Church Army and the NUCSS – the latter, of course, then operating at Lingfield and Starnthwaite. 'The success of these men in "making good" under the severer test of Canadian life,' the report ran, 'shows what excellent colonizing material is going to waste in the mass of the apparently unemployable.'

These sentiments, and the fact that they were so aptly publicised on Empire Day, must have given particular pleasure to one of one of the more colourful CSU figures, its President the Earl of Meath, who was, however, not present at the official opening. The history of emigration to the Dominions, one of several causes vociferously championed by Meath, how the Wallingford Colony contributed to such migration, and how the Colony developed during the first decades of its existence, are dealt with in the next Chapter.

CHAPTER 3
Colony Life, 1912-1933: the 'Hunt Era'

. . . the concept of a universal union of the far-flung British peoples, held together by sentiment, mutual economic interest, imperial defence strategy, and national pride – Eric Richards, 'Britannia's Children', 2004

[Turners Court] dwellings . . . should be ere long the envy of social reformers in many parts of the country - 'Social Service', December, 1912

Reginald Brabazon, 12th Earl of Meath, had been President of the CSU's Council, and a useful 'name' on the organisation's literature, since the late 1890s. As a young man he served in the British diplomatic service, including a term at the embassy in Paris, where he and his wife arrived in October 1870 to find the fires of the Commune still smoking. A few years later, however, he resigned when offered the post of second secretary to the 'remote' outpost of Athens. He and his wife then divided their time between the family's Irish estates (he inherited the title in 1887) and 'the consideration of social problems and the relief of human suffering.' By 1894, Brabazon was already serving on such bodies as the Hospital Saturday Fund, the Dublin Hospital Sunday movement and the Young Men's Friendly Society (later the Church of England Men's Society).

In 1881 he had founded the Brabazon Employment Society, aimed at finding jobs for those who 'from age or ill-health are forced to pass the weary hours in . . . workhouses and infirmary wards'; four years later Lady Brabazon in turn founded the Ministering Children's League, whose members pledged to do at least one kind deed every day. In 1890 Brabazon visited and was impressed by von Bodelschwingh's colony at Bielefeld, which he later described in an article for the *19th Century Review*. The Brabazons together then founded a residence for epileptic women and girls at Godalming, Surrey, and came into contact with the CSU at Lingfield.

A passionate imperialist, Brabazon was a founder of the Empire Day Movement, writing, in 1896, to *The Times*, 'Let the anniversary of the accession of the Queen be made a universal school holiday, the scholars meeting in the morning at the school house to sing the National Anthem and to salute the flag' (the campaign enjoyed some success: by 1923, more than 70,000 schools throughout the Empire reported they were celebrating Empire Day). Brabazon also supported Lord Roberts' campaign for national military service, founding the Lads' Drill Association (later the National Service League) and chairing the Duty and Discipline Movement (aim: 'to combat softness and indiscipline'). He also headed the Legion of Frontiersmen, a more militaristic body than the Boy Scouts, which aimed to provide reconnaissance scouts in war.

Brabazon was an Alderman of the newly created London County Council (LCC) and chairman of its parks committee, arguing vigorously in print and at meetings for more playgrounds and open spaces in the capital. Writing in the *New Review*, in 1894, he argued that the LCC should turn parts of the Thames Embankment into 'a sort of London Champs Elyssées, with alfresco theatres, cafés and restaurants' while fast steam-launches 'would flash over the surface of the waters bearing . . . passengers . . . to water-side concerts and illuminated gardens.' Always a staunch Conservative and Unionist, it would be easy to caricature the Earl as a Blimpish figure[1], but his vision of urban development sounds far from unimaginative.

'Lads for the Empire'

Brabazon's memoirs and other writings fail to mention his role as CSU President (perhaps not surprising in view of the number of other societies and movements he supported). Apart from their shared concern for the welfare of epileptics, however, it would have been the CSU's intention to train colonists for emigration to the Dominions that caught his fancy. He was already both chairman and president of the National Association for Promoting State-Directed Colonization, founded in 1884. He was always ready to, as it were, stick his neck out in support of emigration as a cure for unemployment: at a meeting in Clerkenwell, in January 1887 under the hostile auspices of the Social Democratic Federation (SDF) Brabazon was interrupted by a man shouting 'I should like to cut off your head,' replying that if they could prove to him that cutting off his head would save the starving poor, he was quite willing that it should be cut off.[2]

Mass emigration from England, Wales, Scotland and especially Ireland was no novelty in the 1890s. Shiploads of

---

1. A review in *The Times* (23 Sep 1924) of Meath's second volume of memoirs rather oddly praises him on the grounds that 'There is no corner of his work in which the weed of "jingoism" can grow.'
2. R. Brabazon, *Memories of the 19th Century*, 1923 (London: John Murray) p.222, 337, 232-4. Brabazon's work for the LCC is commemorated by *Brabazon Street* in Poplar, and *Meath Gardens*, Bethnal Green.

emigrants had set sail for North America since the 16th century. By the 19th century, the Antipodes and the Cape were favoured destinations and the number of what we would now term economic migrants was increasing rapidly. In 1826 the House of Commons Select Committee on Emigration concluded that many places in Great Britain (but more especially in Ireland) had 'redundancy' of population; emigration was therefore to be encouraged, although, naturally, without any public expenditure. A Colonization Society was founded as early as 1830, and ten years later the Durham report on the future government of Canada emphasised the need for better facilities for emigrants; its authors urged the government to sell colonial land at attractive prices, 'groping', says a popular history, 'towards a policy of liberal imperialism.'[3]

One study estimates that whereas between 1790 and 1815, around 150,000 emigrants left England and Wales for all destinations, by the 1870s the figure was approaching 100,000 per year; in the decade to 1881, net emigration was about 1.5 million, rising to 1.7 million the following decade – nearly 300,000 left British ports in 1890 alone.[4] The way this tide of humanity was interrupted by the First World War, revived, then declined, is dealt with later in this Chapter.

Institutions such as the Royal Philanthropic Society, the Salvation Army and Dr. Barnardo's were all vigorously promoting emigration as a key part of social policy before

---

3. D. Thomson, *England in the 19th Century*, 1977 (Harmondsworth: Penguin).
4. E. Richards, *Britannia's Children*, 2004 (London: Hambledon & London) p. 118, 180, 280. Another estimate puts Britain's net loss of males through emigration between 1900-1913 at more than double the number killed during the First World War (M. Anderson, 'The social implications of demographic change' in F.M.L.Thomson ed. *Cambridge Social History of Britain*, 1990, CUP, Vol. 2 p.10).

the CSU joined their ranks. To middle-class subscribers, emigration seemed to offer a cost-effective way of 'redeeming a man who had made errors, or had fallen into bad ways, or had descended into debt or indolence.'[5] Other committees were formed specifically to organise emigration – the Female Middle Class Emigration Society, the British Emigration Association, Church Emigration Society, and the Self-Help Emigration Society just a few examples pre-dating the Christian Social Union.

Even so, the great majority of emigrants, whether or not they finished up in what, by the late Victorian era were known as the Dominions, did so of their own choice and largely on their own resources; a 2004 study found that only 7% of all emigrants (and 23% of those emigrating within the Empire) received any substantial financial assistance. And *involuntary* emigration – including transportation of convicts – only ever represented a small proportion of the total movement. An Emigrants' Information Office was set up by the Colonial Office in 1886, but in practice British government policy was generally to leave the level of emigration to be determined by the free market, with a nudge from the voluntary sector. Statistically, most emigrants were not unemployed, but had reasonable employment histories, tended to be slightly

---

5. Richards, *Britannia's Children*, 2004, p.186. See also O. MacDonagh ed., *Emigration in the Victorian Age*, 1973 (Farnborough: Gregg International), a selection of 19th century essays from politico/literary journals such as *Edinburgh Review, Westminister Review*, illustrating almost universal acceptance of emigration as good for Britain.

more skilled and literate than their contemporaries and were generally not traumatised by their expatriation.[6]

Child emigrants were the stark exception to this generally benign picture and have been the specific subject of several studies (although the CSU's role in emigration has until now not attracted much attention).[7] As we have seen, one of the first charities, to establish an inland 'colony', by 1849, the Royal Philanthropic Society, did so with the aim of training boys for emigration. Even earlier, the Society for the Suppression of Juvenile Vagrancy (later the Children's Friend Society) was training boys and girls to be apprenticed as farm labourers and domestic servants respectively, and by 1840 had shipped about 400 children to the Cape Colony. In 1849, 150 boys from the Ragged School Union were sent to New South Wales. The advantage of emigration for child-rescue societies such as these, constantly strapped for cash, was obvious: as one of the specialist studies points out, it cost less to equip, transport and place a child in Canada than it did to maintain the child in a home for one year, adding,

> 'For evangelicals, emigration had another big advantage. Children were not only removed from the morally and physically unhealthy

---

6. Ibid, p. 138, 303. As this book concerns Oxfordshire, it may be worth noting that 8 men from that county were aboard the first convict fleet to Botany Bay in 1787, and an Oxfordshire man, Samuel Speed, was the last known convict to have died in Australia, in 1938 (*Luke & Learn*, Oxon Record Office, July, Oct, 2007).
7. In addition to Richards' *Britannia's Children*, one of the most recent works on child emigration is R. Kershaw & J. Sacks, *New Lives for Old, the story of Britain's child migrants*, 2008, (Kew: National Archives) although it fails to mention NUCSS or Turners Court. See also: J. Parr, *Labouring Children*, 1980 (London: Croom Helm); P.Bean & J.Melville, *Lost Children of the Empire*, 1989 (London: Unwin Hyman); G. Wagner, *Children of the Empire*, 1982 and *Barnardo*, 1979 (both, London: Weidenfeld & Nicolson); D. Hill, *Forgotten Children*, 2007 (Sydney: Heinemann).

surroundings of over crowded cities, they were irrevocably separated from parents considered 'vicious and degraded'. . the advantages for girls . . . were even more apparent; emigration represented the final solution.'[8]

The author's choice of that last phrase puts a chilling gloss on the business of child emigration. By the time the CSU was formed in 1895, the process of taking workhouse or other destitute children and shipping them overseas had acquired a mixed reputation. A number of cases had been reported in the British press where children, especially girls, had been dumped, ill prepared and unsupervised, in remote colonial farming communities and subject to various forms of ill-treatment. Some people suspected that the promoters of such emigration were making money for themselves, without giving much thought to monitoring how their young charges fared in the colonies. New legislation was passed but the Prevention of Cruelty to Children Act, 1894, still allowed emigration to be argued as being in a child's best interests and children could be sent abroad with the Home Secretary's permission.

In the early 20th century the Local Government Board was still encouraging Boards of Guardians to send children overseas, and 'philanthropic abduction' was still a quicker and easier method of separating children from undesirable parents than strict legal process.[9] In the two decades before the outbreak of the First World War nearly 6,000 juveniles were shipped off to Canada alone (Australia and New Zealand would always be less popular destinations not least because

---
8. G. Wagner, *Barnardo*, 1979 (London, Weidenfeld & Nicolson) p. 180-181.
9. Wagner, *Children of the Empire*, 1982 p.147.

it cost more to get the children there). The CSU certainly thought it right to contribute to emigration in general and emigration of boys and young men in particular. Its 1905 fund-raising booklet, *Some Results Achieved in the Farm Colonies and Epileptic Homes* used exactly the same reasoning as had the earlier Victorian societies: by sending men to the colonies for rehabilitation, rather than pay to keep them in the workhouses, the Poor Law Guardians 'recognise they are obtaining a great gain to the ratepayers.'

In 1850, Thomas Beames's *Rookeries of London* had touched on the arguments for and against emigration; then, it was the Chartists who opposed it, claiming that Britain had sufficient land 'if properly cultivated' to maintain a population of up to 150 million. On the other hand Beames heard emigration 'preached up' as not only 'our great national safety valve' but a way of strengthening the colonies with English labourers and artisans.[10] Twenty years on, pressure for and public acceptance of emigration was (as briefly mentioned in Chapter 1) being bolstered by the blossoming of British imperialism; Germany and the USA were now recognised as serious commercial rivals, with Germany also seen as a military threat. In 1870, the historian J.A. Froude published an article under the title *England and Her Colonies*, urging state aid for emigration to the colonies on the grounds that it was needed to counterbalance the growth of the United States which 'have been made stronger, the English [sic] empire, weaker' by the 4 million or so European emigrants who had opted for the USA. And in the 1880s another historian, J.R. Seeley, published his Cambridge lectures under the title *The Expansion of*

---

10. T. Beames, *Rookeries of London*, 1850 (London: Thomas Bosworth) p.260.

Britain, linking poverty and unemployment with the concept of imperial expansion, and the widespread use of pauper emigration to the 'white' Dominions.

The Colonial College, Hollesley Bay (briefly noted in Chapter 1) exemplified this way of thinking. Opened in 1887 by Robert Johnson it aimed to train public school boys for work in the colonies, 'to carry forward the flag of the great mother of Nations, to sustain her good name the world over, to open up new lands, to open up new markets. To create new industries.' An envious French author, whose tract *Anglo-Saxon superiority: to what it is due*, was published in English in 1899, extolled Johnson's plan for agricultural training of 'gentlemen emigrants', saying that this was the process whereby 'the Anglo-Saxon race is gradually taking possession of the world and elbowing out the other races' (including, of course, the French).[11] Emigration, in other words, was not just a Christian charitable reaction to and a political solution for overcrowding, disease and crime (and, as we would add today, no less importantly the *fear of crime*) in British cities, but a positive contribution to making the colonies themselves strong, able to buy British exports and contribute to the defence of the Empire. Episodes such as the initial failure of the British army to get on equal terms with the Boers in South Africa, reports of the poor physical condition of men enlisting in the British army, and the defeat of Russia by the supposedly 'inferior' Asiatic Japanese, all helped to bolster this movement. By the beginning of the 20th century, therefore, the evangelist and the philanthropist had been joined by the imperialist; emigration was seen as a way of populating

---

11. Richards, *Britannia's Children*, 2004 p. 216-217.

the Dominions and consolidating the Empire. 'In an age of imperialism,' writes Harry Hendrick, 'children were seen as investments – human capital in its most elemental form.'[12]

By the time the Wallingford Colony opened, therefore, this attitude was widely accepted. In 1910 a pamphlet appeared entitled *Lads for the Empire*[13] by Thomas Sedgwick, a social worker. In December that year Sedgwick took his first party of 50 lads to New Zealand, having first sent each of them an 'unusually truthful' letter, explaining that the life they would encounter would be 'hard, rough, monotonous and dull' and that beyond one shilling (5p) a week pocket money they would probably only earn enough during their first year to repay their fare. On arrival Sedgwick apparently found no difficulty in placing the lads in jobs, enthusiastically writing that he thought at least 10,000 could be absorbed each year in New Zealand, Australia and Canada. His pamphlet printed letters 'typical', he said, of the opinions of boys who had quickly grown accustomed to their new life:

> 'I could not be more happy, or better pleased with myself.'
>
> 'My employer is a perfect gentleman.'
>
> 'My boss is very good to me.'
>
> 'I have got a good home and situation, and like the work.'[14]

Another well documented and relatively long-lived example of enthusiasm for youth migration in the cause of Empire was that of Kingsley Fairbridge, a Rhodesian of

---

12. H. Hendrick, *Child Welfare in England 1872-1989*, 1994 (London: Routledge) p. 82.
13. Reprinted in *Eight Pamphlets on Migration*, 1914 (London: P.S. King).
14. ibid pp 14, 39.

English descent and a Rhodes Scholar at Oxford. Fairbridge was stirred to action, he wrote, by a vision of 'Children's lives wasting while the Empire cried out for more.' Gathering support initially from the Oxford Colonial Club, in 1909 Fairbridge and some fellow Rhodes scholars set up the Child Emigration Society and three years later, together with his wife Ruby, he acquired 1,000 acres (400 hectares) in the Warren Point district of Western Australia where, in 1913, 12 boys arrived from Britain to be trained in agriculture. Despite considerable financial and political worries the training school survived (Fairbridge himself died in 1924); a separate scheme for girls was set up in New South Wales, and by the 1930s Fairbridge had 365 child trainees.[15]   *The Times* and other journals enthused about this Empire traffic. In 1913, just as the Wallingford Colony was getting into its stride, an article in *The Westminster Gazette* described the welcome accorded to British boys in Australia:

> '. . it is of the utmost importance that English societies with means and influence should cordially co-operate with the invitation to send out boys . . It is an Imperial work of the first magnitude.'

The anonymous author admitted that many of the 'lads' found the transition from London to unpaid apprenticeship on an Australian farm hard to take: 'Of course, they do not like working for no wages, and they resent the necessarily strict discipline; but the best of them realise that they are healthier in body and have better prospects in life than ever before.' The article concluded insouciantly that the lads were

---

15. G. Sherington, C.Jeffery, *Fairbridge, Empire & Child Migration*, 1998 (London: Woburn Press) passim.

'free agents, and can go or stay as they wish,' ignoring the fact that the boys had no money and were several thousand miles from any familiar place or person. Not everyone in the Dominions was equally enthusiastic about the activities of Fairbridge, Sedgwick and others: in Australia the Fairbridges faced political scepticism and local opposition; the New Zealand journal *Truth* commented:

> 'These wretched youths have no friends, they are apprenticed . . . for a number of years at a microscopic screw without having any say in the matter and if they attempt to break from their horrible surroundings, they will be hauled before a magistrate and either sent back to their taskmasters or suffer gaol.'[16]

Recent commentaries show that it was often a miserable existence indeed that faced these boys and girls, 'taken from their parents . . . families, communities and friends and put to work in often Spartan environments . . . subject to exploitation and violence.'[17] Sedgwick and Fairbridge, nevertheless, continued to believe that not only were the emigrants benefiting in the long run, but that it was best to train the boys after they arrived in the Dominions: 'It cannot be alleged that farm training in [Britain] is a sufficient introduction to rural work in the Dominions.' The CSU, however, while subscribing to the 'social imperialist' basis for emigration (the *Westminster Gazette* article was reprinted

---

16. Quoted Bean, Melville, *Lost Children*, 1989. p.79-80. 'screw' was early 20th century slang for wages.
17. Hendrick, *Child Welfare*, 1994, p. 81; David Hill, *Forgotten Children*, 2007, *passim*. Most recently, as this book was being written, British and Australian prime ministers publicly apologised for the treatment suffered by child emigrants up to the 1960s.

in *Social Service,* October 1913) thought, on the other hand, that it was a mistake to take youths from London and other British cities to the far-flung Dominions without first having given them both substantial technical training and, of course, the kind of Christian ethos that it was the job of the Brothers at Lingfield and then at Wallingford to inculcate. A friendly local journalist, writing in *Social Service* (June 1913) about the intention of the Reading Board of Guardians to send an 'unruly' boy to the training ship *Arethusa,* enthused: 'TRAINING! That's the word. Whether on a training ship or a training colony, it is the one they needed.'

The argument continued for decades. A book published after the World War II rehearsed the pros and cons as they had been set out in various inter-war studies:

> 'Opinion in the Dominions was . . . definitely doubtful on these points. It was generally held. . that in the majority of cases training overseas could best be obtained while working for wages in actual employment, whether as farm worker or household help.'[18]

The CSU, however, had no doubts; the training of 'lads' for the colonies had been a key part of Lingfield's (non-epileptic) programme which now switched to the new Colony at Wallingford. As we have seen (Chapter 2), in February 1913, before the first new permanent buildings were ready for occupation, 48 out of the 107 'colonists' already in residence at Turners Court had been 'put up' for emigration. Photographs appeared regularly in *Social Service* showing groups of a dozen or more young men and teenagers, dressed tidily in suits,

---

18. G.F. Plant, *Overseas Settlement: migrating from UK to the Dominions,* 1951 (London: OUP) p.143, 145.

raincoats and, usually, hats, about to set off for Wallingford station to catch the 'Bunk' on their way to Canada, Australia or New Zealand. If farm managers at Turners Court or CSU committee members had doubts about how useful the emigrants might find agricultural training on the slopes of the Chilterns once they had arrived on their colonial farms, they have not survived. Only the success stories got printed in *Social Service* or other CSU publications:

> 'M.N.' A workhouse lad, a problem to the Guardians . . . After a year's training, during which he developed an excellent character, he was sent to Canada and is   doing well.'

> 'K.L.' a young clerk in a position of trust, led astray by gay city life, mis-appropriated money and narrowly escaped imprisonment. Came to Lingfield and was trained for farm work, eventually securing a good position in Canada.'[19]

After the First World War the CSU initially assumed that the Colony's main job would continue to be training youths for emigration to the Dominions and that this would be supported by governments in London and the Dominions. In 1921 Lloyd-George spoke in favour of emigration as a cure for unemployment at home and, following a conference of imperial prime ministers that year, the Empire Settlement Act 1922 gave the UK Government powers to co-operate with those in the Dominions, and with other public and private

---

19. CSU, *Some Results Achieved*, 1905. Not all reformed colonists emigrated: 'S.T. a clerk in an important Government Department, with a sad record of drink, delirium and attempted suicide, was suspended from work, spent 6 months at the Colony, is now restored and reinstated in his old position as a Civil Servant.'

bodies, to assist emigration 'of suitable people', with British taxpayers contributing up to 50 per cent of the cost of any planned emigration scheme. In 1926 the YMCA was reported (in *The Times*, 11 December) to be intending to start a farm colony in Scotland as a contribution to 'training for Empire settlements.' As late as 1932, an academic study commended such emigration which, it said, provided healthy and useful employment for surplus labour and benefited Dominions economies, without harming British industry and agriculture. The author clearly envisaged the traffic continuing:

> ' . . for boys who would ordinarily enter industry immediately they leave the elementary school, 14 or 15 years is the best age for migration. If it is postponed beyond that age, habits become fixed, physical development may be retarded by sedentary or unhealthy employment and both the desire and fitness for emigration may be lost.'[20]

The first post-war party had left Turners Court for Australia in 1921. The following year, out of 220 'colonists', 49 emigrated to Australia (and one to the USA). In 1923, 26 sailed on the SS 'Jervis Bay' from Tilbury to Australia, 'with highest hopes and brightest prospects', wrote Hunt; they were due to be met by members of the Scouting movement (they had worn Scout uniform for their group photograph). In 1927 the Church Army wrote to Hunt about a party of boys who had been placed in their care on arrival in Canada, 'We are very pleased with the boys and farmers are delighted with

---

20. A.G. Scholes, *Education for Empire Settlement*, 1932 (London: Longmans) p. 211.

them. They are what we call in Canada 'a dandy bunch of boys'.[21]

But in spite of the optimism of the 1932 author, quoted above, even in the 1920s nearly as many Turners Court boys (in 1922 it was 37) went to jobs, mostly agricultural, within Britain as overseas. The tide was turning against emigration; an article in *The Times* (January 1925) spoke of growing antagonism in Australia towards immigrants, not only southern Europeans but even 'Pommies.' The total numbers going to Australia and Canada shrank to about half what they had been before 1914.

By contrast, Wallingford Committee minutes (1927) noted 'the demand for boys in English situations is more than we can supply' (although a pencilled addition reads 'some have gone [overseas]'). In 1928, the customary photograph in the CSU Annual Report was of just 6 boys leaving for Australia. The previous year the minutes recorded New Zealand as taking no further trained farm hands, while two Turners Court boys had been turned off the emigrant ship to Canada, one because he had an eye infection, the other because Canadian authorities demanded more information about his past history. Three years earlier, a visit by Australian officials to recruit immigrants was said to have spoken to 'thousands' of unemployed in Southampton and elsewhere, but only interviewed 150, of whom 50 were provisionally accepted. At the end of the 1920s, the CSU Annual Report

---

21. Menday, *Turners Court*, 1998, p.26.

sadly noted 'emigration practically closed down, due to the onset of unemployment in the Dominions.'[22]

Dominion governments, under pressure from their electorates, were becoming less welcoming. When Margaret Bondfield and others visited Canada in 1925 under the auspices of the Commission on Overseas Settlement, they found 'really no close co-operation between the three [British, Canadian, Provincial] governments': of 3,000 children put forward for emigration by Barnardo's, only 30 were eventually accepted by the Canadian authorities.[23] And the 1951 study of the Empire Settlement Act concluded that the record of the various land settlement schemes had been 'far from encouraging,' and that Dominion governments had been sceptical of the value of agricultural training provided by the CSU and others in England: 'Boys who have had such a training . . . have an exaggerated idea of their. . . attainments . . . are less adaptable and less inclined to do as they are told. They also ask for wages which are quite unjustified.'[24]

While industrial depression and widespread unemployment in Britain in the 1920s and 1930s might be thought to have favoured emigration, in practice this was not necessarily the case; unemployment also existed in the Dominions and, if it was bad to be out of work in Wolverhampton, it might be imagined to be even worse in Wagga Wagga. The historians of the Fairbridge school in Australia admit that even in the

22. OCRO, TCYT Box H02, H03: AR, Minutes. Of the 1922 cohort, one joined the army, 6 were in hospital, 25 discharged 'unfit' or 'insubordinate', 7 'withdrawn by friends', 19 absconded, 2 died (*SS* Nov.1925).
23. M. Bondfield, *A Life's Work*, 1948 (London: Hutchinson) p. 258. Virginia Woolf's 1925 novel *Mrs. Dalloway* provides a fictional picture of differing degrees of enthusiasm for emigration; in it, Lady Bruton appears as the only real enthusiast: 'Emigration had become, in short, largely Lady Bruton.'
24. G.F. Plant, *Overseas settlement*, 1951, pp. 114, 143.

1920s 'the climate of opinion in Britain was turning against *all* child emigration'.[25] The birth rate was falling; legislation such as the Adoption Acts 1920 and 1926 and the Maternity and Child Welfare Act of 1918 put a different focus on the welfare of children, as did the growth of professional local authority health and welfare services. One of the major institutions, the National Childrens Home, which, since 1873 had sent over 3,000 young people to Canada alone, ceased its emigration programme in 1931. The CSU had to agree that emigration had become 'more difficult'; only one lad emigrated that year, whereas youths from Turners Court were to be found on all neighbouring farms, 'largely keeping them going'.

The CSU, like some politicians, hoped that this difficulty was only temporary; when Brigadier General Sir Henry Page Croft, MP (Bournemouth, Con.) visited the Colony in May 1933 he sought assurance that the CSU remained committed to emigration; an editorial in *Social Service* the following month admitted that there were difficulties in getting emigrants accepted in Australia, but added, 'We have been surprised in these hard times, when Dominions are suffering in common with ourselves with an unemployed problem, to find how boys trained on an English farm colony have been able to hold their own.' Of course, it could have been true that ex-Colony boys already in Australia were no more likely to be laid off than workers who had been born there, but equally true that Dominion governments would clamp down on further immigration.

---

25   Sherington & Jeffery, *Fairbridge etc*, 1998, p.91. Emphasis added.

'The Making of Men'

Turning aside from the debate over their ultimate destination, what was daily life like for the lads and the Brothers charged with their educational and spiritual welfare in the first decades of the 'Colony's existence? Apart from the couple of Conscientious Objectors whom we have already met, who were these volunteer Brothers and what were they like?

Although the papers of the Turners Court Youth Trust archive contain many news items and descriptive pieces about life at the Colony in the monthly *Social Service* journal, they all originated with the management of the CSU and those responsible for running the Colony. Allowance has to be made not just for the somewhat florid prose style of the journal articles, but the fact that there is virtually no word written by the 'colonists' themselves, except for the invariably commendatory letters written by former colonists and selected – by the Superintendent – to appear in CSU print. Hunt and his colleagues naturally put the best possible gloss on the development of the Colony and the events that took place there; apart from any other considerations, the journal, the Annual Reports and so on had to encourage readers to contribute to CSU funds. For later years it has been possible to track down former inmates and members of staff, and so a less top-down view can be taken. In those early decades – when William Hunt was not only Superintendent but editor and chief contributor to *Social Service* – such evidence is generally lacking.

As Superintendent at Turners Court, William Hunt thought that it would take three years satisfactorily to train a volunteer Brother (although he admitted that 'some men tire in six months'). Around the time of the official opening there were between 80 -100 'colonists' and up to 20 Brothers normally in residence. At that time each Brother received free board, lodging, medical attention and laundry, plus 5 shillings (25p) per week in his first year, rising to six shillings (30p) in the second year and 7 shillings and sixpence (37.5p) in the third. A Brother whom Hunt considered to have rendered 'satisfactory service' (only the Superintendent's own judgement was involved) was entitled to bonuses amounting to £1 per year, paid on leaving the Colony. Some of Turners Court's former farm labourers were kept on by the CSU; once the new buildings were complete and the Colony's organisation settled down, it also employed a Housekeeper, a Clerk, Cook, dining room attendant, laundresses, sewing women and a domestic servant (for the Superintendent's house). The CSU expected the Brothers, both to train the 'colonists' and to train themselves for work, for example as prison or asylum warders, carrying 'the redemptive spirit of Lingfield, with its sweetness and light, into those austere institutions of the state.'[26]

Continuing his practice at Lingfield, Hunt kept a register, (brief extracts from which have already been used in the Prologue) listing, for each of the Brothers, home address, previous job, religion and destination when leaving the Colony. Previous occupations ranged from architect to ship's carpenter, school teacher to butcher (the last oddly also described as 'vegetarian'). For some, at least, a spell at Turners Court looks to have been akin to an extension of (public) school life – perhaps the equivalent of a 21st century

---

26. Paton, *John Brown Paton*, 1914, p.248.

gap year with VSO. Although written after war broke out in 1914, a purported letter from a new Brother to friends in his home town, printed in *Social Service*, has a distinctly peacetime flavour. The writer explains that he had been put to work in Paton Home – the adult male block – because he smokes, a habit discouraged among the boys. Fellow Brothers, including printer, shoemaker, insurance clerk and grocer, are described as jolly fellows 'anxious to do good but not goody goody chaps who sing hymns and recite long prayers all day long.' The alleged letter concludes: 'We had our annual supper a few nights ago, and had a ripping time'.[27]

Some recruits clearly fell short both of Hunt's projected three year term and other expectations. William Brasier, for example, previously employed at Rowton House, and designated 'Assistant House Father' – that is, second in command in one of the two accommodation blocks – only stayed a week. Waged staff, too, could be difficult to keep: Chris Udall and his wife, cook and dining hall attendant respectively, with a joint wage of £45 per year (plus board and lodging) were at Turners Court from March 1917 to June 1923, but Edith Eborn, the laundry maid (£20 per year) only stayed one month in 1914. Some of the comments Hunt wrote in his ledger might surprise today's human resources professionals and indicate the wide range of capabilities of early 'Brothers':

'Fiery. Red-haired. A big boy & erratic. Did well at times.'

'Enterprising. Ill-balanced. His marriage was his downfall. Might have been a considerable success with a little more ballast.'

---

27. OCRO, TCYT Box. H13. The letter is signed 'Alick M.' not identified from Colony records.

'Quite a decent lad. Rather odd views. Came from Letchworth [Quaker Adult School]. Not much use here.'

'Short in stature and in his work, inches tall!'

'A Worker but gloomy and unable to control colonists.'

'Deaf and doubtful. Lacked alertness in handling boys.'

'Active, earnest man. Immersed in Labour politics. Left for domestic reasons.'

'good chap but wholly useless as a Brother . . no control over boys. Left suddenly.'

' . . was going in for musical profession [but] good fellow. Too religious to play his violin although he was a capable performer. Belonged to a peculiar sect which claimed to speak with tongues.'[28]

Soon after the official opening, several sympathetic accounts of the Wallingford Colony appeared in print. In November 1913, the Quaker journal *The Friend*, in a section devoted to The Friends' Social Union (see Appendix II) reported 'an interesting excursion' to Turner's Court; at that time five or six members of the CSU's governing committee and at least one Wallingford Brother were Friends. The article described the site and buildings: 'the dormitories are large and very simply furnished; the Brothers have single bedrooms, partitioned off at the end of each dormitory. The lavatories, laundry, kitchen, cowsheds, stables and stock-yards are all well-planned and well-equipped.' The author, F.J. Edminson M.A., emphasised the 'homeliness' of the Colony, 'due in no small measure to the Superintendent, the Brothers, the staff,

---

28. Ibid, 'Brothers Register', a handsome A4 sized leather-bound volume entirely in Hunt's MS.

their wives and daughters' and concluded that the colonists 'seem happy and they turn out well.'

Earlier, *Social Service* had printed 'The Making of Men: pen pictures of a farm colony' by W.E. Pittuck who, like Hunt, was journalist by training and philanthropist by vocation. Born on Merseyside and, like Hunt, initially trained as a printer, Pittuck was briefly a telegraphist on the Midland Railway before joining the staff of the *West Yorkshire Pioneer*, Skipton. When he got the call to undertake social work, he became an assistant to the Rev. Bruce Wallace of Letchworth, soon after the foundation of that Garden City in the early 20th century. He then joined the Lingfield Colony as a Brother, transferring to Turners Court as book-keeper ('making his weight felt wherever a hand was needed' said his obituarist in *Social Service*, January 1933). After serving in the Royal Engineers during the First World War, Pittuck combined work as Secretary to the CSU London committee with free-lance journalism, before becoming editor of the *Berks and Oxon Advertiser*, one of the local newspapers in which the Colony could, therefore, be pretty sure of favourable coverage. He was also a photographer; several surviving picture postcards of Turners Court in the 1920s bear his name, and there are occasional references to postcard sales contributing to Colony funds.

Like Hunt's, Pittuck's prose style may strike today's readers as flowery. The account of his first visit to Turners Court in Autumn 1912 has him walking across the bridge from Wallingford, through Crowmarsh (the village 'that has a touch of old time things about it') before coming across the 'fine modern buildings' of the Colony; 'The architect's

Oxfordshire Colony

brain, the builder's skill and the management's experience have . . combined to produce a group of dwellings that should be ere long the envy of social reformers in many parts of the country.' Although perhaps not much of a countryman himself, Pittuck spent three days on the land with colonists and Brothers, pulling turnips and swedes ('or was it only turnips – or which was it?') after which his 'enthusiasm was not so very keen' – unlike the 'cutting north wind'. This combined with the heavy soil (the Autumn had been generally wet) unsurprisingly caused grumbling among the boys. Pittuck was also introduced to the dairy farm, the horse stables and 'the mysteries of the dung yard.'

There are hints in both these articles, and the illustrations accompanying accounts of the official opening, that however distinguished their new buildings might be, life at the Colony could be Spartan; away from the excitement of the dung yard, time might hang heavy on the colonists' hands. Beds in the dormitories are packed tightly together, the dining hall offers only the plainest furniture. A picture of the men's day room in Paton Home shows, again, plain deal tables and upright chairs, with no recreation equipment in sight. One well-filled bookcase appears in a shot through the doorway of the Brothers' Library, but another shot seems to show only two books on the shelves of the 'Youths' Library.' Edminson's article in *The Friend* admits that 'the winter evenings are long. . the Colony is three miles from the nearest town [and] Books for the library are in much request,' going on to say that Friends might like to contribute such luxuries as 'a couple of old pianos, a bagatelle board, good framed pictures for the dining hall.'

Pittuck, ever the optimist however, reported hearing 'merry laughter coming from the dining room' on Saturday evening, when a concert was in progress. Other weekly entertainment included lantern lectures, whist drives, dramatic performances and 'debates of a humorous nature' provided by the staff (although the colonists 'occasionally take a turn'). 1914 would see the first of several visits by a Wallingford amateur dramatic company, with 'a smart little comedy' titled 'Artfulness'. Colonists had also been entertained by 'Professor Ward's talking doll' (presumably a ventriloquist act) 'whose bright sallies kept the audience in roars of laughter'. Two pianos had indeed been acquired (whether either of them had been donated by readers of *The Friend* is unknown), one for use at the dining hall concerts, the other in the Youth's Day Room 'for Sunday afternoons and evening prayers'. In 1913, young colonists might have been even more pleased to know that nearly £12 had been raised towards the purchase of 'a cinematograph machine', towards which Pittuck was giving profits from his photographic business. The first annual sports day took place in September 1913, with the Rector of Mongewell presenting prizes and paying tribute to the 'neighbourliness' of the Colonists.

On Sunday the culture was inescapably religious, traditional – and teetotal.[29] On his 1912 visit, Pittuck noted that the Brothers had a Bible class 'of a conversational nature,' while the men and lads were 'busy tidying themselves up' or going off for a stroll before Sunday dinner of roast beef, potatoes

29. The issue of *The Friend* carrying Edminson's article about Turners Court also contained a plea for speakers at Quaker Meetings to refer to the need for the re-introduction of the Inebriates' Bill, a measure designed to deal with habitual drinkers that had been hanging fire in the Home Office for some years; it was eventually overtaken by wartime licensing legislation.

and cauliflowers, followed by 'a good helping of jam tart.' In the afternoon there was a Bible class for Colonists under the age of 21, and Sunday evening service was compulsory for all Brothers, staff and colonists, who were joined by local farm workers and their families: 'Seldom have I heard more hearty singing.' On weekday evenings he was told there were classes on agriculture, bible study, and social service. Four years later, in 1916, one of the CO Brothers described regular evening classes for the less literate boys, encouraging them to write letters home, reading Dickens' 'A Christmas Carol', and discussing prose style:

> 'Every now and then they ask me questions .. after I explained and illustrated the use of the word "simile" one lad ventures the suggestion that "acting the giddy goat" isn't a bad example.'[30]

'Your Country Needs YOU!'

A good deal of Hunt's time was spent touring the country touting for funds. The CSU had considerable debts; as we have seen, the second 'Home' had been left un-named in the hope that a wealthy donor would come along and pay off the £2,000 or so attributable to its building costs.[31] The man who was the source of the CSU's inspiration, von Bodelschwingh, left the reputation of having been able to shake the last *pfennig* from reluctant *bürgers*: Federal Germany's first President, Theodor Heuss, later referred to the Pastor as 'the most brilliant beggar

---

30. *Social Service*, May 1917. Although 'Letters from a C.O.' are anonymous,' acting the giddy goat' was a habitual metaphor (not simile) of Edward Sladen.
31. 'What man or woman is wealthy and kindly enough to give the £2,500 necessary to pay for this Home and give to it a name which shall remain as a fragrant memorial?' (Pittuck, *SS* April 1913).

in Germany.' Hunt, however, found such work hard going. In 1918 – perhaps not the easiest time to raise money - he 'went off to stomp the country again for funds' but had to report 'Five days strenuous effort, over 1,000 miles travelled, £9 expenses and only £1 return.' The parenthetic comment of his successor, R.P. Menday - 'What faith and energy!' – seems hardly adequate.[32]

However, Boards of Guardians, the London County Council and other authorities continued to refer boys and young men to the Colony, and Dominion emigration authorities continued to accept parties. The visitors who had thronged the – rather roughly cut – lawns and inspected the suspiciously tidy dormitories on the day of the official opening, and other visitors during the first year of the Colony's full operations, could have assumed that, subject to raising further capital, the Colony was set fair for a busy and fruitful existence. The outbreak of war, however, a year after the official opening, upset all plans.

1914 had started encouragingly, with a party of boys setting off to Australia; the CSU Annual Report printed letters from some of those already settled there: 'I am getting the highest pay they can pay to a man who came straight out here from the old country. I could only milk three cows an hour then but now I can do ten an hour so you see I have pulled up pretty good.' A further party was due to sail in the autumn. Instead, able bodied Brothers and Colonists left Turners Court to join the armed forces. By December 1915 13 former members of staff and 73 colonists were serving either in the army or navy; 15 out of 45 names on the war

---

32. Menday, *Turners Court*, 1998, p.16.

memorial in the middle of Benson village have been identified as from Turners Court. Most of the young men served either in the Royal Berkshire Regiment or the Oxfordshire and Buckinghamshire Light Infantry, with a handful in other military units or the Royal Navy.[33] Others volunteered for non-combatant services such as the YMCA and the Friends Ambulance Unit. There were letters and visits, for example by ex-Brothers serving in the RAMC who reported that living conditions in army camp compared unfavourably with Turners Court, although presciently they thought the muddy camp might be good training for life at the front.

Some of those who left look to have been missed less than others. In his Register, Hunt noted the departure of Brother H.E.Gibbs, identified as former 'checker' in a Vancouver store, who had started at the Colony in April 1914; Hunt described him as,

> 'Erratic and neurotic. Thrashed a lad with a stick in the Home. When recruiting canvassers came, took a day off to London, got a job for himself and Jarman in YMCA. Their friend Lock at the same time secured appointment at Darenth. All three men left on the morning of Dec 11 [1915]. In their departure they did not in any sense consider the well-being of this work and Gibbs, who had only served 1 year & 8 mos [sic] and was therefore refused the 2nd year bonus, was insolent. They were all 3 weaklings & had been a source of discontent. Gibbs

---

33. A. Jack et al, *The War Memorial & Graves Book of Remembrance*, 1995 (Benson: Skycatcher Press). During the World War II 'Benson' on the memorial was deliberately defaced to confuse invaders. The memorial also carries the names of 10 Benson men killed in that war.

grumbled to colonists! [He] subsequently made several applications to return here.'³⁴

The last available fit Brother left in 1915; the Colony was asked if it could supply labour of any kind to local farmers whose own employees had enlisted (somewhat surprisingly, the local press reported that farmers could apply to the Labour Exchange for the services of soldiers stationed nearby for up to four weeks 'special leave' at harvest time).³⁵ By 1916 numbers had shrunk to 4 Brothers and 60 Colonists: 'it was possible that the Colony would have to close altogether.' As well as staff shortages, the Colony suffered from common wartime problems, including high prices for food and goods of all kinds: the Board of Trade's working class cost of living figure rose by 45 per cent between the outbreak of war and July 1916. Food prices, especially of imports, had risen, and continued to rise even more steeply; at the end of the war a Ministry of Labour table of retail prices showed increases of well over 100 per cent since 1914 for meat, sugar and other

---

34. OCRO TCYT Box. H03. The mercurial Gibbs died in Knutsford, Cheshire in 1923. A friend who sent Hunt news of his death wrote that Gibbs 'often spoke very appreciatively of you and your work.' Jarman, described in the Register as Wesleyan, tailor and 'a very poor Brother, much complained about to the Housemother. . Plenty of talk. Had a useful social side,' became a Trade Union organiser after the war, before returning to the Colony in 1925 as a temporary Brother. He was later appointed minister at Benson Free Church and a J.P. A press cutting pasted on this page in the register carries the photograph of a man in old clothes with a policeman and the caption reads: 'Minister as Casual: the Rev. F.A. Jarman J.P., a Congregational minister of Benson . . receiving a ticket for a free meal and bed at the Salvation Army hostel, Blackfriars Road [London] SE where, to study the methods, he spent the night as a "casual". The cutting is undated and the page in the register is loose, as though torn out then replaced.
35. *Berks & Oxon Advertiser*, 3 Jun 1916; of course, such applications did not necessarily succeed.

products. The Colony's wage bill also went up; by 1918 the weekly wage for Brothers had doubled, to 10 shillings (50p). Work and leisure activities were hampered by restrictions like the 'Lighting Orders' (black-out).

The 'Goods order & received' book for this period illustrates the variety and cost of products needed for the day to day running of Turners Court: one week in 1917 saw the ordering of 9 lb.(4 kg) of shoulder of mutton from the London Central Meat Co. at a cost of just over 10 shillings. Perhaps the local Wallingford butchers could not cope with all the Colony's needs. Rationing, first of sugar, then meat and fats, was not introduced until the end of 1917, but there had been severe shortages for some time before that. On its own, the quantity of mutton ordered sounds small (might it have been for soup?) even for the reduced number of Colonists; the weekly meat ration, when it finally started was fixed at 15 ounces (420 gm) of beef, mutton or lamb per adult. All Colonists, however, might have expected at least a small share of the 27 lb. (14.3 kg.) of 'slab cake', ordered locally. Non-food orders included wool - probably for knitting and mending socks and jerseys - from the Wallingford drapers Pettit's (still trading from the same premises in the early 21st century) which later that year also supplied two pairs of cord trousers for 18 shillings (90p). Another Wallingford store, Field, Hawkins & Ponkin (closed by the late 20th century) supplied 2 dozen pairs of grey socks for 19 shillings (95p), of which one dozen were later returned, as a money-saving gesture.

As would happen again in the World War II, the Colony had to accommodate unexpected visitors. At one time it looked at though it might have been completely taken over for other uses: at the outbreak of war the Home Office asked the CSU to furnish them with suggestions for the establishment of 'concentration camps' - the term coined by the British during the South African wars – for destitute aliens. The plans were apparently made but 'much to the Colony's regret', says Menday, never finalised. Another proposal would have seen Turners Court transformed into a military hospital, as was the case with the University Examination Schools and several college buildings in Oxford.[36] The idea of settling ex-servicemen on the Turners Court land seems not to have been discussed, although the War Department certainly encouraged such 'colonies' and the Small Colonies Holding Act 1916 empowered the Board of Agriculture to acquire land for up to four such settlements, where 'co-operative methods' were employed to help the small holders.[37]

Instead, there arrived at the Colony a handful of the 200,000 Belgian refugees who escaped to Britain in autumn 1914. Some of them were less than enchanted by their new home: one youth, previously billeted on a family in Birmingham, refused to eat, sleep or converse with the Brothers in either English or French but somehow made it clear he did not intend to do any farm work. Another – or possibly the same - young man had to be asked to leave because he was a bad influence on other refugees; 'On Monday morning, rather than do any work, even the lightest, the two youths absconded' and were

---

36. Menday, *Turners Court*, 1998, p.14. The 'German' colony at Ware (see Chapter 1) was transformed into an internment camp (*Herts. Mercury* 6 Oct 2000).
37. *SS*, Apr 1920; by then at least one of the ex-service 'colonies' had failed and the War Department was said to be cutting its losses, sellling off the land and re-settling the ex-servicemen on individual small-holdings where possible.

rumoured to have been seen in prison or the workhouse in Birmingham.[38]

The refugees and the COs whom we met in the Prologue were not the only unforeseen arrivals. The eventual introduction of rationing may have made distribution more equitable, but it also forced the closure of many small restaurants; in May 1918, Daniel Wingfield and his wife, having regretfully closed their London 'dining rooms', took jobs as dining hall attendant and cook at the Colony. They stayed until 1932; five years after the war ended their joint wage was £5 6s 8d (£5.33) per week.[39]

Post-war changes

At the end of the war there were around 80 Colonists at Turners Court. Apart from Horsfall, most Conscientious Objectors left. Some pre-war Brothers, like Pittuck, returned from war service, and new staff were recruited. Finance remained a head-ache: in 1918 the Colony seems to have owed a Wallingford draper (possibly Pettit's) £395 and the annual accounts for 1918 showed a loss of £200. Staff costs and charges to Boards of Guardians both continued to rise. In 1922 there was a total staff of 36 and the weekly wage bill was around £40; in 1929, the weekly wage bill was £66, for a staff of around 50, although 30 of those were only receiving 10

38. *SS*, October 1914. Initially there was widespread sympathy for the Belgians. Later in the war relations were less good; many able-bodied refugees were moved to work in munitions factories at a 'village' in NE England, where there was some tension between the workers, Belgian *gendarmes* and British police. (see I.F.W. Beckett, *Home Front 1914-1918*, 2006 (Kew: National Archives) p.155n.
39. OCRO, TCYT Boxes H08, H12 supplemented by personal information: the Wingfield's daughter, Constance, became the aunt of the present author.

or 12 shillings (50-60p) in addition, of course, to free board and lodging. Frank Horsfall, now the 'Administrator' (head of the Colony office) earned £1.10.0 (£1.50) per week in the 1920s, £3 in 1930; in that year, the Superintendent's annual salary was fixed at £450. It had already been accepted that the Brothers might need more structured training if they were efficiently to care for and work with the boys and young men; regular lessons in the relatively new discipline of psychology were introduced – 'a giant leap forward.'[40]

By 1925 the weekly charge for each man or boy placed by a Board of Guardians had to be increased from 21 shillings (£1.05) to 22 shillings 9 pence (£1.13). Nevertheless, numbers of Colonists rose steadily, from 222, in 1922, to 277 five years later, and 300 by the mid-1930s, with a staff of 31 Brothers including Mr.de Louis, 'a coloured man'. Back in September 1922, the editor of *Social Service* had written, perhaps with some relief (not to say *schadenfreude*) that, by contrast with Wallingford's growth, a charity-run farm training colony for boys at Steinmühle near Frankfurt-on-Main had failed, probably because numbers were too small, and been taken over by the German government 'who no doubt will administer it in their own peculiarly efficient way.'

The replacement, in 1920, of the old Local Government Board by the Ministry of Health (MoH), which took over most existing Poor Law supervisory functions was, we can now see, the first move towards the more active and persistent involvement of government (central and local) with the Wallingford Colony. The new Minister of Health carried more weight in Cabinet than had his LGB predecessor; MoH

40. McLellan, *History of CSU*, c.1963, p. 4; Menday, *Turners Court*, 1998, p.28, 21.

officials were both more numerous and more inquisitive than had previously been the case. By the early 1920s, those officials were making occasional visits to Turners Court ('inspections' is probably too formal a description) and puzzling over the ambiguous status of the Colony: not a 'Certified School' under the existing legislation (Children Act 1908), Boards of Guardians were, however, entitled to send boys there without specific MoH sanction. In any case, the officials decided, most of the boys were over school age, the Turners Court buildings seemed generally adequate, the food nourishing and sufficient, and the lay brothers being trained for social work passed muster.[41]

During the 1920s MoH officials did query Hunt's management on several occasions. Boards of Guardians and, more crucially, MPs, would pass to the new Ministry complaints they had received from individual 'colonists'; some of these concerned the severity of corporal punishment meted out, for example, to boys who absconded and/or caused trouble in Wallingford.. Hunt defended the Colony's practice, saying that only a leather strap was used, and all incidents were logged in the punishment book; further, he pointed out, 'Critics of the Colony forget or do not realise that [it] is intended for and receives only the worst material.' Agreeing to take no action, MoH officials noted that 'The atmosphere is very different from what would be inevitable in an official institution. The disadvantage is that there is a lack of the smartness and regularity to be expected.'[42]

In 1924 MoH was passed a letter of complaint from another of the troublesome 'private' inmates, originally addressed to

41. National Archives (NA), ex-Ministry of Health file MH 57/52.
42. ibid

a 'Mr. Lloyd' - perhaps his guardian or financier. Named as J.H. Mackie, the inmate was said to have 'done brilliantly at Oxford, then taken to drink and. . . . down in the gutter.' Despite having been (he writes) recommended (presumably by Hunt) for 'Brotherhood' at Turners Court, Mackie lists a variety of complaints: poor food, indiscipline, dirt, lack of hot water and finally, 'vice' at 'Woodlands' – the 'branch colony', set up in one corner of the estate, with around 40 adult Colonists and five Brothers billeted in existing farm buildings. Woodlands, Mackie wrote, was 'a hotbed of vice and immorality. . Lots of the Brothers are of a most impossible type;' one of them had been dismissed 'for sodomy', then reinstated. To cap it all, Mackie alleged that the CSU was making a handsome profit out of the 21 shillings per week it charged private clients and Boards of Guardians. After another visit, however, the official dealing with the case simply notes the file, 'On the whole I could find little to complain about.'[43]

A year later, another visit was occasioned by a complaint from several boys to the Paddington Guardians about poor food, bad language, lack of hygiene and sexual misbehaviour at Woodlands. Although, again, no action seems to have been taken, the official report is less complaisant: 'Hunt is an oldish man and does not seem very energetic; he was sitting over his study fire when I arrived at 3.15 p.m. and took me over the house and farm buildings wearing his . . . slippers.' After the tour, the official thought the work 'did not seem particularly well organised and the boys . . . were listless. Everything seems to be run in a slack manner' and the daily menu, involving

---

43. ibid

much bread and margarine, with little meat, did not seem to be enough for boys working in the fields. Hunt admitted that they had no means of dealing with any form of sickness except sending the patient to Wallingford hospital (where the cost of treatment would fall on the local community).

A third official visit, in summer 1927, found fault with the remaining hutted accommodation (beds too close together, beds and mattresses of poor quality), the boys' clothing and the lack of regular medical and dental treatment. Questioned on that point, Hunt 'considered that [the CSU] should not be asked to incur the expense of medical examination or dental treatment for boys who were often at the Colony for less than a year.' On the other hand, the diet was 'fair.'[44]

The Local Government Act 1930 produced further changes in the relationship between Colony and Government. Responsibility for placing boys into the Colony's care finally left the antique Boards of Guardians and rested with County and County Borough Councils. As the new machinery ground into action there was a temporary slowing down in the numbers of referrals to Turners Court. Grown men – the 'unemployables' whom the CSU had once thought would form a majority of Colonists – were now generally no longer sent to Wallingford: 'the emphasis shifted from reclamation to prevention.' Although Menday would write (in his1998 history) that 'in the event little difference was experienced', the stepping up of the regime of inspections by the Home Office, Ministries of Agriculture and of Health, plus the need to work with social service professionals of local authorities

---

44. ibid

– notably the London County Council - foreshadowed a different kind of institution and style of management

Alongside these institutional developments, changes were made to Turners Court's buildings and to the running of the farm. The long-serving farm manager, A.T. Carr (who had started at Turners Court as a Brother) made innovations: Manitoba wheat was introduced; 'Efficiency Badges' were awarded as a stimulus to better farm work; increasing demand for pork meant a new pig house had to be built – and money raised to pay for it. At the end of 1926, with an annual budget of £24,000. the CSU had £1,230 cash in the bank, but by 1929 this had been transformed to an overdraft of £1,291. In the 1930s, water bills 'seemed exceptionally high' (although, oddly, in 1930 the Colony was able to lend £925 to the South Oxon Water & Gas Company at 5% interest). A new bore hole 'proved very expensive' and donors were sought, Lord Nuffield offering £250. The national economy and the weather could both affect the farm's fortunes. In December 1927 and January 1928, after problems had arisen with the dairy herd, and the beet crop rendered unsaleable by the frost, Carr wrote:

> 'One cannot realise or believe the difficulties which confront the ordinary farmer without having the close connection with the selling side of the farming industry which causes anxiety just now . . . it is difficult to sell anything to advantage. Mud seems to be our chief crop at the moment.'[45]

---

45. TCYT Box H02. The Ministry of Agriculture had also queried the quality of the dairy herd.

Nine years later, however, during the Colony's 25th anniversary celebrations, Sir Ralph Glyn, the local MP, was able to refer to good news for the Colony's dairy herd, in the shape of the recently introduced national milk scheme, whereby the Government was to pay £0.5 million per year to see that children at school had milk. The Colony's area was substantially increased by the purchase of, first, the adjoining 300 acre (122 hectares) Mays Farm, then, in 1931, a further 80 acres (32 hectares) of Warren Hill farm. Diversification was planned; a nearby gravel pit was bought for possible extraction.

More accommodation was needed to cater for the increasing numbers of 'colonists', and the CSU records indicate that raising the capital for this expansion was a constant headache, despite the periodic substantial donations from sympathetic industrialists. Soon after the end of the war, in 1921, several army-surplus wooden huts had been bought; one, for enuretic boys, was unkindly named the 'Cory Wet Bed Hut', reflecting a donation recorded in 1922 from Sir Clifford Cory MP, who had already given at least £500 to the CSU's 'Forward Movement' campaign in 1911 (see Chapter 2);[46] the Cory name was later attached to one of Turners Court's larger 'Houses.' Enuretics posed a perennial problem; as late as 1954 their names were still being recorded on a loose page in the Colony register and few Brothers relished working with them. In 1927 the MoH official visitor drew attention to the

---

46. OCRO TCYT H03, CSU AR 1921. The money almost certainly came from a charity established by Sir Clifford's father, the coal broker and philanthropist, John Cory (1801/2-1910), born at Bideford, merchant and founder of Cory Brothers, shipowners, coal exporters and mine-owners. At his death he left nearly £800,000, much of it to be distributed to non-conformist, missionary and other charities.

'offensive, insanitary conditions of the 'Wet Bed' hut, where the boys slept on a sheet over bare boards, with urine running across the floor; Hunt promised to open a second such hut, presumably with better facilities.

In 1923 the second – hitherto nameless – accommodation block was officially opened as 'Basden House' by the opera singer Dame Clara Butt, who lived close by at North Stoke and who later gave a concert which raised £416 towards a new granary; a new bakery and kitchen were also added in 1923. In February 1929 an appeal by Sir John Martin Harvey[47] on BBC radio raised £270, and later that year 'Albright House'[48] opened at an estimated cost of £6,000 (at that time the CSU had some £1,300 in reserve and there were nearly 300 boys in residence). 1930 saw the opening of the new assembly hall, the Ogilvie Hall, named after (and largely funded by) William Maxwell Ogilvie,[49] a recently deceased Scots-born businessman, and 1931 saw the completion of the open air swimming pool. In 1932 there was yet another appeal, to raise £2,000 to pay off a debt on the recently opened sanatorium; in September that year a report in *The Times* claimed that £75,000 had so far been spent on land and buildings, of which £10,000 represented an outstanding mortgage.

---

47. 1863-1944; his most famous role on the stage had been that of Sidney Carton in 'The Only Way.'
48. Named for Arthur Albright, 1811-1900, Quaker, founder of Albright & Wilson chemical company in Oldbury, Birmingham, pioneers in manufacture of (safer) red phosphorus.
49. 1852-1929, originally from Dundee, he is said to have made most of his money as a merchant in Valparaiso, Chile.

'Life at the Colony was no sinecure'

What sort of life might a Wallingford Colonist have led before he left for the Dominions or, as was increasingly the case, a British farm? As at Lingfield, initially the colonists – both men and boys - were grouped into gangs of six or seven, each with a Brother who worked alongside them in the fields, 'teaching them the beauty of work and the use of the tools'; the Brothers also sat alongside Colonists at meals and during whatever social life existed in the evenings. The quotation from Menday's 1998 history at the head of this section looks like an understatement; Menday himself then quoted from the account by W.E. Pittuck of life in the Colony's early days:

'5.30 a.m. rise. Work begins at 6.00 a.m. and goes on till 8.00 a.m. breakfast. Work again from 8.30 a.m. until 12.30 p.m. dinner. 1.20 p.m. until 5.30 p.m., in hay making or harvest until 9.00 p.m. or dark. With the evening comes the service, classes, study, probably recreation duty . . . they are days crammed with hard laborious toil. Some [Colonists] are almost incapable of work . . and a Brother's chief aim. . is to get these men to see the sacredness of labour. [He] learns how to plough and sow other than wild oats . . . he must rub shoulders with pigs in the sty and have a knowledge of garden and orchard produce. . he must take charge of twelve others. . cook and mend for them and keep the house in apple pie order. And woe betide him if the meals are late in appearance.' [50]

---

50. Menday, *Turners Court*, 1998, p.11-12 (Pittuck's account was originally published in *Social Service*).

Apart from work on the farm, the gangs of Colonists and Brothers were, in the early years, engaged on forestry, in the gravel pits, the layout of roads and adaptation of the original houses and other buildings of Turners Court. Additional trade training was introduced; after the First World War 'a discharged soldier experienced in the work' was hired to train Colonists in mending their own boots, instead of sending them to Reading for repair.[51] Boys and Brothers trained and worked in a new carpenter's shop; a laundry was also added, but this was staffed by local girls. There was a small cash hand-out to Colonists each week for good conduct; Pittuck explained that 'the stoppage of this . . . gives rise to much comment, especially between the sufferer and the Brother responsible,' (that something more physical than mere 'comment' could be involved will be suggested later). The stopped money was put into a recreation fund. Cash was also used to encourage pest-control: one penny was paid for the tail of a rat, two pence for that of a mole; Pittuck alleges that Colonists discovered that the skin of a rat's tail, dried, cut into sections, pressed and coloured with boot blacking, could pass for mole (it hardly sounds worth the effort, but these few pence were the only cash most Colonists had).

Pittuck's visit to Wallingford in the early days also suggested that Hunt and his Brothers had brought some ideas for leisure activity with them from Lingfield. Healthy outdoor activity was always emphasised; from the outset the

---

51. The crucial importance of serviceable footwear to the working man often crops up in Victorian and later social surveys; Maud Pember Reeves' 1913 Fabian study, *Round About a Pound a Week*, reissued in 2008 in the Persephone paperback series, notes that Lambeth workmen typically put by a few pence a week for boot repair, and would spend much of their evenings mending the children's boots.

Colony had a Boy Scout troop – as had Lingfield. The District Commissioner, inspecting Turners Court Scouts in 1924, 'expressed his pleasure at their strength and smartness.' The practice of summer camps began at the end of the First World War: in 1918 a Scout camp was held on the banks of the Thames (a plea for money to equip the troop with bugles and drums might not have gone down well with local residents, had there been any within earshot).

During the 1920s, more distant locations were chosen and the pattern established of two summer camps, one for Scouts, one for non-scouting boys, which continued until well after the World War II. In 1921 the Scouts camped at Kimmeridge in Dorset, while non-scouts used a site at Warborough in Oxfordshire. In 1922 both camps were held on the estate of Gordon Selfridge at Hengistbury Head, near Christchurch. In 1933, 60 scouts camped on the Isle of Wight (the GWR provided a special coach on the train from Cholsey to Southampton)[52]; the same year an un-named 'lad', looking forward to the non-scouting camp, wrote in Famous Five style in *Social Service*:

> 'Once again we think of camp time and make ready for a real holiday... Games we shall want and we could have good fun in tracking, rounders, handball and early morning exercise for those who want to take part.. Things to seek are fishing tackle, lemonade, chocolate, bottles of ginger pop, novelty bags.. Food is what we all think of and a light lunch for the mid day meal and a good dinner at tea time will be all the better for everyone, for you can't play games on a heavy dinner. Sunday we don't do much and a service in the marquee couldn't do any harm.

---

52. OCRO TCYT H03, CSU Annual Reports.

.. Swimming 3 times a day with a Brother in charge. . . A concert on the last night with a mouth organ band . . will be tip top.'

Other excursions reflected the Colony's agricultural and Dominion interests. In 1924 there was an outing to the British Empire Exhibition at Wembley, returning 'without any absentees'; William Hunt's son Henry, who was to die in a swimming accident in 1931, served at that year's Wembley Jamboree. The same year the Colony won several prizes at the County Dairy Competition. In early summer of 1918, Hunt had issued a plea for well-wishers to donate games equipment – cricket, tennis, croquet and bowls: 'Cash or kind! New or second-hand!' - and in June that year a set of bowls was indeed received, 'particularly appreciated by the more "aged" members' of the Wallingford community. By 1927 a national press article reported the Colony fielding 12 football and 6 cricket teams against local village sides (later, in 1933/34, a hard tennis court was built.). Sports days, held in August or September each year, were always generously reported in *Social Service* and CSU Annual Reports. The 1927 article also referred to the cinema, billiard tables, concert and dramatic society; it sounds complimentary, although Hunt complained that it had not brought in a penny by way of donations towards the new buildings.[53]

Apart from the cinematograph equipment (which was updated several times during the Colony's history) and the religio-educational evening classes already mentioned, there seems to have been a variety of entertainment throughout the year, although it is not always quite clear whether this

53 SS June 1927; the newspaper is not identified; possibly *Daily Mail* or *Daily Express*.

was geared more to the taste of the young Colonists, or to the Brothers and other staff; the hard tennis court, like the set of bowls, was certainly for the latter. The wireless set with amplifier, bought in September 1924, would have had universal appeal; it had sufficient volume to be used for dancing in the 'recreation hut' (presumably one of the temporary post-war buildings): 'the Savoy Bands on the air were much appreciated;' the 1998 history wonders 'where the girls came from.' A billiard table was also bought around this time, from Figgis, the architect; it cost £25 (perhaps £800 at 2010 prices).[54]

Each year *Social Service* would carry an account of Christmas festivities at Turners Court. In 1920 there had been a party of carol singers, the Colonists had attended morning service before dinner of roast beef and Christmas pudding. The Brothers took tea with the Superintendent and his wife and then beguiled the odd minutes before supervising the Colonists' tea with a 'hilarious' game of Up Jenkins. In the evening 'High revel was held in the dining hall' when the farm staff joined Colonists. There was (writes Hunt) 'plenty of tobacco, apples, crackers, sweets and chocolates for everybody,' well mixed up with 'songs and stunts and round games' before being brought to a close with hearty carol singing. Members of the staff came in fancy dress which 'greatly delighted the younger members of the family [sic].' No intoxicating liquor was served.

The journal and Annual Reports also carry references to percussion bands and exhibitions of paintings by Colonists and Brothers. The Boy Scouts gave occasional concerts, and

---

54   Menday, *Turners Court*, 1998, p.24.

by 1925 the Colony Dramatic Society was active. As well as this home-grown talent, Turners Court continued to receive visits from professional and amateur dramatic companies. An early example of these visits, and one of the best reported, saw the return of the former temporary Brother, Edward Sladen who, in 1919, had taken up a teaching post at the YMCA's George Williams College in London. In November 1920 he brought a small concert party of fellow 'Centymcans' for a week-end's 'entertainment and service.' If the anonymous Colonist's plans for summer camp, quoted above, evoke Enid Blyton, the account[55] of this 1920 visit rather echoes the style of Jerome K. Jerome:

> 'The party paraded at Paddington soon after mid-day. . in full marching order under the command of Sladen. Having commandeered a compartment, Harry and George disappeared for their 'lunch'. . .Gunn and Ainsworth nearly wrecked the expedition by approaching the station in rushing taxis from opposite directions. Sladen heroically read some intellectual review; Harry explained the beauties of socks, while Evans, Gunn and Ainsworth tried to behave like gentlemen. In the course of a change at Reading, we nearly got into the wrong train, but didn't – though some of us seemed to get into the wrong class of compartment. The fun really started on arrival at Wallingford – except for Ainsworth . . . his bag – the most conspicuous of the lot – vanished, the mysterious disappearance being naturally attributed to the tricks of. . . other members of the party. The humour of the situation became rather tragic when, half an hour before the concert, it became evident that the bag was missing – including most of the music! Thanks to the efforts of one of the Colony staff and a

---

55. Originally published in *CentYMCA Bulletin*, reprinted in *Social Service*, Dec.1920. Anonymous, but content and style rule out Sladen as the author.

push-bike it was eventually recovered from underneath the seat of a trap three miles away back at Wallingford . . . the audience got its concert and Ainsworth got his pyjamas and tooth brush.'

'Of the concert,' the account goes on, 'modesty prevents us saying much'; the programme looks to have consisted mainly of male voice solos, duets and 'quartettes', with the audience of Brothers and Colonists apparently joining in hearty choruses to provide an 'absolute "night out" for the Central's humorists.' As we shall see, whatever the talents of the YMCA artistes may have been, the organiser was sufficiently encouraged to return each year until the late 1930s. Again, as with bowls, tennis and the heavy programme of Christian instruction, it looks as though the retro-Edwardian flavour of the concert party would have been more to the taste of the staff than of the involuntary Colonists. The CSU's publications, like those of any institution, naturally highlight good things going on, whether new buildings, better equipment, 'jolly evenings' with concert parties and other activities, or the success stories of former Colonists, a selection of whose letters to William Hunt were published in each CSU Annual Report:

'I was very pleased to get a letter from you and was pleased to hear that you are keeping in good health, as I am at present. I am now busy clearing some land for fallowing. We are waiting for rain to start seeding as we have not had any rain for some time and the farmers want to start seeding. Thanks for the trouble that you went to in writing to the Salvation Army and asking them to find my brother. I have wrote him a letter and trust that he will answer it. Please let me know what it cost you for finding my brother as I would be very glad to pay you for the trouble in writing and sending me his address' - West Pingelly, WA, April 18 1921. [*From a youth formerly in Fulham Workhouse.*]'

'Just a line to let you know that I am getting on fine. I am in an exceedingly good position, and hope to remain so until I have sufficient capital to deposit on a little farm of 90 acres I have in view. I am very sorry I have not written before, but I always was a poor correspondent. If it was no troubling you I wish you would send me different views of the [Turners Court] farm and buildings. W H B 'c.o. R. Thomas, Fish Creek, South Gipps, Victoria, May 27th 1925 [*From 'a boy sent to Wallingford from Whitechapel Board of Guardians, who went to Australia in 1922'. Several writers ask for photos – taken by Pittuck - of staff, buildings, animals etc at Turners Court*]'

'I hold you very high in my estimation, and have a real warm spot for Turners Court in my heart. On September 3rd I shall be married to the girl I have had now for five years. I have gone safely through the depression and am doing better than ever. Please know that if you or yours ever come out here for a trip, that you are welcome at our home ... I still hope as one of my cherished dreams that I shall one day attend a further Sunday afternoon service which I miss so. Please tell the boys at your next meeting that they will never regret those meetings, and that they will be a wonderful help to them through life. Also get them to sing 'God be with you till we meet again' the farewell hymn we sung before departure. I still see Mrs. Carr at the piano and Ben the collie. Yours sincerely C A K [*1932, from 'a bank manager's son' – presumably a 'private patient' – six years in Australia*]'

'Pleased to say I still write to B. who went to Australia about 8 years ago. I must admit he's had a rough time and somehow or other doesn't seem to keep his jobs long. I have told him more than once to try and stick to a job and keep it for a long time, as it will do him more good than to keep changing. I have enclosed a P.O. 3/- asking if you would be kind enough to send me Social Service for the next 12 months. I find Mr. Carr's articles very interesting indeed, and I'm quite sure when he goes round visiting the Colonists it brings good cheer to them. F P [*From 'a lad in Sussex' 1935*].'

It would have been understandable if Hunt had simply destroyed any less complimentary letters and, in any case, the 'failed' Colonists and those with miserable memories of Turners Court are unlikely to have written in the first place. On the other hand, there is no reason to think that these examples are other than spontaneous. Perhaps the most they can tell us is that some boys, at least, believed they had benefited from the 'rough and ready' agricultural training at Turners Court, and their memories of living there – even of the compulsory Sunday afternoon services – were generally happy.

The less rosy side of Colony life only appears sketchily in CSU publications. Throughout the Hunt era (and afterwards) men and boys continued to abscond, although such absconsions never represented more than a small minority – generally less than 10 per cent – of all Colonists. Adult Colonists, walking away from Turners Court (there was no other way of leaving) were written off without much comment; boys caused more concern although there was little that the CSU could do to trace them, still less to persuade them to return. In the mid-1930s the Committee was told that absconsions were continuing and some of the missing boys had been seen at military camps and 'have probably joined the army', perhaps suggesting a somewhat casual approach to the problem. Others, with no source of income and no testimonial from Turners Court to show, almost certainly lapsed into crime. Even apparent 'success stories' could turn out sadly; in 1934 Hunt had to report that a boy who had left the Colony some 3 years before and had 'done exceptionally well' (almost certainly on a British farm) was in prison awaiting trial on the charge of causing the death of his employer's niece, whom 'he was apparently courting.'[56]

One less rosy account of life in the Colony under Hunt was published, in 1941 by the Quaker and former Colony Brother, David Wills, in a book mainly devoted to the 'Q Camps' experiment of the late 1930s. Wills records arriving at Turners Court, aged 19, in 1923, and being greeted by Hunt ('a great man') who peered at him through thick glasses and bushy eyebrows before asking 'Are you afraid of boys, Mr Wills?' Wills, who had previous experience working in boys' clubs, said that he wasn't, but quickly found he was mistaken: 'In less than a week I was reduced to a state of despairing terror.' He asked to be moved to a different (unidentified) House where he inaugurated a reign of terror:

> 'I began by saying I would report any boy who broke the rule forbidding the wearing of boots in the dormitory. Fifteen boys were fined the routine 2d. from their pocket money. The paste-board slips that appeared in their pay envelopes explaining the absence of the 2d I found stuck on my cubicle door. These I collected with care and duly returned each to its owner. The procedure was to say politely,

---

56. OCRO, TCYT Box H02: Wallingford Colony Committee Minutes.

'Yours, I believe?' and as the victim took the card from my right hand I delivered a vicious blow to the side of his head with my left . . . Often my blows were returned . . . but in terror I pursued my chosen way and discipline was achieved. How sweet then to walk in the rowdy day room and with one glare produce a solemn hush. Supper was consumed in silence, prayers which followed in a deeper silence (once during supper a boy tried to carry more mugs than my regulation number, so I knocked him down, cocoa and all).'[57]

Hunt's assumption, that if Wills (or any other Brother) was not frightened of the boys, then he would not feel the need to terrorise them to keep discipline may or may not have been good psychology. Wills' later 'experiment' at the 'Q Camp' in Essex was based on voluntary attendance, consensual management, freedom of expression and a free choice of activity in the camp; his obituary contrasts this permissive regime with the 'punitively oriented' style of the Farm Training Colony (without actually identifying Turners Court). More importantly, perhaps, if Wills' recollection is true, it suggests – as did the MoH official's report, quoted above, that Hunt was either not aware of or turned a blind eye to much that was going on in the Houses and the dining hall at the Colony.

William Hunt, who had been severely affected by the death of his son in 1931, retired from the Colony at the end of 1933 and died in February 1934. There followed a period of just

---

57. D. Wills, *The Hawkspur Experiment*, 1941 (London: Allen & Unwin) p. 34-35. Wills, always vague about dates and places, does not identify the site of his 1936 'Q' camp, and I am grateful to several correspondents who have placed it at Great Bardfield, Essex. See also Marjorie E. Franklin, *Q Camp: an epitome of experiences at Hawkspur*, c. 1942, published Howard League for Penal Reform.

over 20 years which saw four Superintendents/Wardens (one of whom lasted only a matter of weeks); the initial impetus having perhaps faded with Hunt, the Colony began to look as though it had lost its way, while the restrictions of the World War II would once more make life difficult for the management.

Oxfordshire Colony

1920s photo, printed as a Christmas postcard, showing the Colony's first two residential blocks, with Colony offices between them

War memorial in Benson village, carrying the names of 45 'colonists' from Turners Court who lost their lives during World War I, and 10 in World War II.

Memorial at Lancaster Gate, London, London, to Reginald Brabazon, Earl of Meath, 'Patriot and Philanthropist'; during Brabazon's time as President, emigration to the 'Dominions' was a key feature of Christian Service Union policy

Colony Life, 1912-1933: The " Hunt Era "

(undated) photograph showing Basden and Albright Houses after mid-20th century refurbishment (*courtesy Turners Court Youth Trust*)

cadets being inspected at Turners Court during World War II (*courtesy Turners Court Youth Trust*)

Oxfordshire Colony

Ronald Menday, the Warden (left, wearing earpiece) and Sir John Hunt, conqueror of Everest and a substantial supporter of Turners Court, at the official opening of the Boys' Club, January 1957 (*courtesy Turners Court Youth Trust*)

unnamed 'lad' on tractor at Turners Court in the 1960s (*courtesy Turners Court Youth Trust*)

two lads enjoying perhaps rare moments of leisure in the 1960s, during the Wardenship of Col. Menday (*courtesy Turners Court Youth Trust*)

Colony Life, 1912-1933: The " Hunt Era "

Director John Wiles (left centre, bearded) with the cast of *Battle of Agincourt*, the first 'Arenascope' production at Turners Court, 1957 (*courtesy Turners Court Youth Trust*)

Hunt House, named for Sir John Hunt, today a private residence at 'Oakley Court'

The view today across 'Carr's Meadow'

CHAPTER 4

Colony Life, 1935-1954: Interregnum

'confusion developed, followed by a period of enlightenment'
– Menday & Wiles, 'The Everlasting Childhood', 1959

'I shall always think of Turners Court as my home and the starting place of my career as I have never regretted being there'
- letter from former 'colonist', 1940

It is always tempting to write history as a series of discrete chronological packages. In that style, William Hunt's retirement as Superintendent in 1934 and his death soon afterwards, might be ticked up as marking a discernible break in the way of life of Colonists and staff. R.P. Menday, who would occupy Hunt's place in the 1950s, writes in his 1998 history of Turners Court, as if 1935 were indeed the end of one era and the start of another, less well organised and less productive. In an earlier work largely based on his own time at Turners Court, Menday and his co-author John Wiles contrast the rule of Hunt (that 'great man') with what followed: a succession of Wardens (the title now changed from 'Superintendent') and 'confusion . . . as to the true nature of the place.'[1]

But this was not, of course, necessarily the way those living at Turners Court at the time saw things. The organisation and daily life of the Colony, and how it was perceived by the world

---
1. R.P. Menday & J. Wiles, *The Everlasting Childhood* 1959 (London: Gollancz) p. 111.

outside had already undergone substantial change, especially in the later years of Hunt's reign. Successive pieces of legislation set a firmer agenda for institutions like Turners Court. By the Children and Young Persons' Act, 1933, Victorian 'reformatories' and 'industrial schools' were finally abolished; new juvenile courts for those aged under 17 had powers to send young offenders to 'Approved Schools' including those run by philanthropic societies. The Home Office Children's' Department extended its powers of inspection; 'the concept of training by alteration of the environment permeated the Act.'[2] A year later, the Local Government Act 1934 ('Chamberlain's Act') instituted the dismantling of the 1834 system of poor relief. Unemployment became a national responsibility under the Unemployment Assistance Board (UAB); the 'Union' system of parish relief was finally abandoned, although the name and unsavoury reputation of the workhouse remained alive for at least a further decade.[3]

The dream of Tinling, Paton, Sutter and their contemporaries, of grateful 'colonists', saved from a life of unemployment and dissolution on the city streets, learning to work alongside their tutelary Brothers before being packed off to till antipodean soil, was rapidly fading. Menday himself noted that, following the 1933 Act, the Colony catered only for boys, 'and very difficult boys at that: homeless, deprived and maladjusted. The boys of whom everybody despaired.'[4] In the mid-1930s the Colonists still included up to 50 adult unemployed (in the 'Woodlands' spin-off colony); in 1935 one civil service visitor was surprised to find one 'private' colonist

---

2. J. Heywood, *Children in Care*, 1959 (London: RKP) p. 130.
3. See e.g. N. Longmate, *The Workhouse*, 2003 (London: Pimlico) p.12.
4. Menday & Wiles, *Everlasting Childhood*, 1959, p. 111.

aged 56. The emphasis, however, was plainly on the control, re-education and motivation of teenage boys and their eventual placement in employment – mainly agricultural, mainly within Britain. Politicians and public alike no longer looked to emigration as the panacea for economic ills, although it would remain on the agenda of Turners Court and some, at least, of the Colony's supporters for several years yet.

After Hunt's 22 year stint at the Colony, during which, Menday says, 'he came to know more about the administration of farm colonies than any other man in England,'[5] it is true that the next 20 years saw four wardens come and go (one of them only visible for a few weeks) before Menday himself was appointed in 1955. Hunt's immediate successor was a retired army officer, Ronald Grant, a man who Menday accuses of always having been at odds with his committee and his staff, and of enjoying an acrimonious relationship with his chairman (it is not clear whether Menday was referring here to Duncan Basden or to Sir Herbert Read,[6] a former civil servant and colonial governor who took over the chair in 1936, remaining until the end of the World War II).

With the Warden's job, Grant also took over the editorship of *Social Service* although he did not have Hunt's journalistic training (or his flowery style): 'No doubt articles were hard to come by for a new man for it certainly lost some of its flair'

---

5. Menday, *Turners Court*, 1998, p. 30.
6. 1863-1949. Read had retired in 1930 immediately after a short spell as Governor of Mauritius. His other interests included the Imperial Cancer Research Fund and the Society for the Preservation of the Fauna of the Empire. When Duncan Basden died, in 1944, he left £250 to the CSU provided that outstanding loans were paid to his heirs; Edward Sturge duly paid off the £1,000 needed. The Wallingford Committee minutes seem to be silent on the alleged acrimony.

comments Menday.[7] It became the custom to write about the CSU 'family', meaning the three colonies at Lingfield, Starnthwaite and Wallingford; most issues included a *résumé* of news from each of them, but there were fewer articles about social policy and practice, and fewer borrowings from other periodicals than in Hunt's day. Around this time the journal changed format, printed on cartridge rather than coated paper and with fewer pages. During the World War II it shrank further, appearing only quarterly with 'Wartime Edition' under the title and finally ceased publication in 1951.

Grant retired in May 1943; Menday's 1998 history alleges that Grant was 'asked to leave' by the committee, but the surviving records do not support this. His successor was to have been another military appointee, a far more shadowy figure, Captain Tune, who had scarcely moved into the Warden's house when he was charged with fraudulent conversion at Wokingham magistrate's court (the case was not connected in any way with the Colony). Tune was given leave of absence by the Committee and, 'after a great deal of trouble' finally left Turners Court in September. Meanwhile an acting Warden was found in 'Major' Hinton who, with his wife, had already served as 'housefather' before the war. Hinton, who had been on active service, asked if his wife (a former 'housemother') could occupy a Colony cottage until he could be released from the army, but was refused. On the departure of Tune, Hinton took over as Warden for the remainder of the World War II and the first six post-war years.

Menday is dismissive of Hinton's claimed rank, showing it only as 'Captain' in his 1998, history; successive Army

---

7. Menday, *Turners Court*, 1998, p.31.

Lists show him as 'War Service Capt.', but contemporary press reports, including an obituary in the *Oxford Mail* – Hinton died in 1973 – often promoted him to Lieutenant Colonel. Apart from the army, Hinton's interests were horse-riding (he had been District Commissioner of the South Oxfordshire Pony Club) and boxing, for which sport he served as an official at the 1948 Olympics in London. As well as questioning his military status, Menday claims that Hinton spent eight years of inactivity at Turners Court (his boxing expertise surely involved the Warden in some of the leisure time activities covered later in this chapter) and was then (like Grant) 'asked to leave'. Again, this may be a slight over-simplification on Menday's part: available records do not help. Hinton had certainly been unwell and absent from his office for a couple of months; when committee members visited the Home Office they were told by officials that 'a greater degree of co-operation might be expected 'if the office of Warden were in the hands of a younger man.'[8] Major Barlow stood in as Acting Warden in summer 1951. Hinton was then succeeded by a civilian, G.N. Manley, previously a District Inspector for the Department of Education, whose plans for a post-war change of direction at Turners Court are dealt with in due course.

As the changes that had taken place while Hunt was in charge happened gradually and piecemeal, so at the time they were not necessarily viewed as heralding any major change of direction; nor was the change of Warden seen that way. In 1934, the year Hunt died, the CSU and its supporters might quite reasonably have thought of Turners Court as a continuing

8. OCRO TCYT Box H01, Executive Committee minutes 29 May 1951. The Committee voted Hinton a leaving present of £2,000.

success story, set for a stable future. With the purchase, first, of Mays Farm, then Warren Hill Farm, the Colony was at its greatest extent – almost 1,000 acres (400 hectares). By the late 1930s the Colony's buildings comprised four Houses or Homes – Paton, Albright, Basden and Cory – plus the Ogilvie Hall, sanatorium, swimming pool, administration building, laundry, bakery, carpenter's and boot repair shops, all of which were grouped around the open space now named 'Carr's Meadow', together with the old 'Woodlands' army huts, and a number of staff houses and cottages.

In the middle of the decade there were usually around 300 colonists in residence; 1934 saw 156 arrivals, 107 trained colonists sent to situations. The number of 'absconsions' continued at 10 per cent or less (boys were, naturally, less able than adult Colonists simply to walk away from the site). The 1935 Annual Report claimed that the previous year had been 'notable for the number of lads applied for farm and domestic situations . . . the demand exceeded the supply.' Letters continued to come in from farmers expressing their appreciation of the lads 'and the debt they acknowledge to the Colony for its training and moral influence.' Two years later, in 1937, it was claimed that, apart from the teenagers sent to the Colony by local authority children's departments, there was 'a mass of letters . . . from parents to ask if the Colony would take in "a difficult son" for training.'[9]

At the annual open day in the summer of 1936 – an occasion when CSU committee members, supporters and other VIPs could inspect the work of Colonists and Brothers – a keynote speech by Col. Sir William Campion, reported

---

9. Menday, *Turners Court*, 1998, p.34.

in *The Oxford Times* (10 July), expressed his 'amazement' at what he had seen by way of good farm training at the Colony; 'everyone present would agree', he went on, that Britain needed to be 'an A1, not a C3 nation', a reference to the number of recruits to the armed forces currently rejected on medical grounds. Set piece occasions, like the open day, continued to get friendly coverage, even after Hunt's death, not only in the local press, but national newspapers, notably *The Times*, whose report (4 July) on that 1936 annual gathering mentions an 'excellent' display of physical training, concluding:

> 'It is the attention devoted to character building which gives to the scheme a special place among organized efforts on behalf of unemployed boys. The lads are accommodated under the "house" system . . Sometimes there is a case of home-sickness, but it is rarely that a boy loses interest in the full life which a stay in the colony means.'

Eighteen months later, *The Times* (8 November 1937) devoted half a column to a new appeal, the largest yet, aimed at raising £40,000 (a target which was to prove over-ambitious) towards new buildings. Grant, Warden since 1934, now worked mainly in the CSU's London office, where the Duchess of Marlborough chaired the appeals committee. Hinton taking charge as Deputy Warden. The following year there was a further publicity boost, a visit by the Duke of Gloucester, who was entertained by a display of the physical

Oxfordshire Colony

training regime, originally designed, the Duke was told, for turning those C3 Army recruits into Grade A1 'in about six weeks' and now adopted at the Colony with great benefit to newly arrived boys. The local press (the pen could well be that of Pittuck) was also enthusiastic:

> 'It was really extraordinary to be sitting there, watching these clean, bright, alert looking boys, in their smart gym kit, and to realise that they had arrived there almost entirely through the public assistance committees from various parts of the country.'[10]

CSU Annual Reports continued to print occasional extracts – briefer than in the past – from the letters of former colonists, which, allowing for judicious editing, seem to show that some, at least, of the 'lads' retained some affection for the Colony. Two examples, printed in the 1940 report, suggest nostalgia may have been enhanced by the then inevitable transition to army service (records show that it was not uncommon for boys who had left Turners Court to join the armed forces to return on leave – in some cases, no doubt, because they had nowhere else to go):[11]

> 'Just a line to let you know that I am getting on very well. Will it be O K to come up and see you, I will be pleased to see you before I am called up for the Army. I do not want to forget you. Good luck and all the best from your pal . . . [*From a farm boy who left theColony 5 years ago*].'

---

10. *Berks and Oxon Advertiser*, 11 May 1938.
11. In the mid-1930s one UAB official wrote (presumably after speaking to the Warden) that it was not uncommon for ex-colonists to spend their holidays at Turners Court [NA, AST 10/6].

'I shall always think of the Colony as my home and starting place of my present career as I have never regretted the day I went there . . . I still see some of the lads who left and are in my regiment. I remain your true friend . .[*From a Private in the Royal Berks, in India*].'

The number of boys emigrating was now small: January 1935 saw three boys off to Australia, but only because finance was provided from the 'Warden's Fund', a cache of donations intended for special needs. The following month a further three were set to follow, with the Public Assistance Board paying half the fares; the boys apparently passed the medical examination but were then rejected by Australia House, with no reason given. Grant worried that Turners Court was 'not looked on favourably' by the High Commission; he met High Commissioner Bruce who 'assured me we were not in bad odour, but would get a fair deal with other Training Colonies.' Sir William Campion (a former Governor of West Australia) concluded his 1936 annual gathering speech by saying that 'he ventured to prophesy that before very long emigration would be resumed,' implying that, for the present, emigration was not an option; as it turned out, this would continue to be the case up to the outbreak of the World War II.[12]

'The worst elements . . . have been got rid of'

All of these signs – capacity numbers in residence, availability of jobs, good reports in the press, at least some public finance and the hope that emigration would one day resume – might have suggested that Hunt's legacy had been generally benign, and that little change was needed. Wallingford Committee

12 Wallingford Committee minutes, OCRO, TCYT Archive Box. H01

minutes, however, show that Grant saw the need for further change. 'Twenty years on [from the official opening],' he wrote, there was confusion over its aims; lack of finance for emigration, and the smaller number of boys emigrating, meant that too high a proportion of the boys were going onto local farm work – more varied training should be provided. The mixture of 'mental' and 'backward' boys was undesirable and, in the light of the 1933 Act, the original mix of 'unemployable' adults and 'difficult' boys could not be sustained; having placed the remaining men into a separate house, Grant recommended that no more adult colonists should be taken in.[13]

Grant thought the amateur status of Brothers unsatisfactory. In writing about 'lack of discipline', which, among other things, he judged 'largely responsible for bed-wetting cases' as well as consequent difficulty in placing individual boys into employment, he gave priority to ill-discipline among the Brothers: 'Bad manners, slovenly habits and . . . a lack of a sense of responsibility are very grave handicaps and until those responsible for the direct control of Colonists learn to discipline themselves we cannot get the results we deserve.' The first priority was to improve the quality of the Brothers, speeding up the transformation of the semi-amateur and philanthropic nature of the Colony. At that time - summer 1934 – it seems that a number of Brothers had drifted away, perhaps because of Hunt's departure; some opted to train for work in mental health institutions; one, who had given no reason for leaving, was spotted working as a parachutist during an air display at Lingfield. The Colony's future staff,

---
13. Ibid.

Grant suggested, needed more careful selection, after which they must be properly trained for social service work. It was around this time that the job title of 'welfare officer' began to be used alongside, or replacing, the old appellation of 'Brother.' [14]

The new style reflected the rapid growth of interest in and reliance on the new expertise of industrial welfare officers by British employers as a whole between the two world wars. Stimulated partly by major changes in the workforce, notably the increasing numbers of women in employment during and after the First World War, it became common for employers to employ professional welfare officers and to provide such amenities as canteens, workplace medical facilities and even crèches. The Industrial Welfare Society (later the Industrial Society) lobbied effectively for facilities of this kind, and for statutory paid holidays which became a reality at the end of the 1930s.[15] By summer 1935, after what seems a commendably short time at the helm, Grant was able to report that discipline was 'distinctly improving,' with 'a general atmosphere of cheerfulness among the boys.'

The management structure was also revised, with separate finance and farm work sub-committees. In future Brothers would be engaged on three-year contracts. Houseparents' salaries were raised. Four years after Hunt's death the total weekly-paid staff was around 65, with a wage bill of up to £106/week, and many – perhaps seasonal – staff taking home £1 a week or less. A minor example of military-inspired

---

14. Ibid
15. See e.g. A. Russell, *The Growth of Occupational Welfare in Britain*, 1991 (Aldershot: Avebury). Russell suggests that post-1917 some employers embraced 'welfare' provision to stave off industrial unrest.

efficiency was the completion of a card index system of all Colonists, showing names and sponsoring local authority of all new boys; sadly, that does not survive, although later, in 1943, it became routine to record this information in Wallingford committee minutes. In passing, this is probably the place to record the installation, in 1941, of a new President of the CSU, the office having apparently been left vacant since the death of the charismatic Earl of Meath in 1929. The new President was the historian and former fellow of Queen's College, Oxford, Lord Elton,[16] who had served on a number of government and quasi-government committees; it may have been his secretaryship of the Rhodes Trust which brought him into contact with the CSU.

More pertinently, so far as the running of the Colony was concerned, the Wallingford Committee recognised (the decision may have been taken before Hunt's departure) that a properly organised system of after-care should be put in place. In May 1934 a Committee member, Squadron Leader Gordon, visited 58 ex-colonists now working in Dorset and Sussex, reporting 'all well with the great majority.' Such visits became regular, sometimes with brief extracts from the reports printed in *Social Service*, like the following from 1937, one of them signed 'F.A.S.H' (Hinton, the future Warden).

'G.D. Steward near Wantage doesn't seem quite settled down. He says he wants to do the milking but it is all done by machinery. His boss is very pleased with him. He will be alright [sic].'

16. Godfrey Elton, 1892-1973; created Baron 1934. Elton had fought and been captured in Mesopotamia during the First World War before taking up his Fellowship at Queen's. Several times an (unsuccessful) Labour candidate between the wars, he followed Ramsay Macdonald into National Labour obscurity.

'J. Pinder at Edenbridge looks fit, he has been at his job some time now and seems quite an experienced hand with poultry.'

Occasional reunions of former colonists living and working in the same part of the country were also arranged, perhaps with a member of the current Turners Court taking part. After-care tours continued during the World War II; *Social Service* (Jul-Sep 1941) reported that two members of staff, Mrs Wright and Mr Osborn, had managed to save enough petrol from their ration to get at least as far as Tidmarsh, Pangbourne, where they found ex-colonist J. Cowley not only 'doing very well' but commendably having saved money and bought himself a cycle 'not on the hire purchase system.' One further example of the kind of change in status that Grant wished to bring about was the introduction, later in the 1930s, of a psychological advice service, initially provided by Dr. R.W. Armstrong (Oxfordshire County Council's mental health superintendent) and Miss St. Clair Townsend.

The rather ill-defined, arms-length relationship between Turners Court and Whitehall, evident in Hunt's time, continued. Soon after he took charge, Grant wrote to local MPs and others interested in social questions, seeking their 'support'. In terms of hard cash, results were moderate. In 1936 the CSU applied to the Ministry of Agriculture and the Development Commission for £23,000 to increase Wallingford's capacity to 350 by building one more permanent Home (to replace the army huts on which several MoH officials had commented adversely), new staff cottages, plus improved bathing facilities in all the existing buildings, and to set up an 'endowment fund' of £10,000. Approving a grant of just £4,000 for farm building and other improvements, the Commission pointed out that while they appreciated the social work done by the CSU, they were only able to contribute to specific agricultural projects.[17]

It looks as though civil servants were still finding it difficult to place the Colony in the scheme of things following the passage of the Unemployment Act, 1934 which created the Unemployment Assistance Board (UAB).[18] On the one hand, officials thought that because the bulk of the 'colonists' were 'able bodied' the Colony might have become the responsibility of the UAB, at least as regards informal advice, but definitely not for finance! On the other hand, since most Turners Court residents were aged 14-16, they did not fall within the scope of the 1934 Act. There was then prolonged correspondence between UAB and Ministry of Health as to whether, since the Colony was not a 'designated training centre', 'normal' unemployed boys aged 16-18 could be sent there. Not until August 1939 was it formally agreed that the UAB could pay for youths to be trained at Turners Court.

While the formal relationship was being debated, MoH and UAB officials continued to visit the Colony. 1935's visits produced conflicting evidence. UAB officials minuted that Grant seemed to have no real knowledge of farming or farm training. Financial accounting was judged poor: 'no one can say with any confidence what is the profit or loss separately on the farm, dairy, poultry or piggery.' The officials found 'no attempt at further education or handicraft training'; illiterates, they thought, might be helped 'but there is no system.' While the new sanatorium was described as 'excellent', there were

---

17. NA, D4/371.
18. Material for the following paragraphs from NA files: MH 57/3/10; MH 57/52; AST 10/6.

serious defects in other buildings: too few showers for the boys, and the dining hall too small, necessitating two sittings for meals. There was a need to look at 'recreation and cultural and intellectual activity in the evenings' and medical attention seemed poor or non-existent, with (as we have seen) no trained staff on the premises.

In Grant's defence, the UAB officials found that the mental capacity of many of the boys precluded them from effective training and the local authorities should never have sent them to Turners Court. Grant's own suggestions for changes in administration were being 'greatly hampered' by the 'reactionary "Christian" committees' of the CSU. Some indication of Grant's own background (and that of the civil servants he dealt with) and his aptitude for the job appear in a letter he wrote to officials about a boy called Duffy from Bolton who, he wrote, exemplified the 'lower type of boy' sent to Turners Court by local authorities. Officials minuted, without comment, that Grant was convinced that such boys were affected in their behaviour at the time of the full moon,

> 'He has considerable experience in Africa and says that he can recognise in the boys many of the primitive characteristics of African tribes.'

Ministry of Health officials wrote more sympathetically. Grant was, they thought, 'dealing intelligently with the duties of his post.' Whether or not he was being obstructed by the CSU committee, they approved his plans to reduce the period of training, get rid of all adult colonists, fix 19 as the maximum age, and take in boys as young as 11 to 'arrest the deterioration of mental ability and character which otherwise often occurs'. Priority was being given to improving discipline and 'manners' after complaints from employers about the behaviour of boys who left the Colony to take jobs in the catering trade. The improved after-care service was noted: 'The Colony is particularly successful in placing youths in employment . . . very few are returned as unsuitable.'

By 1938, some things had improved. Maximum capacity had been reduced to 300 (almost all of them sent by local Public Assistance Committees) lessening pressure on accommodation; although bath and shower facilities were still inadequate, the enlarged dining hall meant speedier service, if not necessarily better food, as we shall shortly see. Hinton, as Deputy Warden was, officials thought, 'heart and soul in all the details of . . . training and general welfare. The boys were now kitted out with grey flannels and sports coats for weekends, and oilskins for wet weather work on the farm. The pocket money scale was revised and made dependent not on the particular job being done – previously a source of discontent - but the age and overall skill of the boy.

Food, almost universally the second most pressing interest of adolescent males, was a continual source of worry and complaint. 'I was disappointed with the food' wrote one of the first UAB officials to visit, in 1935. Grant assured him that the Colony was trying to provide three cooked breakfasts each week. By 1938 it was thought that advice on diet from the Ministry of Health had produced 'considerable improvement' but Whitehall continued to receive complaints from local public assistance committees on the subject. A

UAB visitor sampled the boys' lunch of sausages, Yorkshire pudding and potato, followed by jam roll; the sausages were thought unacceptable because 'the content is so uncertain.' Duffy, the boy from Bolton whose 1936 letter to his local authority had led to Grant drawing comparisons with African tribespeople, had complained, among other things, about 'porridge tasting only of water,' and alleged that he had been beaten or kicked out of the dining hall for complaining about stale bread. Grant assured the Ministry that no boy was ever treated in this way, and that the quality of the bread was good, but then rather undermined his case by admitting that it was regular practice for the staff to prepare the breakfast the night before by cutting up the allocation of bread and spreading it with margarine.[19]

Civil servants' concern about the provision of recreation and cultural activity was echoed in *The Everlasting Childhood*, the account of the work of Turners Court published in 1959 by Menday and Wiles, which paints a gloomy picture of life at the Colony in former times, a picture which the reader is invited to contrast with the regime of the late 1950s when Menday himself was Warden. Like David Wills, whose account of his brief and brutish term at Turners Court was quoted in the previous Chapter, Menday and Wiles can be mildly irritating, neither citing references nor identifying which decade they are describing. Writing about unspecified 'early days,' they say:

---

19. Turners Court was, among other things, a dairy farm. In Chapter 7 a comparison will be made with attention to bread at another 1930s institution, the Hawkspur Camp.

'. . there were few facilities for recreation, and none for leisure activities. In the evenings, the boys remained in their houses, seated at long tables, and with nothing to do. They had to ask permission to use the lavatories, and were frequently accompanied to make sure they did not run away once they were outside the room.'[20]

If 'early days' was taken to mean the first year or so of the Colony's existence, then the description could ring true, although there the evidence is scanty. At that time an obvious disciplinary model would have been the workhouse where no form of enjoyment was permitted, and 'silence [was] the norm during meals and work.'[21] But this extract from Menday and Wiles' book is in the middle of a longer passage about the 'succession of wardens' which followed Hunt's death, and the nihilist picture is difficult to square with what has been seen of leisure time activity even in the 1920s – the evening classes, film shows, swimming and sports sessions, Boy Scout troops and so on. In the 1930s that pattern continued, although an editorial in *Social Service* (January 1937) admits that boys newly arrived at Turners Court might find life dull after the constant excitement and crowds of London (from where a sizeable proportion of boys came): 'Here is boundless space; they must walk two and a half miles to the nearest town [Wallingford], and that is to them the tamest affair, with the cinema as the one bright spot.'

A photograph printed in the same journal in late 1941, towards the end of Grant's Wardenship, is captioned 'Recreation in Cory Home'; it shows boys playing bagatelle, billiards and so on under the eye of the House Father and (probably) the

20. Menday & Wiles, *Everlasting Childhood*, 1959, p.111.
21. P. Wood, *Poverty and the Workhouse*, 1991 (Stroud: Sutton) p. 101.

House Captain. The atmosphere certainly differs from that of the smoke-filled billiard halls and other venues that boys might have aspired to in London and other big cities, although some allowance has to be made for the time-exposure needs of the photographer (Pittuck). If direct evidence from the boys themselves is lacking, there is minor confirmation that for adults Turners Court could indeed lack excitement. A 1944 typescript account[22] written by anonymous members of an RAF unit which occupied part of the Colony grounds before D Day runs: 'Life at Turners Court was decidedly much more quiet than at Hendon.' The only palatable entertainment for the airmen, it seemed, was Wallingford's single cinema (the Regal, where the programme was changed twice weekly) and the public houses.

A steady trickle of news items suggests the Colony's management was doing what it could to provide diversion, perhaps after learning of the civil servants' criticisms. Complementing the improved physical training regime, parties of boys were being taken to Aldershot to see the military displays. On their 1937 visit officials noted that the 'new and up to date Talkie Cinema is proving to be very popular with Colonists and Staff.' Money for the new equipment (the old projector would have been a silent one) came partly from the Warden's Fund (which we have seen being raided for emigrants' fares) and partly from expected profits of the 'Tuck Shop,' a public school-inspired innovation, memories of which will recur later in this book; turnover was estimated at £900 per year (over £30,000 at 2010 prices). Cricket and football matches continued to be played against local sides.

22. 'Our Share: No. 1 Company 15 Air Formation Signals.' OCRO TCYT Box. H06.

By the mid-1930s there was, according to *Social Service*, also an organised winter social programme:

> 'Events seem to follow on each others' heels with alarming rapidity. Woodlands [spin-off colony] opened the ball with a very jolly evening. Mrs Osborne [house-mother] excelled herself in the manufacture of good things to eat and there were most amusing games, frequently of the 'practical joke' variety . . . Mr Osborne and his staff put on their very popular and inimitable sketches. Albright Home followed . . . in their excellent parody of the broadcast 'In Town Tonight'. Paton was next with their tea in the Home and the entertainment following in Ogilvie Hall.'

Home-grown drama was a regular feature: the 1937 'dramatic season' concluded with a staff production of a thriller called *Five at the George* by Stuart Ready, a prolific author of mainly one act plays for amateur groups and repertory companies from the 1930s to 1960s. Visiting performers, amateur and professional, ranged, in 1935, from the Army Physical Training School from Aldershot to the London Mystical Players who put on two religious plays, and at least two other visiting concert parties. One of the latter, in the winter of 1935/36, saw another return as impresario, apparently for a 12th successive year, of the former World War I Brother, Edward Sladen. He came this time with a party from Swindon, where he was now head of the Commerce Department at The [Technical] College:

> 'They have braved snow storms and fog in years gone by, but this year they had a pleasant journey. 'The Late Christopher Bean'

[by Emlyn Williams] was this year's choice for the evening. It was followed with rapt attention and the players' efforts were greeted with overwhelming applause at the close. The Colony audience is unique. Mirth just bubbles up almost without provocation. The members of all visiting parties assure us that it is a great pleasure to perform on the Colony.'[23]

It could well be that lads from inner London would have found much of this well-meant entertainment 'tame'. The Lancashire songstress Gracie Fields might have been more to their taste than the high-minded offerings of the London Mystical Players but sadly what was described as her 'hurried' visit to the Colony in July 1937 does not seem to have included an actual performance (she was appearing that week at Oxford's New Theatre). Discounting the enthusiastic tone of *Social Service*'s contributors, however, the picture painted by Menday and Wiles seems unfairly bleak.

In the summer of 1936, the enclosed rural life of Turners Court was briefly touched by events in the wider European political scene. The incident was first dealt with by the Colony's Finance Committee (Grant, the Warden, was away at the time) chaired by Edward Sturge,[24] the Quaker, who

---

23. *SS* March 1936; Hunt's editorial style seems to have survived his death. 'In Town Tonight', mentioned in the first extract, was a popular BBC wireless magazine programme, broadcast on Saturday evenings throughout the 1930s and 1940s.
24. 1872-1951. Member of a prominent Birmingham Quaker family, Edward Sturge worked in marine insurance, from 1913 as a Lloyd's underwriter. Apart from his long involvement with Wallingford (and Lingfield) he supported charities linked to temperance, adult education, housing and social welfare in Hoxton and elsewhere.

would begin each committee meeting with a few moments of 'silent preparation' (up to the 1940s, other chairmen would opt for spoken prayers). On 30 July a report was made to this committee 'with regard to unrest on the Colony which was being caused by Dr. Tioli, an Italian who had lately resided on the Colony.' The committee moved that two members of the staff, Martin and Horsfall, should visit Scotland Yard with a view to getting the authorities to 'effect the speedy removal of the man from the country.' Whether that visit took place is not clear, but by September the Committee was told the matter had been resolved:

> 'An attempt made by George Tioli – who had been a voluntary helper and two Brothers (then under notice) co-operating with a ~~Communist~~ camp at Wallingford to spread ~~communist~~ propaganda amongst the boys. This was admirably handled by Mr Horsfall, Acting Warden, who immediately discharged the two Brothers and one Woodlands [adult] Colonist. . . . Tioli has left the country.'[25]

The word 'communist', twice struck through on the Colony typewriter, was perhaps felt to be in itself so inflammatory that it could not be allowed to stand in the record. The offending camp is easily identified as one organised by the Oxford Trades and Labour Council (OTLC) for the benefit of unemployed men. Such camps were not uncommon during the slump of the mid-1930s. An Oxford Unemployed Camp Committee had been formed in 1935, with a £5 donation from the OTLC; it was also supported by, among others, the South Wales Miners Federation, the National Union of

---

25. Minutes, OCRO TCYT Archive Box H.12

Vehicle Builders, the shop assistants' union and the Oxford Co-op. Figures from the university, including Patrick Gordon Walker and Frank Pakenham, also served, somewhat fitfully, on the committee and a camp was held for four weeks that first summer, at Clifton Hampden.

In July 1936, camp was pitched at Bow Bridge, on the bank of the Thames between Wallingford and Moulsford; further camps were certainly planned for later years, including 1939, although their sites are not known. Again, the OTLC voted to contribute £5 (this was later increased to £5.15s.0d - £5.75). Pertinently, as we shall see, the OTLC also voted for a £5 donation to the National Council of Labour's Appeal for Spanish Workers (a collection for that Appeal at St. Giles's church in Oxford in September that year raised £1.15s.7d. - £1.72).[26]

This kind of impromptu holiday was part of a much broader - and largely non-political - 1930s trend. Influenced partly by practice in continental Europe (including the 'Strength Through Joy' movement of Nazi Germany) there was a burgeoning of 'healthy athleticism' – cycling, hiking, hostelling and rambling holidays; by 1939 the Youth Hostels Association had nearly 80,000 members, the Cyclists' Touring Club over 28,000. At Bow Bridge the unemployed men (their wives presumably left at home) spent the time in walking, swimming and other sports, singing round the camp fire in the evenings and so on, in much the same way as did the Turners Court boys on *their* annual camps. Much the same pattern was followed at the annual 'school journeys' organised by the London County Council and other major education authorities, which organised sea-side and

26. OTLC Minutes, OCRO ACC 5639 box 6 (formerly held at Ruskin College, Oxford).

Oxfordshire Colony

other camping trips for sizeable parties of school children - and continued to do so certainly up to the 1950s when, jumping ahead somewhat, Turners Court boys and London schoolchildren holidayed simultaneously at St. Mary's Bay, Kent, with the better endowed schools parties inviting the Colony boys to film shows and dances: *Social Service* (Apr-Jun 1950) said the Colonists were given 'complete freedom . . . to go anywhere and do anything they wished, within the bounds of good behaviour,' and claimed camp authorities and leaders of the school party paid tribute to the boys' 'good behaviour and polite manners.'

Individual supporters of the 1936 unemployed camp included a small number of those who might reasonably be portrayed as Communist sympathisers, among them the barrister D.N. Pritt, Labour MP for Hammersmith North, who would later number Ho Chi Minh and Jomo Kenyatta among his clients. The use of 'communist' by the Colony management, however, probably does no more than reflect their suspicion of the left in general and left-wing students in particular.[27] There is, however, no doubt about the identity of the man accused of having tried to subvert the Colonists. George (Giorgio) Tioli was an English-speaking Italian, possibly a journalist although this is not certain, whose presence in England that summer is otherwise frustratingly unrecorded. His presence at the Colony was also mentioned by Duffy, along with complaints

---

27. Frank Pakenham, later Lord Longford, then a junior lecturer at Oxford, had only recently been converted by his wife to the Labour cause from traditional conservatism. Left wing activism by undergraduates was periodically reported in the press: in June 1936 Basil, son of Professor Gilbert Murray, was fined £2 with 3 guineas costs for disrupting a British Union of Fascists meeting. But according to the official history of the University it was hardly representative: 'Earnest left-wing causes . . . evoked a deflating humour or even indignation from those who viewed high-minded crusading as bad form . .' (B. Harrison ed. *History of the University of Oxford VIII,* 1994, Oxford:OUP, p.96.)

about food and ill-treatment, in his letter to the Bolton Public Assistance Committee. When this letter eventually filtered through to the Ministry of Health, it suggested that initially Tioli, who produced references from the YMCA and others in Italy, had been employed by Grant as a 'Dr. of Pedagogy' to help examine 'difficult' boys, but disagreed with staff on methods of treatment and was asked to leave.

It is possible (the correspondence is unclear on the point) that Duffy, already marked as 'difficult' and anxious to get away from Turners Court, had been inspired by Tioli with the idea of going off to fight in Spain against Franco's rebels: other boys nicknamed Duffy 'comrade.' Meanwhile, Tioli's passport was said to have expired; it was also claimed that the Italian government was trying to get him back to Italy to serve in the army. 'All these things combined seem to have produced in Dr Tioli a violent hatred of one of the most experienced house-fathers [unnamed] and persecution mania', although, oddly, he is then said to have left 'on the best of terms with Colonel [sic] Grant.' If Tioli's reasons for being in England, and his precise activities in Oxfordshire remain ambiguous, his subsequent fate is, sadly, rather more certain. In August 1936, having made his way across France (whose authorities seem to have accepted his passport) he crossed into Spain at the frontier town of Port Bou, along with the Englishman David Marshall and joined the Tom Mann 'Centuria'. Sometime later that year he was taken prisoner by (Communist) special police in Barcelona and by

July 1937 had disappeared from view, possibly murdered by his captors.[28]

Refugees, rations and 'disgracefully large profits'

The structure of the Colony and its scale of operations were now in a steady state. Provision for adult Colonists was phased out (the Woodlands Home was closed in 1941). Most boys now arrived aged between 14 – 18, and could expect to spend between one and four years in training. The majority were what the Colony management termed 'difficult' lads; about 5 per cent were privately placed, all the rest came via Public Assistance Committees. By the end of the 1930s international politics was intruding into the life of Turners Court in more serious and more prolonged fashion than the alleged recruitment drive of the Communist Tioli. The army cadet force was now competing with the Boy Scouts for the boys' leisure time; by 1941 all 16-year olds had to register and were pressed to join either the Cadets or A.T.C. (Air Training Corps). Grant recommended enrolling *all* boys who were physically fit into the Cadets which, along with the

---

28. R. Baxell, *British Volunteers in the Spanish Civil War*, 2004 (London: Routledge) p.54; J.Newsinger, 'The Death of Bob Smillie', *Historical Journal 41.2*, June 1998, p.575-578. NA, MH 57/310. A photograph taken in September 1936 shows Tioli, somewhat inexpertly grasping a rifle, with other members of the company. He also gets a kindly mention - 'George Tioli . . .a great friend of ours' - in George Orwell's *Homage to Catalonia* (1980 edition, p.144). During his imprisonment he is said to have smuggled out police files relating to the earlier capture and death of other international brigade volunteers. 70 years on, his brother in law was still trying to establish precisely what happened to Tioli (private letter to the author, 29 Aug. 2007). Marlene Sidaway, Secretary of the International Brigade Memorial Trust, confirmed Tioli's arrival in Spain with David Marshall who, she says, described the Italian as 'a bit mysterious' (private e.mail, Nov.2008).

Home Guard, he wrote, 'already had a definite steadying influence on those who have enrolled.' He proposed setting aside periods each week for drill and physical training under a 'drill sergeant', preparing the older boys for their likely conscription into the armed forces although, as farm workers, some at least could claim exemption: in the last two months of 1941, out of 25 boys leaving the Colony, three went into the army, seven to farm jobs, four into domestic work, and three absconded (the remainder were either referred to the Courts or withdrawn by their public or private sector sponsors).[29]

August 1939 saw the Warden and staff preparing for the expected air raids. Stirrup pump, pump trailer (to be towed behind his private car) black out material and gas masks were acquired. Air raid practice involved the evacuation of the Turners Court buildings, with boys and men taking cover in nearby woods, women and children descending to cellars of the older houses; in fact very few bombs ever fell locally (unlike Lingfield, which later in the war suffered heavy material damage, although no loss of life, from unmanned V1 weapons). It was found that, unless the wind was in the right quarter, it was impossible to hear the nearest ARP siren at Benson; later it was arranged that the wardens would telephone the Warden when the alert was sounded and Turners Court then activated its own siren.

Even before this, however, as in the First World War, the Colony had to deal with an influx of refugees. The first reference to this appears in January, 1939, when the CSU agreed with the directors of Royal Dutch Shell to take up to 100 Jewish and other refugees from the Central Refugee

---
29. Minutes, OCRO TCYT Box H 01.

Committee for training, when vacancies occurred. Shell was acting as sponsor for this work; initially it looks as though they agreed to pay three shillings (15p) per boy per week, compared with the then going rate of 25 shillings (£1.25) paid by local authorities and others. The Annual Report provides some clarification:

> 'A radical change . . . in our work was caused by an offer made earlier in the year [1939-40] to the Committee for Jewish refugees to receive refugees from the anti-Jewish States [sic] for agricultural training . . . an Agreement was made with the Movement for the Care of Children from Germany [MCCG] to take 100 boys. . the Movement have   established a training camp of army huts on the Colony.'[30]

This temporary camp, alongside the Colony but with its own staff of adult refugees, was given the name Chiltern Emigrants Training Camp. By early 1940 around 45 boys were in residence. The Annual Report is diplomatic about the problems, saying that it was 'unfortunate' that initially the refugees comprised mainly boys who had been apprenticed in Germany and Austria to various non-agricultural trades and 'did not take kindly' to rural life, although some of them were able to exercise their own trades during construction of the camp. When this first batch could be placed in outside jobs they were replaced by boys who had definitely opted for farm training and the camp ran 'fairly smoothly' although 'a considerable amount of tact' had to be devoted to dealing with the boys' personal problems, including the inevitable worries about the fate of relatives still subject to the totalitarian regime

30. AR 1940, OCRO TCYT Box. H02.

in Europe and uncertain prospects for their own onward migration, for example to the USA.

By spring 1940 the number of refugees had risen to 75, mostly but not exclusively Jewish, who (unlike the ungrateful Belgians of 1914) were 'behaving excellently'. The Colony's administration seems, however, to have had a variable relationship with the refugee charities: the MCCG, based at Bloomsbury House under the firm hand of the redoubtable Lady Reading (famously the dominatrix of the WVS) is described as having a 'very complex administration.' By the end of 1940 it had been decided to disperse as many as possible of the refugee boys from the Chiltern Camp because of the 'precarious position' (meaning the risk of invasion). The few remaining refugee boys moved into the Colony itself and were paid for – whether by the MCCG or others is unclear – at the normal rate of 28 shillings (£1.40) per week. *Social Service* later noted that of some 70 refugees, 36 eventually got jobs in agriculture, 24 in other trades, with the remainder either joining the armed forces or emigrating.

Soon after the Chiltern Camp closed, the RAF took over its wooden huts; in 1944 it became a transit camp for troops *en route* to the invasion of France. RAF personnel were able to provide Turners Court with both practical and spiritual assistance: air force artisans instructed the lads in hut-building and similar work, while the padre took occasional church services in Ogilvie Hall. Later in the war other troops occupied temporary camps on the Colony and used parts of the estate for exercises, sometimes co-operating with the Home Guard.

In November 1939, two months after war was declared, *The Times*' agricultural correspondent paid a visit to Turners Court and reported favourably on the professionalism of the agricultural training provided and the apparent ease with which the boys could get jobs on British farms (emigration being no longer an option). Apart from thus improving job prospects for the trainees, the war obviously had other major consequences. Demand for home-produced food soared; in November 1941 Warden and farm manager reported that the farm was making 'disgracefully large profits' and asked the Wallingford Committee for suggestions as to how money from these 'fat years' could best be used for the future well-being of the Colony. The farm manager, Osborne, asked to be paid commission on sales of produce, without success - he got an increase in salary, and bonuses.[31] The move towards a more professional and better trained staff was halted by an inevitable increase in wartime staffing problems. Able-bodied instructors and other staff could not always gain exemption from conscription. New employees sometimes turned out to be less than satisfactory: a married couple engaged as head cook and typist in November 1941 had both given in their notice by January 1942. Costs, too, rose in wartime: practically all weekly salaries had been raised 'considerably' in late 1941, and would see further rises before the end of the war.[32]

The Colony had the benefit of growing foodstuffs for its own consumption, but fruit and vegetable crops on their own were of little use. Early in the war, in May 1940, a good rhubarb crop was reported, but no sugar was to be had for preserving it: 'I fear 50 per cent. . will be wasted.' Six months later,

31. Ibid.
32. Minutes, Jan 1942, OCRO TCYT archive box H01.

stores were already presenting 'increasing difficulties . . . our usual suppliers often cannot supply sanctioned requirements'. Cake and cheese were available only in small quantities and 'the position is likely to get worse rather than better.' An application for Colonists to be allotted the higher 'agricultural' ration of cheese available to adult farm labourers was turned down. Although cattle and pigs continued to be successfully reared, they had to be slaughtered elsewhere; Colonists, like all civilians, were mainly dependent on rations.

Successive Warden's reports continue to note shortages in this and other respects. In January 1941, perhaps partly due to the severe weather, deliveries of meat over the previous four weeks had fallen 723.5 lbs (328 kg) short of the entitlement; only half the usual quantity of sausage meat had been delivered and over 15 weeks, the bacon ration had fallen 380.5 lbs.(175 kg) short. Four months later, the meat delivery was found to be adequate for the staff, but the boys got only reduced rations. Liver, currants, sultanas, prunes, dried apples, figs, dates, suet, syrups and marmalade were all said to be unobtainable. Non-food shortages also hit hard: 'No soap, stockings or shoes are obtainable' in late 1940, although by early 1942 'Clothing questions seem to be gradually sorting themselves out. . we have received a large stock of coupons', although prices of some (unspecified) items were claimed to have risen by up to 400 per cent.[33]

By September 1941 Grant was able to report some easing of the food shortages: 'There has been a definite improvement in the catering, judging by the boy's [sic] comments and

---

33. In mid-1942 the index of clothing prices reached a peak of 195 (with 1939 = 100), but then fell back to around 170 for the rest of the war. (Hargreaves & Gowing, *Civil Industry & Trade*, 1951, London: HMSO)

comparisons drawn by visiting soldiers and sailors between our feeding and that in the Services.' Home-grown food would be much more abundant during the summer, of course, and it is not too surprising that former colonists who turned up on leave should say they preferred Turners Court food to that served in barracks. Apart from that comment, letters again confirm that Turners Court was seen as a place in which to spend precious leave from the forces.'[34]

Whatever the truth about the standard of cuisine, underlying problems remained. In 1942, in the middle of the war, an *ad hoc* 'Catering and Supplies' committee was formed; it recommended decentralised feeding, with all meals taken in the individual Homes. The Wallingford Committee minutes give an indication of what must have been a general deterioration in the fabric of the Colony's buildings: 'Apart from other considerations, the dining hall is inadequately lighted in the black-out and its general condition is such as to make it almost impossible to keep clean and sanitary.'[35]

The 1930s range of leisure activities continued throughout the war, with some additions. Whist drives and dancing lessons (a wartime innovation which stuck and, as we shall see, would be recalled with particular affection by post-war colonists) were organised for the boys, sex education lessons for the staff. Also popular were the wartime dances 'to brighten the black out' – for staff only – to which up to 100 guests might be invited from local RAF, WRAF and Canadian sappers: 'A most excellent and energetic band was provided by three of our staff,' ran one report in *Social Service*. Despite the Hall's shortcomings, the Dramatic Society continued to

34. AR, OCRO, TCYT Box H02.
35. Minutes, Jan 1942, OCRO TCYT Box H01.

operate. At the beginning of 1945 a mixed cast of staff and boys performed the Edgar Wallace thriller *The Case of the Frightened Lady* at the Colony and other venues, including Wallingford Grammar School and the Boro Court Mental Hospital, although scenes from religious plays, including those of Dorothy L. Sayers, were more commonly chosen. Each Christmas boys, staff and wives, mounted a traditional pantomime; 1943's *Ali Baba*, was described as,

> '. . . a really great show . . . the cast included twenty boys. Mr C. Steynor taking the part of Ali Baba was a joy to behold and to hear. He also played Mukkadam and in both parts brought the house down. Mrs Sowerbutts was magnificent in her make-up and part as the shrewish wife of Cassim. . . Mrs. Clifforth sang charmingly and Mr. Islwyn Rees was excellent in his part of Hamid, and in the dances with Miss Barrett and Miss Day (who cycled all the way from Reading to take part). The band . . . came up to their usual excellent standard in providing lively and suitable accompaniments.'

Although in retrospect it might pale in comparison with the productions we shall find being tackled in the 1960s, it probably offered a welcome interlude of light and light-heartedness during the black out – the last time this particular burden would have to be born: on 17 September 1944 it was replaced by the so-called 'dim-out' when, *Social Service* lyricised, it was possible again to see 'the lights that portend Peace', lights which, a decade earlier, had been somewhat fancifully compared with those of a large liner passing inshore.[36]

Visits by outside companies to the Ogilvie Hall also continued through the war; a few months after VE Day the Belfry Players of London, a group made up of amateurs, semi-professionals and professionals which had spent the war years touring garrison theatres, hospitals and AA gun sites, brought their production of *Ladies in Retirement*, the Victorian gothic drama by Edward Percy and Reginald Denham, staple fare for amateur dramatic societies over the decades but, again, perhaps on the tame side for an audience of 'difficult' teenage boys.

'restrictions and looming crises hung over them like a fog'

As peace returned, with Hinton as Warden, Turners Court, like the British people as a whole, might well have hoped that bright times were just around the corner. In Spring 1945 there were 260 boys in residence, originating from every part of England, from Devon to Stoke on Trent, from Monmouth to London. The number rose to over 270 that summer (the Annual Report claimed there was also a long waiting list) and it looked as though the Colony's future might be secure: 'It had been hoped that after a short period of peace ... the future would be brighter for the Colony.' January that year saw the opening by Edward Sturge of the new Home/House that bore his name – 'in recognition of his long and devoted service to

---
36. *SS*, Jan-Mar 1944. Nov 1936: the comparison with the pre-war liner is not by-lined but seems unlikely to have been written by the then Warden, Col. Grant.

the Christian Service Union and this Colony.' Smaller than the earlier buildings but built in the same style, Sturge House catered for 28 boys, mainly what were termed 'special cases', including the always problematic enuretics.[37]

Even under the allegedly *fainéant* Hinton, therefore, some innovations took place. On a more light-hearted level, in 1946, Paton Home introduced a wall newspaper, a 'not too serious commentary on incidents in the Home', almost certainly Turners Court's first internal medium of communication, as opposed to the journal *Social Service*, which was mainly intended for outside consumption. Lingfield, by contrast, had a hand-written and duplicated *Chronicle* as early as 1914; whimsical in style, it carried news of church services and other events. There seems to have been a running joke about Lingfield staff sloping off to London to enjoy themselves: a column headed 'Witty Bits by Witty Wun' claims 'It is rumoured ... that the L[ondon] B[righton] and S[outh] C[oast] Rly. contemplate running special Excursions to London for the benefit of Colony Staff.' No such references to excursions from Wallingford appear in Paton Home's short-lived wall newspaper: it featured an agony column, tips on better football tactics – 'Soccer Secrets' – a series of caricatures of staff and boys and, in deference to the Colony's evangelical roots, 'Wayside Pulpit', pictures and texts emphasising the spiritual side of life. Around the same time came an appeal for funds for the Chapel library to buy suitable spiritual books which could be read, in the library, in what was now styled a quiet hour between 6 and 7 p.m. each day 'under the supervision of a trusted boy.'[38]

37. Menday, *Turners Court*, 1998, p.36; AR 1945, OCRO TCYT Box H03.
38. OCRO, TCYT Box H 02.

Three years later a more formal publication was launched, with management approval. This was *The School Review*, 'being the Magazine of Wallingford Farm Training School.' The first issue, dated April-May 1949, consisted of 12 quarto typed and duplicated pages, with an attractive black-and-white illustration of a country scene on the front cover.[39] Reminiscent of the magazine of a minor public school, it reflected the largely unchanged ethos of Turners Court since pre-war days. Articles touched on such subjects as the celebration of Holy Week, the boys' Bible Club and Young Farmers' Club, the still-popular dancing classes, athletics, inter-house football, and work-related issues such as 'What the boss wants from me.' There were two pages of 'House Notes' covering what were now the five accommodation units – Albright, Basden, Cory, Paton and Sturge. The prose style suggests that the boys themselves wrote little, if any, of this material: 'The advance summer has been welcomed by Paton boys, in numerous country walks, evenings and weekends, which have been greatly appreciated.' There was also news of 'Old Boys' [sic] including Ron Hewitt ('taller than ever') and Ken Martin, both of whom had spend embarkation leave at Turners Court before leaving for military service overseas.

Having apparently done well during the war, the Colony's farming activities continued to predominate. In 1947 the name of the institution was changed to Wallingford Farm Training School, belatedly reflecting the alterations that had taken place in the 1930s, not just in the training that was offered, but in the way the institution wished to be thought

---

39. The same illustration, unattributed but probably the work of a member of staff, was re-used on the cover of the *Turners Court Magazine* (see below, Chapter 6).

of by its 'customers' the local authorities. Annual Open Days returned, but shifted to September. The local press report on the 1949 Open Day enthused about the boys' performance in contests such as sheaf pitching, poultry plucking and dressing, sheep husbandry and tractor driving. The minority of 'lads' who 'do not take to farming and all its aspects so readily' were able to show their skill in handicrafts, including boot and shoe making and repairing, some 'beautifully made wool rugs and woodwork articles.'[40] The Young Farmers Club flourished and Colony boys took part in annual agricultural competitions. Evening lectures were given on topics including artificial fertilisers and watercress management. CSU Annual Reports, much briefer than in pre-war years, continued to print extracts from letters by former colonists:

> 'I am grateful for everything you have done for me. I have learned my lesson and am going to be a man trusted by people [1945]'

by employers:

> 'I am pleased to say Leslie is quite happy. He is a very nice lad and seems interested in his work [as under-gardener] in which there is evidence of good training [1944]'

and by LA children's officers, like this one from Bury (Lancs) County Borough:

---

40. Berks & Oxon Advertiser, 30 Sept. 1949.

'I was pleased to find William in such good condition and profiting by his stay with you. He has certainly gained in every respect and is a credit to your care and attention [1950].'

With more accommodation it was hoped that satisfied local authorities like Bury would place more children in care, but, as with other institutions, the hopes were not realised. Rather, as the novelist Susan Cooper lugubriously put it in relation to Britain generally, in this 'Age of Austerity', 'the mood was . . . one of bleak resignation . . . at the restrictions and looming crises that hung over them like a fog.'[41] The Colony's underlying problem remained the one that had haunted Hunt - inadequate finance. Despite the modest annual profits made from farm operations, in 1945 the mortgage stood at £12,300, cash in hand £10,000, an apparently viable position. But by the beginning of the next decade circumstances had combined to leave the Wallingford committee with an overdraft of £20,000, a figure which increased to nearly £25,000 by 1959 before, under Menday's wardenship, the sale of Mays Farm once again reduced it to £14,000 (see Chapter 5). New farm machinery was needed, at 'awesome cost', to replace machines which had worn out during the war. More capital had to be injected in the hope of making the market garden profitable. Far from increasing, as had been hoped, the number of trainees started to fall. Fees were increased, but local authorities were reluctant to see them rise to a level at which the School would break even. In 1949 the School showed a trading loss of £3,000. The bank had forced the CSU to sell War Loan to

---

41. S. Cooper 'Snoek Piquante' in M. Sissons, P. French eds, *Age of Austerity*, 1986 (Oxford: OUP) p.30.

reduce its indebtedness. That same year 60 head of cattle were sold off, raising £3,000 cash.[42]

The changes introduced since Hunt's day meant that the Training School needed a larger and better qualified teaching staff, all of whom had to be paid nationally agreed salaries: the days of the lay Brother who might serve his three years for £1 a week or less, plus board and lodging, were long gone. The original CSU colony at Lingfield found itself in the same boat: 'recruitment of staff and the adoption of salary scales more in line with those in comparable fields of work taxed the resources' of the CSU.[43] Regular inspections by Home Office, Ministry of Health and individual local authorities, notably the LCC, were welcome in that they underlined the status of the School, but also often resulted in calls for extra expenditure: at the beginning of the 1950s, for instance, the Home Office insisted that individual chairs, rather than Victorian-style benches, should be provided in the dining hall at a cost of £500, and that recreational space should be increased. The local and national authorities now expected Turners Court to provide more by way of non-farming education, including literacy and numeracy classes and special provision for 'backward boys.'

A publicity leaflet dated July 1950, aimed at local authority children's departments, confirms that boys were now taken only between the ages of 15 (school leaving age) and 18. It emphasises technical training in agriculture, forestry,

---

42. AR, audited balance sheets, OCRO TCYT Box H03.
43. McClellan, *History of the CSU*, undated, p.5. After the World War II it had initially been thought that Lingfield might become part of the National Health Service, but eventually it was decided that an epileptic colony was outside the NHS' scope and the considerable programme of building and modernisation there continued as a voluntary enterprise.

market and other gardening, along with boot and harness-making, and includes such ancillary subjects as Citizenship, 'Getting on with People', 'Choice of Friends and Value of Friendship.' More general education was limited to classes run in conjunction with Oxfordshire County Council for 'backward and illiterate' boys. Total capacity was now put at 230, in five houses still publicised as being 'on the public school system', each with Housemaster, his wife and a staff of welfare officers responsible for the 'discipline, recreation and character training' of the boys. Each boy now received pocket money of 6 shillings (30p) per week – enough, perhaps, for one visit to the Wallingford cinema plus some fish and chips on the way back to Turners Court, with a few pence left to spend at the School Tuck Shop.[44]

As peace returned, the traditional concentration on farm training may well have seemed the best way forward. The raising of the school leaving age (to 15), the automatic deferment from National Service given to agricultural workers post-1945, and the apparently good prospects for employment on British farms, meant that a full course of farm training could be given to boys in the two or three years they could expect to spend at Turners Court. Unfortunately, automatic deferment was removed in September 1951, at the end of Hinton's time as warden. The prospect of boys being called up for National Service soon after their 18th birthdays meant that they had to be placed in employment while still aged 17, so that they could settle into their farms, have a 'home base' during their two years service, and a job to return to on demobilisation. 'Inevitably', notes the 1952/53 Annual

---

44. Menday, 1998 (p.39), says it was 5 shillings (25p) in 1951, but he may have been writing from memory.

Report, explaining why Cory House had now been closed, this shortening of the age range and of the average length of the technical training period considerably reduced the total number of boys in training, at a time when agricultural employment was, in any case, already on the decline, thanks, partly at least, to rapidly increasing mechanization.

In some cases no doubt the Turners Court regime did help smooth the transition both to National Service and then into civilian employment. A clipping from a local newspaper – unnamed and undated, but internal evidence suggests the mid-1950s – carries an interview with Mike Shaun, an orphan from Chesterfield, Derbyshire, who passed through a succession of orphanages and teenage jobs in domestic service before being dismissed and sent to the Wallingford School. 'It steadied me up a bit' he says. 'I became the best scrubber, the best sock-darner, the best milker, the best gardener and a Company Sergeant Major in the college [sic] Army Cadets.' His two years in the army were, says the report, 'Mike's happiest days', perhaps because the daily routine was, like that of Turners Court, strictly defined. On demobilisation he not only got a job as motor mechanic (although he doesn't say that this was one of the trades he worked at while a colonist), appeared on Hughie Green's TV show 'Opportunity Knocks' and was signed up for a recording date by Oriole Records.[45]

Less happily, the decline in numbers of trainees, along with the steady increase in costs, which had begun under Hinton, continued under his successor, G.N. Manley, a former schools inspector and the first professionally qualified person to take charge of Turners Court. In 1951 there were

---

45. OCRO TCYT Box H06.

150 boys in residence – little more than half the total capacity. Fees to local authorities had to be raised to 73/6 (£3.66) per week; weekly charges were raised again a year later, and in 1955 (by which time Menday had taken over as Warden) they reached £4.19 shillings (£4.95), plus £50 per year for clothing. Oxfordshire County Council found these charges 'fair and reasonable'; only 6 out of the more than 500 children 'in care' in Oxfordshire under the provisions of the Children Act, 1948, were at Turners Court; Oxfordshire was by now also 'supervising' boys placed there by other local authorities, whose views on the charges are not recorded.[46]

By 1954 annual expenditure was out-running income by nearly £10,000 and the overdraft, as we have seen, was approaching £20,000. In October 1953 12-15 acres of Potters Farm was sold to the aggregates company Grundon for gravel extraction on a royalty basis.[47] The fabric of Turners Court was causing concern; in April 1954 a management sub-committee noted that no exterior painting had been carried out since 1939, while the School's motor car – a gift from Edward Sturge – and the office typewriter (each of them apparently unique) both needed replacing.[48] Manley instigated various cost-cutting exercises, including a reduction in staff. This in turn meant that fewer boys could be accommodated, and for shorter periods. A draft letter dating from 1954 from the Warden to a (unidentified) local authority explains that 'because of severe shortage of staff' he must ask them to

---

46. Oxon CC Quarterly reports, OCRO ACC 4544; the Duchess of Marlborough had been co-opted as a member of the county Children's Care Committee.
47. Minutes, OCRO TCYT Box H01.
48. The typewriter, at least, was duly replaced with a second-hand model costing £21.10 shillings (£21.50 – something over £300 at 2010 prices).

remove Stanley Jones who had been at Turners Court since January 1953 and 'in my opinion is sufficiently trained.'

There was some disaffection among remaining staff about salary levels and the lack of a pension scheme: in mid-1953 the Wallingford committee minuted concern over the handling of 'widespread discontent' among the welfare staff (no longer, apparently, commonly called 'Brothers'); the committee set up an 'investigating sub-committee' to interview staff members, while expressing its confidence in the Warden. Manley protested about the sub-committee's report being sent to the staff concerned without any input from him and the episode looks to have contributed to his decision to leave Turners Court the following year.

Meetings with Home Office officials were not encouraging. Among child-care professionals and politicians the view was gaining ground that the ideal environment for the troubled child was a small home, staffed by married couples, for a small number of children, rather than the four or five barrack-like blocks of Turners Court. Menday writes that 'the impression gained was that the Home Office was beginning to lose interest in the School and there was a suggestion of closure.' In his own internal memorandum of late 1953 or early 1954 on 'The Future of Turners Court', Manley, reporting these trends, wrote that he doubted whether any independent non-profit making body could now exist, cut off from direct Government financial support. His own preferred option for the future of Turners Court was that an ESN (Educationally Sub Normal) school, perhaps to be named 'Cory House School', should be set up with Ministry of Education support for boys up to the age of 16, after which they would pass on to vocational training, which would continue as a parallel stream on the same site. Manley claimed that the ESN boy 'is a large factor of modern times' but there was as yet no educational-cum-vocational establishment catering for such boys.

Manley's plan was never formally accepted by the committee. During the summer of 1954 he handed in his notice while absent on holiday, and in August Colonel Royston was appointed Bursar and Deputy Warden, to hold the fort until a new Warden could be recruited. Minutes suggest that, not for the first time, there had also been tension between the farm manager and the central administration of the School; the management committee thought it necessary to put on record Royston's overall authority over Farm Manager. In September Royston put his name to a report urging the committee to make a choice between somehow improving the quality and quantity of traditional vocational training (and securing more local authority report) or opting for Manley's ESN boarding school, which assumed Ministry of Education Finance. Eventually, in 1955 under the new Warden, the ESN plan was finally dropped.[49]

Although Manley seems to have grasped the necessity of some radical change, if Turners Court were to continue viable, there is some sense that things had been allowed to drift, and that the original philanthropic, informal and slightly unformed remit had not yet been fully replaced. Perhaps nothing illustrates the long overhang of this legacy so well as the story – heart-warming on a personal level - of Charles William Hunt, who had come to the Colony from Clapton, East London, in 1920 as a teenage boy, severely handicapped

---

49   Minutes etc, OCRO TCYT Box.H01.

by infantile paralysis (so he was a genuine and unfortunate 'unemployable'). What was supposed to be a 'short visit to enjoy country air' lasted 29 years, nobody at Turners Court having had the heart to send him back to, in the first years, the workhouse or then the local authority. 'Charlie' was equipped with an electric wheel chair and became a familiar figure[50] around the Colony, and as far afield as Wallingford. He was given some office work and sent on errands: 'his attention to business was amazing', claims the report in *Social Service* announcing Charlie's death in 1949, 'as also was his cheerfulness, his shrewd wit, and good humour.'

Although the management committee seem to have accepted Manley's legacy in the form of his plan for the ESN school, a provisional opening date of October 1955 had to be postponed; in the interim a new Warden was found in Lt. Col. R.P. Menday, who took over on 1 January 1956 and would have very different plans of his own.

---

50. The present author recalls seeing Charlie setting off to the shops in his electric buggy during WWII.

CHAPTER 5
Colony life, 1955-1967: the 'Menday era'

Unreadiness for employment is frequently due to unreadiness for life
- R.P. Menday, J.Wiles, 'The Everlasting Childhood'

Following Manley's departure in 1954, the CSU Wallingford Committee's first choice of replacement was Captain Johnson, headmaster of an Approved School on the Wirral. Johnson is said to have visited Turners Court, seen the dilapidated state of the buildings and insisted that £10,000 would have to be spent on new staff quarters. As the committee plainly could not command anything like this sum, Johnson turned down the job. The committee's second choice was Lt. Col. Ronald Menday, who accepted. This choice may look no more than the easy option of another retired officer to head this institution for 'backward', 'unstable' or 'deprived' boys. Menday, however, differed not just from the journalist Hunt and the educationalist Manley but also from previous ex-army wardens (although the latter may not have merited the dismissive verdicts Menday dished out in his own 1998 history of the Colony). On his appointment Menday says he asked that his military rank should not be used: 'far too many colonels and senior ranks had been involved which seemed to him not a good advertisement for one running a child establishment.'[1] Nevertheless, press reports and CSU publications continued to identify him as 'Lt. Col.' throughout his wardenship, and

---
1. Menday, *Turners Court*, 1998, p.42.

some of those who spent time at Turners Court in the early 1960s recall a distinctly parade ground manner as being one of Menday's trade marks.

Born in 1913 in the Buckinghamshire village of Buckland (the family later moved to Kent) Ron Menday could reasonably claim (in his 1998 history of Turners Court) to have a 'basic knowledge of farming from birth.' Although his first job, after leaving school at 16, was as an apprentice draughtsman with British Thomson Houston (BTH), he returned to work on the family farm after developing TB and later ran his own poultry farming business. He also served in the (Buckinghamshire) police and, crucially, worked at boys' clubs in Aylesbury, Bermondsey (contemporaneously with Clement Attlee), Chelsea and Scunthorpe. After enlisting (in the military police) in October 1939 he trained as a commando officer and served with distinction in the D Day landings, earning the Military Cross for his 'great vigour and determination' while in command of assault troops at Ouistreham in Normandy on 6 June 1944; later, he writes, he had the Croix de Guerre pinned on him by de Gaulle.

After demobilisation in 1946 Menday became the manager of a boys'club in Welwyn Garden City, with particular interest in drama. He then spent about a year in the British zone of occupied Germany, dealing with Eastern European displaced persons, where he met his Swedish wife Inga, also concerned with United Nations relief work. Returning to Britain, Menday became Social Development Adviser and Chief Administrative Officer for the new towns of Welwyn Garden City and Hatfield. He also resumed the -unpaid - wardenship of the Welwyn boys' club and became a committee member of the

National Association of Mixed Clubs and Girls' Clubs; there he met the South African John Wiles, who would play an important part in Turners Court's cultural activities and collaborate with Menday on *The Everlasting Childhood*.[2]

While waiting for Menday to take over, Royston continued in charge as Deputy Warden; Inga moved into the Warden's house and Menday visited at weekends before taking control in January 1955. Menday's view of the state of the training school in those months is described in *The Everlasting Childhood*, published four years later: 'twenty years of arrears of maintenance of buildings, and a lack of happiness over all' which, he says, nearly drove him away again. He was, he said, assured on every side that the school was 'on its way out; that it was only the dumping-ground for boys of whom even the children's officers had despaired; that the day of the larger group home was definitely over; that the farm would not pay; and, in fact, that the sooner he closed it down the better it would be for all concerned . . .Children's officers . . thought of the school as a work colony, where Dickensian charity and discipline went hand in hand.'[3]

Royston, writes Menday, told him that the run down condition of the school, and the relatively poor pay that could be offered, made it difficult to recruit staff: many of those in post were, he said, 'awful, producing no leadership;' small wonder, then, that Menday summed up the prospect as 'a daunting task.' Menday's own recall of the details of this task may sometimes vary slightly; his 1998 history of Turners

---

2. For Menday's pre-Turners Court career see *To a Peak and Beyond* (1995), a privately published autobiography written with the press and TV journalist John Hartley.
3. Menday & Wiles, *Everlasting Childhood*, 1959, p. 112.

Court cites the number of boys in residence at the time of his arrival as 100, whereas *The Everlasting Childhood* puts it at 130 (by mid-1955 it is shown as 161, reaching a maximum of 168 in 1968). But there seems no reason to doubt the overall picture he painted, to the CSU committee, of the condition of the buildings and the lack of imagination in the boys' regime. The boys were living, he said, in 'horrific conditions' where all WC pans were cracked or broken, metal beds had sagging springs, grey blankets and no sheets. 'Because of lack of supervision or lack of money in the past, certain things are rapidly falling into disrepair.' He was dismayed to find boys being kept indoors every day to scrub floors, an economy made necessary by the colony's inability to pay wages for domestic staff.[4]

Menday and Royston estimated annual running costs at £40,000. Menday then says he calculated that with only 120 boys each paying the current rate of four guineas (£4.20) per week, annual income would be only £26,000, leading to an obvious Micawberesque conclusion. His 1998 history reads as if he had made this calculation on first arriving at Turners Court, in the Autumn of 1954; but this seems odd, since there were then around 160 boys in residence; Menday also wrote, with apparent envy, of the time when Hunt ('a wonderful man') had managed to boost the number of colonists to around 300. It does not seem likely, however, that in the 1950s serious thought was given to a return to those days; quite apart from the difficulty of raising those

---

4. Menday, *Turners Court*, 1998, p.43; OCRO, TCYT Box. H.01. Turners Court was far from unique in using boys for domestic chores; the private boarding school attended by the present author in the late 1940s depended on pupil help with daily cleaning, washing up etc.

numbers from the local authorities, fire regulations and other practical considerations would have ruled out that kind of increase; indeed, an unofficial Home Office limit of 160 boys was already in place, although it was briefly exceeded at the end of the 1960s.

More importantly, however, Menday seems to have hit upon Turners Court's underlying financial instability – lack of capital, inability to borrow cheaply, and the reluctance of local authorities to pay fees high enough to make the colony viable; '. . . the constant lack of funds is a crippling handicap', Menday and Wiles would write in *The Everlasting Childhood*. Indeed, given the enthusiastic tone with which Menday, in his 1998 history, recalls his arrival at Turners Court, the 1959 book reaches a surprisingly pessimistic conclusion: *no* voluntarily funded organisation can offer the full range of services at the top quality in the way that statutory bodies can do; '. . . what the voluntary organisation can do the statutory authority can do so much better'.[5] Manley had, of course, reached much the same sort of conclusion, the exact opposite of early CSU publications which consistently extolled the superiority of voluntary effort over inefficient state institutions.

In January 1955 there was certainly room for pessimism: the bank overdraft stood at over £18,000 and there were various small debts to local traders. The 'disgracefully large' profits achieved by the farm in wartime seem to have melted away; the reported profit for 1954 was £2,000, 'a matter of great concern to the committee.' Menday suspected the farm manager of siphoning off money; a year later he was

---

5. Menday & Wiles, *Everlasting Childhood*, 1959, p.209.

dismissed; a deputy house-master had been asked to resign soon after Menday's arrival, as were the cook and his wife, charged with taking food from the kitchen.[6]

Even before he had officially taken up the Wardenship, Menday prepared for the Wallingford committee his 'Temporary and Immediate Plan' for the future of Turners Court which should, he wrote, concentrate on 'character training and the production of a boy who, in addition to being a fully trained man in any particular branch of farming, market gardening or bricklaying etc, will also be generally fitted for life.' Menday thought that in the past too much emphasis had been placed on the farm as an end in itself, rather than as the 'servant' of the school. He also expressed concern at the preponderance of farmers on the committee. As Menday had alleged about Grant, relations between Warden and committee may have sometimes been less than perfect: about a year after Menday's appointment, it was recorded that information seemed to be leaking from the committee to the outside world; Royston 'categorically denied' being responsible, and the culprit never seems to have been identified. For the national CSU committee Menday seems to have had little time, describing it to a visiting Home Office official as 'four octogenarians meeting once a year in London.'[7]

Menday did, however, welcome the appointment to the committee of Major John Hedges, head of a Wallingford

---

6. Menday, *Turners Court*, 1998, p45-47; OCRO, TCYT Box H13.
7. OCRO, TCYT Box H02; NA, BN 62/3222. Royston sounds unlikely to have been scheming against Menday; although 2 years older, an Indian Army veteran, civil servants wrote: 'In spite of age and rank he appears relatively youthful . . . is pleasant and correct and gets on easily with staff and boys' (BN 62/3222).

Colony Life, 1955-1967: the "Menday era"

law practice and member of the family which had bought Wallingford castle grounds from the Crown in the 19th century. Hedges went on to serve as chairman of the Wallingford committee for nearly 20 years. Like Menday, Hedges said he wished his military rank to be disregarded: at that period, four of the other 12 committee members are usually identifiable as retired officers; the military flavour of Turners Court around this time is also exemplified by the programme for Menday's first annual sports day, which shows him as referee, Lt. Col. Royston as Chief Field Judge and Major L.C. Lacey as the Official in Charge of Athletics and Physical Training.

Menday and Hedges agreed on the need for drastic change, and for an injection of new money. Among the specific changes Menday proposed was the provision of a dedicated Further Education Centre in Cory House, replacing Manley's plan for an ESN school, but with capacity to take in boys when they left other ESN schools. The Houses should be organised to offer each boy an individual progression through different stages of training, starting with a reception and assessment period in Sturge (the smallest of the Houses, opened in 1945). There needed to be more evening activities of an educational kind, better facilities for recreation, improved after-care, a modernised canteen, more realistic pocket-money allowances and a less restrictive regime for outside visits, with week-end passes to Wallingford 'provided boys co-operated.'[8]

His plan also mentioned up-dated discipline. Menday said he intended to break up the canes, (which had replaced the Brothers' original leather strap); he wished, he said, 'the boys

---

8. Menday, *Turners Court*, 1998, p.42-43, OCRO, TCYT Box H02. For most of Menday's wardenship the 5 houses were Albright, Basden, Cory, Paton, Sturge.

to smile when he met them.' Menday's attitude to physical punishment, along with his management style, was called into question some five years later when a letter of complaint from one of the boys reached the Home Office, alleging that the Warden 'rages at them and strikes them with his fists.' After visiting Turners Court, one official found that, 'Generally there is a friendly, free relationship between Warden and boys and Warden and staff.' A second visitor, however, wrote: 'I think it likely that Mr Menday "rages" at boys . . . I have recently heard that former staff have alleged that [he] could become hostile to boys or staff who were not going the way he wished, but I have no direct evidence.' Minutes on the Home Office file sum up the Warden thus:

> 'Major [sic] Menday . . . is a man of ideas with the necessary drive and enthusiasm to carry them out. He knows how to manage publicity. His public manner to visitors, staff and boys is friendly . . . He appears, however, the kind of man easily precipitated into anger and hostility with [staff and boys] who are not going the way [he] would like. At times such differences could become violent. There is a spirit of interest and enthusiasm for the changing school. There is, however, the impression that all members [of staff] are not entirely happy with the Warden's dynamic rule.'

One specific cause of unhappiness was Menday's insistence on dealing with all casework, disciplinary or otherwise, himself; civil servants noted that the contribution of even senior House staff to 'social training' – on which Menday himself put much emphasis – was very limited. Less seriously, perhaps, the civil servants noted that Menday's use of a hearing aid could make communication 'difficult' and might affect his understanding of people and situations; in 1962 he had an operation and dispensed with the aid.[9]

The civil service visitors seem to have agreed with Menday that without considerable change, including change of personnel, Turners Court could fail. Many of the individual ideas he put forward were building on or improving changes that had been put in hand by previous Wardens. But while the military background of Grant or Hinton may have contributed to good order and discipline among the colonists, no previous Warden had Menday's experience of and contacts with bureaucrats and businessmen, through his work in the new towns and boys clubs, and perhaps also his post-war work with the control commission in Germany. He displayed a particularly useful talent for identifying, button-holing and influencing the kind of public figure who could prove helpful to the future of the colony. The most illustrious example of this talent would be the installation in 1961 of Sir John Hunt, conqueror of Everest, as 'President' of the School. but useful contacts were also made early on in both central and local government.

The first such was the Assistant Secretary grade head of the Home Office inspectorate, Miss A.M. Scorrer, alleged by Menday to have the reputation of 'a real dragon'. In autumn 1954 the Chief Inspector was, he writes, preparing a report to recommend closure of Wallingford Farm Training School, 'even though it was desperately needed.' It is not clear, first, under what powers the Home Office would have 'closed' the <u>entirely indep</u>endent Turners Court, although officials could,

9   NA, BN 62/3222. Menday attributed his deafness to commando battle training (*To a Peak*, p.61).

of course, have strongly influenced local authorities against sending boys there. In the event, invited to visit the School, the reputed dragon seems quickly to have been won over by the Mendays (Inga providing 'an excellent Swedish dinner'); Menday says she assured him that, 'updated and properly run, there was a good future for the School and for thousands of boys who needed training' and mentioned the possibility of Home Office financial assistance under Section 46 of the Children Act, 1948, assistance which was to be crucial to the continued viability of Turners Court.

A second example of Menday's shrewd acquisition of supporters was the head of Oxfordshire County Council's Children's Department, Mrs V.J. Kahan, who became a useful supporter of Turners Court. Better relations with local authorities in general had featured on Menday's introductory memorandum: '... one hears far too many stories of Children's Officers having been insulted at Wallingford' he wrote. Nationally, the number of children taken into care under Sections 1 and 5 of the 1948 Act was increasing rapidly: from 55,000 in 1949 to 81,000 ten years later; virtually all the 170 boys at Turners Court now came via this route.[10]

Menday also made use of links with wartime comrades. When the committee launched an appeal for funds, he called in Rupert Curtis, former RNVR Lieutenant Commander whom Menday met during landing-craft training before D Day (Curtis would receive the DSC for his leadership of the flotilla at Sword Beach). Curtis was now partner in a successful advertising agency (among its better known commercial clients at this time was the up-market shirt brand Van Heusen).

10. Menday, *Turners Court*, 1998, p.44; OCRO, TCYT Box H01. S5 of the 1948 Act related to children referred to local authorities by the courts.

Curtis duly produced, free of charge, a new prospectus for Turners Court which breezily outlined the current training course – 'a week or two to shake down, a full four seasons' experience of . . . farm work, and an additional two months . . specialised to suit a boy's aptitudes'. Curtis also produced a fund-raising leaflet which seems to have raised £550, better than Hunt's 1,000 mile trek for £1 (see Chapter 3), but not enough to make much of a dent in the overdraft.[11]

Modernisation

By the end of 1956 the various initial changes instituted by Menday and the Wallingford committee, most importantly the change of farm management, seem to have put the farm, and the school as a whole back into the black ('the Committee expressed delight at the result of the year's working', wrote Menday). Weekly charges had been raised to £6. 9 shillings and 6 pence (£6.45) per week, plus an annual charge for clothing without antagonising too many local authority clients. The London County Council was a major provider of new colonists, supplementing the visits of Home Office officials with visits by LCC officers. By the early 1960s Menday claimed there were over 1,000 visits by local authorities and others each year; most visitors now arrived by car and the considerable increase in road traffic became a matter of concern to the committee, in the first place as a danger to boys walking into Wallingford. The increasing availability of motor cars also proved a regular temptation to

---

11. Menday, *Turners Court*, 1998, p. 47. Lovell & Rupert Curtis, advertising agents, continued in business into the 21st century, although by 2008 their telephone had apparently been disconnected .

Oxfordshire Colony

boys, a steady trickle of whom, from the 1960s onwards, were charged by the police, both in Oxfordshire and further afield, with taking and driving away: one, resident at Turners Court in 1964-1965, remembers that, bored with weekend visits to the Regal cinema in Wallingford, he and another lad hitched a lift to Watlington, where they stole a Mini van to drive back to the Colony. The police were summoned and identified the culprits, who seem to have escaped without penalty in this instance.[12]

By 1959 the total number of boys in residence was 165, of whom 150 were the responsibility of local authority Children's Committees (two from Kilmarnock, the rest from all over England, with a pronounced London weighting). Of the remainder, 7 were paid for by Education Departments, 6 by various national charities (including one sponsored by the Actors' Orphanage) and two 'private cases' - boys sent by parents ('one or two of whom were well known public figures', claims Menday) who could afford to pay the fees.[13] This level of occupancy should have produced an annual income of around £57,000, more than covering Menday's original estimate of running costs. Those costs, however, continued to rise. Staff had to be replaced; houseparents, Menday thought, wanted to stay on too long and became 'out of touch' with the continually changing population of boys who now arrived 'with more sophistication.' An age limit of 60 was instituted ('even this was too old, but faithful service had to be acknowledged', wrote Menday); Miss Rider,

12. Ibid, p.52; OCRO, TCYT Box H12; telephone conversations with 'JC', various dates. 'JC' also claims that the boys owned up to taking some questionable magazines from the back of the van, but this part of the story was disbelieved by the police, he claims, because the van was owned by a vicar.
13. OCRO, TCYT Box H02; Menday, *Turners Court*, 1998, p. 79.

who had replaced Horsfall as Bursar, was reluctant to retire even at 65. In 1966, towards the end of Menday's era, a Mr Pritchard would retire after 50 years service; he was given a 'wonderful party', the committee awarding him £1 for each year of service: lack of a realistic pension scheme must surely have been a key factor in the reluctance to retire (and, indeed, to work for the CSU in the first place).

New staff were recruited, in some cases from among those known to Menday from his work with boys clubs and in the New Towns, and the committee was persuaded to raise salaries and wages, which Menday and Royston agreed had been 'lamentably low.' Not all new recruits lived up to expectations; in 1962, a Mr Way, hired as a deputy house master, was discovered to be an alcoholic: 'inevitably', the minutes note, 'he failed the chance of making good' and had to be dismissed.[14]

To further the initial upturn in Turners Court's fortunes, in 1959 a sub-committee was set up to look at the longer term organisation and financing of the school. It determined that the original size of the Colony was too large, and that the way forward was to sell off a substantial portion of the land, using the proceeds of the sale to modernise and add to the buildings and equipment, with more varied trade training, including catering, and better workshop facilities. When this had been done, it was argued, the number of boys could be reduced to a more realistic 120, with better living conditions for both boys and staff; 'Current thinking of local authorities and the

---

14. OCRO, TCYT Box H02. Spiritual rather than physical attack on the boys was the charge when, after committee discussion in March 1965, a (named) member of the Cory House staff was warned to stop 'promoting' Seventh Day Adventism (TCYT Box H13).

Home Office was that far better results could be achieved by having boys in small groups for living and . . . training.' New staff cottages were also needed. It was proposed to raise fees to £8. 15 shillings (£8.75) per week (£455 per year).[15]

Concurrently, a substantial change took place in the legal and operational structure of Turners Court. The remit of the Christian Service Union had already been re-defined as 'the maintenance of homes and schools for handicapped children,' and by the 1960s the CSU was increasingly entrusting responsibility for both day to day operations and strategic planning to the three committees – Lingfield, Starnthwaite and Wallingford. On 1 January 1962, Starnthwaite, by now an Approved School for younger boys, became fully independent. The following year Lingfield Hospital School was reconstituted as an independent voluntary school for epileptic children (and continues thus into the 21st century as St Piers Lingfield).

Around the same time it was proposed (it is not clear by whom) that Turners Court should also become an Approved School. Menday was strongly opposed to this – and managed to convince the Wallingford committee, on the grounds that the colony would no longer be able to select which boys to admit; the Home Office (he argued) would be getting a new Approved School on the cheap, and the move would run counter to Menday's own philosophy of dealing with prevention, rather than cure. A questionnaire (no copy of which seems to have survived) was mailed to children's' departments and others and apparently showed that 85% of boys had not offended since leaving Turners Court, whereas it was said that 80% of

---

15. Menday, *Turners Court,* 1998, p. 62-64.

Approved School leavers re-offended. The committee then agreed with Menday's assessment and opted for Turners Court remaining independent. In September 1963 an Extraordinary General Meeting of the CSU formally changed its name to 'Turners Court', with a revised constitution as a company limited by guarantee, with its own board of management and new articles of association. After almost 70 years, and several changes of name, the Christian Service Union ceased to exist, leaving, its historian wistfully concludes, 'many events and much devoted service . . . not recorded.' The former style of 'Training Colony' and 'Farm School' were now dropped in favour of 'Turners Court', the name by which most local authorities already recognised the institution.[16]

Menday's argument for prevention rather than cure were developed in *The Everlasting Childhood*, a book, 'ghosted', Menday says (in *To a Peak*), by the South African Wiles, from raw material provided by Menday himself. Although he says it got 'rave reviews' in the press the book was also the cause of what sounds to have been a moderately serious breakdown of discipline. One review, in the *Sunday Pictorial*, was headlined 'Outcasts'; it implied that, according to the book, this was what Turners Court boys became, thanks to lack of supportive family life. The boys, Menday says, took exception to the word, and a number of them downed tools and vanished into the woods surrounding Turners Court; there is some suggestion that a few may have gone further afield before he was able to pacify them and persuade them to return. There is now no telling how many Turners Court boys had actually read the book; any who did so might indeed

---

16. Ibid, pp. 78, 83; McClellan, *Christian Service Union*, c.1963, p.6.

have been less than pleased with the graphic descriptions of inadequate home life that it contains. In the event Menday says he got the boys to write to the *Pictorial*'s editor, who replied, apologising 'and honour was restored.'[17]

Having abandoned the idea of Approved School status, and achieved operational autonomy, the future size and direction of the newly independent Turners Court were now effectively determined by two key financial decisions. The first of these was the successful sale of around 800 acres (320 hectares) of Potters Farm and Mays Farm. Future policy – as Menday and the committee had previously agreed - would be to concentrate entirely on grassland, with one dairy herd and a flock of Clun Forest sheep, together with a more non-agricultural training. The sale brought about an immediate improvement in the colony's finances: from carrying a heavy mortgage, Turners Court was in a position, by 1967, to lend more than £20,000 to Oxfordshire County Council, at 7% interest. On its new smaller scale the farm also seems to have returned to profitability, reporting a profit of £4,867 in the year 1963-64.[18]

The second, and larger, financial boost came from Home Office grants totalling, some £56,000 during the years 1960-65. Just how far Inga Menday's Swedish cuisine may have influenced that friendly 'dragon' Miss Scorrer on her first visit to Turners Court is debatable, but under Menday's leadership the former Colony seems better prepared than before to make a winning case for this kind of financial aid. The grants, under Section 46 (1) of the Children Act, 1948, had to be

---
17. Menday, *Turners Court*, 1998, p.60-61; Menday & Hartley, *To a Peak*, 1995, p.197; OCRO, TCYT Box H12.
18. NA, BN 62/3222.

used for capital improvements – buildings and equipment.[19] They were supplemented by a number of substantial private donations: one anonymous gift of £10,000 in 1963 went towards the new covered and heated swimming pool, which would feature largely in future publicity for Turners Court, and would be made available to schools and other local users – another possible example of Menday's political and networking sense. A former resident recalls a dinner hosted by Menday for Elton (still CSU President), Sir John Hunt[20] and other sponsors who had contributed to the pool fund. £5,000 from a retired Essex electrical manufacturer called Stapleton, originally also earmarked for the pool, was diverted to modernising Paton House, with the implication that the building might be renamed for the donor. A grant from the Gulbenkian Foundation, in 1966, was devoted to providing a new office building. Contributions in kind were also received, some more successful than others; the gift of an 'adorable pony' in foal, with another at foot, went well for about a year, but Menday admits, 'with the changing boy population the idea did not work out' and the ponies had to be returned.[21]

Over the five years 1958-1963, therefore, Turners Court underwent what Menday, with pardonable pride, would term an 'enormous' reconstruction programme. The four large houses or homes (Albright, Basden, Cory, Paton – later re-named Stapleton) were modernised and re-opened with the

19. Ibid; the grants would have to be repaid if, within 7 years, Turners Court had ceased to be a voluntary controlled school.
20. 1910-1998, led the Everest team 1953, knighted, retired from army 1956, director Duke of Edinburgh Award scheme, created life peer 1966; Menday first met Hunt during commando training in WWII.
21. Menday, *Turners Court*, 1998, pp.82, 89, 77; Menday claims he reeled in Stapleton at one of the fund-raising events of the Henley Midnight Matinee Committee.

old dormitories transformed into small family-style living units; oil fired central heating and modern plumbing were installed; cooking and lighting facilities were improved. 1960 saw the opening of the smaller-scale Hunt House (named for and funded by Sir John Hunt, who succeeded Elton as President of Turners Court the next year). In *The Everlasting Childhood* Menday paints a word-picture of the now vanished buildings - 'Three-storied, clean of line, with gable roofs and dormer windows' - lining two sides of 'Carr's Meadow' – the colony's central open space. The smaller Sturge House became the reception and assessment centre, with the sanatorium behind it. The offices, chapel and kitchen stood between Cory and Paton, with the stores and laundry behind them. On the third side of the square was the boys' club (of which more shortly), with its school-like clock tower and double doors. Houses and cottages for the staff and their families were scattered between these main buildings, and in other parts of the colony.

On his arrival, Menday had bemoaned the 'barrack-like' dormitories and his plan was to reduce the maximum number in each 'House' to 30. In this he was following a national trend towards smaller, more domestic style accommodation for both boys and staff, providing lounges and quiet rooms for the boys and replacing the 'dun-coloured interiors' which dated from the time of William Hunt, with 'bright contemporary colours and textiles.' New furniture was bought for all the boys' houses, staff cottages, and the Warden's house. Six new workshops and classrooms were built, farm buildings modernised and new farm machinery installed. Externally, an entirely new sewerage system was put in, along with surface water drainage and improved surfacing for the colony's roads. The old army huts, some of which had been acquired after the First World War, were finally demolished and the approach to the main entrance prettified with rose bushes. On the farm, around 40 acres (16 hectares) of scrubland was pulled out and converted to pasture. Menday's report on the 5-year improvement programme concluded that the improvements in physical conditions enabled more training programmes to be introduced and to higher standards, with consequent improvements to end of term reports and the 'bearing, manners and attitudes to others' of the boys. The next stage should see more improvement of training techniques in the various vocational workshops, and more scientific study of the boys as 'cases'. The new Occupational Assessment Centre (formerly Sturge House) involved more stringent study than hitherto of what sort of trade would be most likely to suit each boy on arrival; there would be a full time case worker and improved psychiatric care.[22]

One consequence of acquiring government grants was a more regular programme of visits by civil servants. In general their reports suggest that the refurbishment – finally estimated to have cost £84,000, of which about £28,000 came from the sale of Mays Farm – was proving good value for money. A 1960 progress report praised the newly opened Hunt House, 'a delightful conversion; the four bedrooms each have 3 beds . . . bedside lockers and lamps. The decoration and furnishing throughout are contemporary and pleasant.' By contrast, Sturge House, opened in 1945, was 'a most unpleasant and depressing bungalow' with primitive sanitary

22. Menday, *Turners Court*, 1998, pp 80-81, 87, 93. The rose bushes were dug up in 1981.

accommodation (the showers flooded the area immediately in front of the urinals). At that stage total capacity seems to have been around 140 boys: 12 in Hunt House; 38-39 each in Basden and Paton; 19 in the insanitary Sturge and 26 in Cory, with Albright House still undergoing conversion. Five years later, in January 1965, a final report confirmed that Sturge House, having been deemed incapable of conversion to acceptable living accommodation, was by then serving as workshops and the assessment centre; Home Office inspectors were not initially impressed by this innovation, which they thought had 'unqualified though experienced staff' and a 'loosely planned' curriculum.[23]

With the capital programme thus taken care of, increased revenue from local authorities was used to improve staff salaries and the boys' pocket money, which went up to between 15 and 25 shillings (75p to £1.25) per week, roughly in line with what was received by those in homes run directly by local authorities. In 1963 the annual charge was once more raised, to £525 (equivalent to £10 per week, compared with around £11.75 per week at Approved Schools) without, Menday reported, any significant reduction in the number of boys being referred. The 168 boys in residence in 1968 – the year after Menday left - would, however, prove to be the high point; from then on numbers would steadily decline.

By this time the proportion of boys leaving to work on the land, as opposed to non-agricultural trades, was dropping - although agricultural training was, Menday thought, 'good therapy' for the boys and the farm was now making a profit; some part-trained boys were sent to complete their training

---

23. NA, BN 62/3222, BN 62/3223.

on local farms. Few Turners Court boys now went to jobs in Australia, New Zealand or South Africa, although the concept of child emigration was not yet quite dead: in the late 1960s enquiries about emigration of orphans and other children were dealt with by government departments from, among others, the Fairbridge Society (see Chapter 3) and the Loyal Order of Moose. Illustrating the shift in public attitudes to child emigration during the 20th century, however, civil servants also received, in 1965, a complaint by a Samuel Gibson against the National Children's Home for having sent him and his brother to Canada over 50 years earlier, in 1908; officials suspected that the NCH had failed to get the necessary consent of the then Secretary of State but went ahead and sent the boys anyway. 'In general', officials noted, we do not [now] favour the emigration of an unaccompanied child for institutional care overseas' and even the Fairbridge Society now more commonly dealt with the emigration of single parent families, rather than individual youths.[24]

Writing in 1959, Menday and Wiles argued not only for improvements in the training programme but also a change in the whole system of referring boys to places like Turners Court, and the length of time they could spend there. Menday had been impressed by a visit he made to the William Baker Technical School, run by Dr. Barnardo's just outside Hertford, which provided a range of vocational

---

24. NA, BN 29/1329 (1965), BN 29/1319 (1968), BN 29/1321 (1969). The Loyal Order of Moose had wanted children to emigrate to Mooseheart Village, outside Chicago, USA. And see Chapter 3, note 17.

and academic training for boys aged between 13 and 21.[25] Menday considered, rightly or wrongly, that unlike Turners Court the William Baker School was not one for 'awkward boys' – the disruptive, damaged children with low IQs. Early in the 1960s he 'drew the committee's attention to the fact that there was now a tendency for local authorities to offer training at Turners Court to boys who had been concerned in larceny or house-breaking which was unprecedented.' He also claimed that local authority child care officers were putting in applications for boys to be sent to Turners Court against the boy's will or desire, 'causing a resentment to be set up by the boy and . . . making the start at the School very difficult.' From this he argued for tightening up the vetting of applications – and also the after-care visits to boys when they left the colony.

In the longer term it may be that this understandable wish to pick and choose among boys offered to Turners Court was a factor in the gradual decline in referrals by the local authorities. In the short term, of course, Menday and the other staff had to deal with the more disruptive boys, and the changing economic and social background. Although Menday argued against the Juvenile Courts as a process for taking children into care – he and Wiles wrote that the decision should be left to local authority children's' officers[26] – at this time some 40% of Turners Court boys had been before the courts, 20%

---

25. Menday & Wiles, *Everlasting Childhood*, 1959, pp.207-209. The William Baker school opened in 1922 and closed in 1967. A less complimentary view of the school, looking back to an earlier era, is in Frank Norman's memoir *Banana Boy* (1969, Secker & Warburg). Norman berates Barnardos' quality of training, mind-numbing regime of drill, marching, physical training and cold showers, and under-estimation of boys' intelligence.
26. Menday & Wiles, *Everlasting Childhood*, 1959, p.222.

more than once. In the section of Menday's 1998 history which deals with the period of his own wardenship, there are references to absconsions, petty theft, drug use, solvent abuse and sexual misbehaviour both within the colony and in the surrounding area: around 1964 there was, Menday writes, 'a spate of offences by men picking up boys by car at weekends' – typifying the new, mobile, relatively affluent society outside Turners Court (references to road traffic accidents also increase in this period). In 1957 a boy was found in the house of a Reading prostitute, and returned to his local authority in Lincolnshire; the latter incident was included among several case studies (the boys' names, of course, were withheld) of boys' sexual activities featured in *The Everlasting Childhood* in a way which previous superintendents or wardens would hardly have contemplated.[27]

Other and less sensational case studies of Turners Court boys feature in Menday's 1998 history and *The Everlasting Childhood*. Early in their residence at Turners Court the Mendays were faced with an irate local farmer whose property had been set on fire by one of the boys (unidentified, except as 'a mental defective'); the farmer is placated after he and his wife are given supper in the Warden's house. More typical, perhaps, of the class of boy which Menday accused the local authorities of palming off on Turners Court was 'George' (Menday identifies the boys only by pseudonym) who came with a history of petty thieving, and was then accused of stealing a bottle of fruit squash from another boy's locker. Affronted, 'George' absconds, is found, pleads his innocence, is exonerated and, on leaving Turners Court, says that

---
27. Ibid, p. 138; OCRO, TCYT Box H13.

Menday was 'the only person in his whole life who had ever believed in him.' Another boy, 'Peter', disciplined by being sent back to his House after throwing a chisel at the carpentry instructor, is later found dancing with Inga in the Mendays' kitchen. 'Peter' claims he is upset by not having heard from his mother; Menday gives him a lift in his car back to his alleged home address in Birmingham which, it transpires, is fictitious (possibly along with the mother) and 'Peter' is at last forced 'to come to terms . . . with the facts of life' with presumed good effects on his temperament.[28]

Annual reports from the final years of the CSU (now entitled 'Homes and Schools for Handicapped Children') and the early years of Turners Court as an independent charity no longer contain the kind of letter from former residents which William Hunt and his immediate successors had liked to publish, although Menday told the Wallingford Committee that they were still received. By contrast with earlier periods of the colony's history, some anecdotal evidence is available from those who were there as boys under Menday's leadership. One, who still lives in Oxfordshire, describes the year (1963-64) he spent there as, overall 'not bad'; living in Albright House was 'brilliant' and even the institutional food 'OK'. The agricultural training he received – he remembers how to treat cattle for the bloat after they had eaten too much kale – proved of limited use: he worked for a while part time on a farm, but most of his working life was spent in factories or driving heavy goods vehicles. Forty years on, however, he still uses the cobbling skills he also acquired at Turners Court to mend his family's shoes. Another ex-Albright House resident

28. Menday, *Turners Court*, 1998, pp. 54, 63, 87. OCRO, TCYT Box H12 'Events of importance' book.

writes that the housemaster – 'perhaps another commando' – and his wife 'did a grand job' even though on the whole he now thinks his time at Turners Court was wasted; he also went on to work briefly on a farm before spending nine years in the army. A third old boy, at Cory House in 1960, also thought the training of little value, but remembers the Club: that Menday-inspired innovation (see below), along with the already existing school shop, were the main features recalled by a fourth informant, who arrived at Turners Court in 1967, at the end of the Menday era, and now thinks the Colony was 'a great place . . . I made a lot of friends and. . . did not want to leave.'[29]

'Arenascope' and other diversions

Menday's enthusiasm, his ability to draw on previous experience and enlist useful outsiders, are all illustrated by the leisure time activities available to the boys at this period. While the gloomy picture he painted of soulless evenings spent in idle quietude under previous administrations may have been overdone, it is true that during his wardenship a more varied and imaginative programme was developed for the boys' free time. Not everything was a novelty: Turners Court sports teams continued to compete in local competitions; summer camps continued much as before (in 1960 a new site near Chichester was made available); the 1957 summer Open Day had features that would have been familiar in Hunt's time - demonstrations of farm work, machinery maintenance, tractor driving, a parade of working horses, scarecrow making

29. Private telephone conversations/e.mails 'JC', 'KC','MH', 'JS' June 2006-June 2008.

and morris dancing – but it was thanks to Menday's interservice contacts that incidental music was by the band of RAF Benson. The Young Farmers' Club reformed in 1955; the next year it acted as host to the Oxfordshire YFC Federation's annual rally, a substantial county event, with a dance in the evening.[30]

Morris dancing which had featured back in the 1930s was now revitalised; soon after Menday's arrival, in April 1955, the Turners Court Youth Club performed with credit at an Oxfordshire County Youth Folk Dance festival, repeating their success in Oxford town hall in 1957. And an account of Christmas festivities sometime in the 1950s, written some 30 years later by a former Cory Housemaster, sounds as though William Hunt might have felt at home during the celebrations:

> 'Cory House looked very festive . . . House staff and the twenty-six boys had been busy preparing for Christmas, going round the estate gathering holly etc, making paper decorations and dressing a tree . . . On Christmas Day, after a late breakfast, the boys changed into their best clothes – blazer and flannels – and sat around playing games, reading (no T.V. in those days) and helping to set tables. The staff saved up small amounts over several weeks in order to provide a modest gift for each boy. . . After large helpings of turkey and traditional fare, everyone rested during the afternoon. After tea, the highlight of which was a Christmas cake made by the House staff and iced by a talented lady who was Housematron in Basden House, parties took place in all the Houses. Staff visited each House in turn for a drink where games were taking place. A popular game was "Spinning the Plate" which

---

30. Menday, *Turners Court*, 1998, p.77; private letter Mrs B. Bunyan, Nov 2006.

consisted of a person placing a plate on its edge, spinning it round and calling out the name of another person who then had to rush forward and keep it spinning. It got very boisterous and also very boring after the first hour. The day usually passed without mishap and everyone enjoyed the 'family' atmosphere.'[31]

The year being described is not stated, but references to 'blazers' and lack of TV suggest the early years of Menday's wardenship. By 1962, boys were sent home to their families for the Christmas holiday (and again at Easter and in the summer) as if from boarding school. A few, who had no families or who were rejected by them on arrival for the holiday, had perforce to stay at Turners Court where, the 'Events of Importance' register notes tersely, 'Staff coped.'

The blazers and grey flannels came into their own when Menday used wartime contacts to get parties of boys used as unpaid stewards or ushers at events such as the Aldershot military tattoo and the Henley regatta, where they (and he) might catch the eye of potential donors or supporters. The Henley connection proved fruitful; apart from the retired entrepreneur Stapleton, Turners Court also benefited from the fund-raising efforts of the Henley Midnight Matinee Committee, fronted by the actor Richard Todd; Todd was present to hand over a cheque for £1,250 from the Committee when the refurbished Basden House was re-opened in 1962.

Menday made use of his prior acquaintance with Sir John Hunt to arrange that Turners Court should be one of the pilot establishments chosen to test standards for the Duke of Edinburgh's Award, of which Hunt was appointed

---

31. *Turners Court Magazine*, (see Chapter 6), Dec. 1987. Menday had ordered the blazers from the London clothier Mackness, an old Welwyn Garden City contact (*To a Peak*, p. 166).

Oxfordshire Colony

director in 1958; Turners Court was specifically involved in testing outdoor and survival activities. In later years boys won several medals. By the end of the 1950s Turners Court had a permanent headquarters at Nant-gwynant in North Wales, where a small cottage was equipped to sleep a dozen boys at a time, useful, Menday and Wiles write, for weekend expeditions – not something that would have been possible in the days when the Colony boasted only a solitary motor car. Menday, himself a keen hill-walker, was enthusiastic about the impact of climbing on hitherto 'difficult' or uninterested boys:

> 'It is difficult to know what it is that attracts men to mountains, but one thing is quite certain: no one is quite the same after climbing. It is more than a feeling of having been "away from it all"; it is the sensation of being at one with the spirit of the universe.'[32]

In January 1957 John Hunt performed the official opening of the Turners Court Boys Club, at the rear of the Ogilvie Hall, which was to play a central part in Menday's plans. One of his earliest appointments had been that of W. E. ('Bill') Smewin to run the Club (he later became Deputy Warden). One Turners Court resident of this era describes the Club as 'brilliant'. In what must have seemed to some on the committee a rash move, Menday suggested the introduction of local girls for dances and other social events 'to provide more fun in the Club', but a former resident, from 1959, asked whether there were any girls around the School, could

---

32. Menday & Wiles, *Everlasting Childhood*, 1959, p.193. Menday also writes about the soothing effect of hill-walking while he was debating whether to take on the challenge of Turners Court.

only recall the 'very attractive lady – probably the wife of one of the staff' who had partnered him at the ballroom dancing classes which continued from the previous regime, adding, 'her name, I am mortified to say, escapes me.' An equally popular amenity, an informant says, was the school Tuck Shop, run in premises at the back of the Hall by the veteran 'Pop' Hansen, described by one Home Office official as 'an elderly gentleman of independent means' who also ran stamp and jigsaw clubs for the boys, and would split packets of cigarettes so that they could be sold singly to cash-strapped residents.[33]

As we have seen, drama and music had been present even in the pre-war era, although some offerings, like Edward Sladen's concert parties and Hugh Walpole's *The Old Ladies*, must have been more to the taste of staff and their families than of teenage boys. A more ambitious and inclusive arts programme now began. Menday's belief in the arts as part of the character-forming work of boys clubs was evident before his arrival at Turners Court: in May 1950 an article by him about youth club arts festivals ('one of the most valuable activities of . . . voluntary youth organizations in this country') was published in *The Times,* celebrating the success of the Welwyn Garden City club, of which Menday was then warden, in gaining honours for its performance of what was said to be the first opera to be entered in a regional festival of this kind. And the literature produced for Turners Court by Curtis highlighted the work of the Drama Group which, it was claimed, helped

---

33. Menday, *Turners Court*, 1998, p.53; private e.mail, Jun 2008, 'KC'; telephone conversations, 2006, 'JC'; NA. BN 62/3222. The shop may sometimes have been known, affectionately or not, as 'The Robbers Nest.'

instil 'unself-consciousness, team work and concentration'; the words are probably those of Menday himself.

The revived Turners Court drama club began modestly, with the production of a scene from *The Merchant of Venice* at the Oxfordshire Rural Community Council drama festival in 1955. The next year a pantomime, perhaps not dissimilar to the one that had delighted the wartime audience, was produced. In 1957 Menday and his wife were both involved in directing scenes from *King John* plus *The Pie and the Tart*, the latter adapted from a 15th century French 'booth' play, which won an award at the National Association of Boys Clubs' Southampton arts festival. Each Turners Court house also put on a short play at Christmas. In 1959 Menday himself directed a play called *The Seventh Man*, which took first place at the Oxfordshire Youth drama festival in Henley.[34]

By far the most ambitious and creative innovation of the Menday era, however, was the half dozen grand scale drama productions put on by boys and staff as part of the summer Open Day, mostly under the direction of Menday's collaborator, John Wiles. Wiles, born in Kimberley, South Africa in 1924, had come to Britain after the World War II; his novel *The Moon to Play With*, (Chatto & Windus, 1954) set in his native country, won the John Llewellyn Rhys Award (for a first novel by a writer under the age of 35) although, like his other novels, it has now slipped out of sight. Drama was his main interest: his play *Act of Madness* was taken by the London Theatre Group to the 1955 Edinburgh Festival; five

---

34. OCRO, TCYT Boxes H06, H12. Much of this detail, with photographs, comes from an album apparently compiled by Menday; a note pasted on the cover reads: 'Very few records could be found before [1955]' but Menday also often failed to date or identify items; *The Seventh Man* was probably the one-act play by Michael Redgrave, based on a story by 'Q'.

years later his satirical *Never Had It So Good,* 'an attack on the present state of Coventry' was performed by the famously stage-left Theatre Workshop in East London. Acting editions of some of his plays are still advertised on the internet but Wiles' main claim to popular fame was his work for the BBC, as producer, director or writer on episodes of such popular series as *Doctor Who, Dixon of Dock Green,* and *Poldark.* It was as a member of the Arts Advisory Committee for the NABC, and a keen advocate of mime drama and dance for young people, that he came into contact with Menday and Turners Court.

The first of these large scale productions, for which Wiles coined the name 'Arenascope', took place at the 1957 Open Day (Sir John Hunt, as guest of honour, presented the annual awards for agricultural and other classes). Entitled *Battle of Agincourt*, this was a grand scale outdoor production by Wiles and Ronald Johnson, employing a cast of over 120 boys, 30 staff and five or six shire horses (as against an audience of around 170). Wiles' idea was, he wrote, to combine speeches of great poetry with 'extensive virile movement, which would interest the least drama-minded boys.'[35] Scenes from Shakespeare's *Henry V* provided a central core, with the professional actor Cyril Wentzel (then a regular on BBC radio's 'Saturday Night Theatre') carrying the narrative, but the emphasis was on action: the play opened (the printed programme explains) shortly before dawn on the morning of the battle and concluded with the firing of the barn and the withdrawal of forces from the field. The martial theme was probably to the taste of most boys, while 'Carr's Meadow' in

---

35. Menday & Wiles, *Everlasting Childhood,* 1959, p.187.

the centre of the colony afforded a 'stage' 200 yards long; the availability of reasonably docile horses and skilled handlers gave Wiles and his helpers plenty of scope for spectacle. The programme gives prominence to 'Major Lacey's superb effort in making the magnificent armour'; staff wives had been expected to help out with costumes and refreshments. Advance publicity, probably also down to Wiles, included photographs of the boys rehearsing in the *Sunday Pictorial* and *The* [London] *Star*.

Although 1957's outdoor production gave such scope for military and equine spectacle, the summer's appalling weather determined Menday and Wiles to site future productions in the Ogilvie Hall. The following year's production of *A Fable of Baghdad*, by L. du Garde Peach, directed by Inga Menday was not on such an epic scale; Wiles seems to have been there only to present the annual awards. In 1959, however, after the first part of Open Day afternoon had seen a harvesting demonstration, Wiles' 'Arenascope' production was *The Trojan Horse*, mimed to the music of Sibelius, and performed 'in the round' in the hall to audiences totalling around 400. Programme notes explained that the play was 'not a strictly literal explanation' of the siege of Troy, but 'a convenient peg on which to hand a free and creative interpretation of an exciting legend,' continuing,

> 'The method used is founded on Alan Garrard's work in mime-drama... Because movement forms the basis of the production, acting has become for these boys not a question of posturing and affectation, but an activity closely associated with physical education... creative

movement is, therefore, both therapeutic and instructive. For our boys it has also been vastly challenging.'[36]

Wiles was again successful with advance publicity: illustrated reports in the [London] *Evening Standard* and *Evening News* emphasised the 'immense number of costumes', designed by the play's producer, John Wiles, and, inevitably, made by the wives of the school's instructors. The *News* report also indicated the scale of the setting which transformed the Ogilvie Hall into the market place at Troy with scenery which included 'a vast wooden ramp down which will be drawn the 12 foot high wooden horse containing three Greek soldiers, built by the boys during their carpentry classes.'

Wiles produced similar mimed epics in the following years: *King Arthur* in 1960, and in 1961 *The Crusaders*, marking the 750th anniversary of the so-called 'Children's Crusade'. There were six public performances of *King Arthur*, with a total paying audience of 1,389; ticket sales amounted to £600, total costs around £1,000. *The Crusaders*, with Menday and Wiles again risking an outdoor production, gave the director scope to deploy satisfyingly large bodies of both infantry and cavalry and played to total audiences of around 2,000.[37] 1964 saw Wiles and a cast of around 100 tackling *Alexander the Great*, miming the action to the music of Stravinsky, Carl Nielsen and Shostakovich. '. . . we have dramatised the spirit,

---

36. OCRO, TCYT Box H06, *Trojan Horse* programme note; Alan Garrard, later County Drama Adviser for Buckinghamshire, had worked with secondary school children in Essex. He and Wiles described this type of drama teaching in *Leap to Life, an experiment in school youth drama* (1970, Chatto & Windus).
37. Scenes either from this production or *Agincourt,* were captured by an anonymous cameraman on one of several – undated - films now in the Oxfordshire County Record Office [OCRO TCYT Box H04].

a kind of *essence* of the main events . . . what alternative is there, when actuality demands a cast of tens of thousands and a stage 20,000 miles long?', ran the programme note.

Alexander, the 1964 'Arenascope' production, seems to have been the first for which female actors were used, with Christina Eketorp (either a staff wife, or perhaps a friend of Inga ?) taking on the role of Statira, queen to the Persian monarch Darius. Five years earlier, programme notes had robustly defended the all-male cast of *Trojan Horse*: 'Helen has no part in our story; neither has Cassandra . . . we have been concerned simply with youth's idea of nobility and our view of the nobility of [male] youth. If honour is ageless, so too is adolescence.' In 1966, the last in this series of historical epics saw two girls imported: Lynn Royston (daughter of the Deputy Warden, perhaps) and Susan Cooper, who played Aztec priestesses in *Gods of the Sun, a story of the Aztecs*, one of the few productions of which colour photographs exist.

The book which Wiles wrote around this time in collaboration with the teacher and educationalist Alan Garrard extols the virtues of this type of drama for boys who are 'inarticulate and emotionally disturbed.' With no scripts to read, or lines to learn, the Turners Court boys, 'proved they could run, jump, fight with a shield and sword, wrestle, leap from a Wooden Horse; could, in short, act with complete enjoyment.' The Turners Court annual play, Wiles wrote, had made a name for themselves among local authority children's officers, who would make an effort to see each production; for the later shows, up to ten performances had to be scheduled to meet the demand. But, Wiles concluded,

'. . more important than this is the tradition they have made at the School itself so that new boys arriving are indoctrinated by the other boys and not by the staff. When recruits are called for to cast a new show never less than ninety of the possible hundred and twenty volunteer to continue the tradition.'[38]

With numbers of boys at a high point of 168, the large building and refurbishment programme almost complete, the Boys Club and other leisure activities in full, not to say dramatic swing, Ronald Menday may have thought – although his 1998 history is not explicit on the point – that his work at Turners Court had reached a peak, for in 1968 he resigned. His decision was almost certainly inspired, partly at least, by the death of Inga two years before: he may have simply felt unable to continue alone with the kind of residential, 24-hour involvement that the colony demanded. According to his own account, he was then invited to meet the Minister of State at DHSS, Alice Bacon, to work on details of new legislation (the Children Act, 1969). He received an MBE for his work at Turners Court and elsewhere, and after his spell in Whitehall, served as Chief Administrative Officer for Cwmbran Development Corporation from 1971 to his retirement in 1978.

Ron Menday died in 2003; his privately published *History of Turners Court* provides an invaluable resource for other historians and a suitable memorial for Menday himself.

---

38. J. Wiles, A Garrard, *Leap to Life,* 1970, p.145-6.

CHAPTER 6

The End of Turners Court: 1968-1991

Children in community homes should be allowed much the same degree of freedom as children brought up in a well-regulated private household.
  -'Children in Trouble' (Cmnd. 3601) 1968
'Thus came to an end in 1991 the dream of Pioneers in 1911 . . . [but] the Spirit lives on' - R.P. Menday, 'Turners Court', 1998.

Menday's successor as Warden (from 1970 known as Principal) of Turners Court was John Howells, who had been first deputy head then head of an Approved School, and also the superintendent of a remand home. Without discounting at all the commitment, experience and varied qualifications of his predecessors, including the educationalist Manley, Howells, with post-graduate qualifications in education and social science, might reasonably claim to be the first professional social scientist to head the former 'colony.' A former Welsh rugby football player, Howells is said by one former resident to have cut 'an impressive figure'; another says that he was known among the boys as 'Boss Hogg', after the character played by Burt Reynolds in the popular TV series *The Dukes of Hazzard*. The Deputy Principal was Bill Smewin, succeeded by Mike Cornfield (one informant describes him as 'a cross between a private detective and a football manager') who went on to become Turners Court's last Principal.[1]

In Howells' first year the number of boys stood at 168. This figure would never be approached again; instead, the records show a steady decline through the 1970s and 1980s, until by the 1990s the number in residence had fallen to 25 or less. At the same time staffing costs were rising: more and better trained full-time teachers and instructors had to be found, more sophisticated equipment installed and better living quarters provided for the increasing number of married staff. Another major change was also taking place in the legislation governing treatment of boys in need of care, which in the end seems to have had the (unintended) effect of further edging Turners Court out of the mainstream of child care and education provision. The Children and Young Persons Act 1969, which came into effect in 1970, substituted non-criminal procedures for 10-14 year olds who would previously have been criminalised. More generally, the Act accepted the correlation between deprivation and crime, and the need to adopt a more comprehensive 'family' approach to welfare work.[2] Supervision of Approved Schools and the equivalent voluntary institutions – like Turners Court – along with most other child care responsibilities, was transferred from the Home Office to the Department of Health and Social Security (DHSS), created in 1968 after the Fulton report on the civil service.

---

1. Private e.mails, Jun, Aug 2008, 'IOC', 'AP'. As Principal, Howells continued to take part in academic life, necessitating occasional absences from Turners Court when Smewin or Cornfield deputised for him.
2. See e.g. H. Hendrick, *Child Welfare in England 1872-1989*, 1994 (London: Routledge) p. 231-236.

In terms of day to day management, most Approved Schools now became the responsibility of the newly organised 'Social Service' departments set up by local authorities following the 1970 Seebohm report. The 1970 Act, an article in a professional journal explains, set up a basic framework of 'Community Homes', a difficult concept, whose success would depend on persuading the local community to accept the change.[3] Only a handful of institutions had sufficient independent funds to remain wholly voluntary – the former Philanthropic Society farm school at Redhill, for instance, passed to the London Borough of Wandsworth in 1973. In that same article Howells, perhaps from experience of dealing with local Oxfordshire residents, wrote that there was likely to be difficulty in persuading communities to accept the concept of the 'community home': 'Staff . . . will have to meet local people to gain their confidence.' He concluded that it would be better for Turners Court to remain at present outside the community homes scheme, instead used, as in the recent past, by local authorities as 'a specialised establishment with a well-proven formula.' Over the next two decades, Turners Court would discover how difficult such an independent existence might be.

This changed legislative background – almost unrecognisable to the original pioneers of the 'Colony' – is exemplified by the wording of S46 (of the 1969 Act) which, in permitting local authorities to take over former Approved Schools and run them as 'community homes', said children should be allowed 'much the same degree of freedom as those brought up in a well-regulated private household', making

---

3. *British Hospital Journal & Social Science Review*, 30 Jan 1970.

use of educational, health and other services locally available; in other words, children taken into the local authority's care should mix with those of other families whenever possible.

The net result of these changes was that by 1977 'community homes', with some 40,000 places between them, represented the lowest, or least restrictive, tier of establishment to which young offenders and others could be sent (that is, behind Borstals, Junior Detention Centres and Remand Homes). By this time about one-sixth of children in homes or hostels were in those run by voluntary organisations, like Turners Court, but those transferred to local authority control, or in voluntary/local authority partnerships, were more likely to benefit from DHSS financial support. Underlying all this was the unspoken drive for cost-effectiveness. One contemporary commentator suggested that at the time child care professionals were concerned that central and local government would not put enough resources into making the 'community home' plan work.[4]

Although Menday and others claim that many of the ideas realised in the 1969 Act had been floated by him – for example, in the book *The Everlasting Childhood* which he wrote with John Wiles – it now looks as though the shift away from the inclusive, residential-cum-training establishments like Turners Court and towards the small 'community homes' and use of training facilities was a key factor in the decline

---

4. See E.R. Bryant, *Some attitudes towards the treatment of children who appear in court etc,* 1970, unpublished thesis, Bodleian library HV 9146 A5 BRY. Commentary on the 1969 Act is from *Children and Young Persons in Custody,* 1977, the report of a NACRO working party chaired by Peter Jay. Apart from the types of institution listed, the Act also envisaged the creation of Youth Treatment Centres, for the most disturbed children or those convicted of serious crime; only one, at Brentwood, existed by 1977.

and ultimate closure of the 'Colony'. The final chapter of this book will suggest that perhaps Turners Court, now without any parent organisation, had missed a trick in not becoming such a partnership 'community home'.

Meanwhile, however, a new promotional brochure appeared in the mid-1970s, aimed at local authorities. The now independent Turners Court was described as a 'Voluntary Society, set up to provide special help for difficult or backward boys' (it also mistakenly dated its foundation to 1910). Fees were set at £1,666 per term, with a three-term year; most boys no longer stayed at Turners Court between terms, returning either to their families or to local authority-provided care. The old 'Houses' – Albright, Basden, Cory, Hunt and Stapleton - with their public school image, were now described as 'Living Groups', each accommodating between 12-24 boys, looked after by residential Social Workers. The tradition of training in agriculture and horticulture continued to feature, although the farm was now reduced in size to just 400 acres (170 hectares). Equal prominence was now given to vocational training in engineering, motor vehicle maintenance, bricklaying, carpentry and joinery, painting and decorating, and catering. At the beginning of this period there were between 15-20 full time instructors, falling to half a dozen by the 1990s. Overall, John Howells explained in a promotional video made in 1986 (see below), the aim was to offer an 'integrated curriculum' comprising vocational, academic and 'social' instruction – what Menday had called 'readiness for life.'

Oxfordshire Colony

Further education continued to be provided in Sturge House. Only a passing reference is made to religious observance - 'primarily Anglican in character' – and by the 1980s another long-standing tradition, that of the annual harvest supper, was thought to be becoming anomalous, although the wife of the Motor Vehicle Instructor, at Turners Court 1969-1989, fondly recalls the festival as,

> 'fantastic . . we sat down with the boys and . . John Howells would be dressed as a headmaster, complete with mortar board and hand out rewards to the boys who had done well that year."[5]

A later brochure, published in the mid-1980s, illustrates the change that had taken place in the post-war decades: pictures of farming and horticulture no longer predominate, outnumbered by shots of catering, vehicle maintenance, carpentry and metal-working. The text emphasises the independence afforded the boys; they travel to and from Turners Court on their own and a 'small unit offering independent living' is said to be under development, to give 'young people' (it is possible that co-education was still under consideration) experience of living on their own before being decanted into the wider world. Tellingly, most of the illustrations show them singly or in groups of two or three, training, in the bedrooms or in the day room of one of the accommodation blocks. The groups of men and boys working in the fields, or posing in suits before leaving to catch the emigrant ship were a distant memory.

---

5. Private letter, Mrs J Busby, Oct. 2006.

As well as vocational training the brochure emphasises the need to equip boys with basic skills for any type of work; there was also a broad Arts programme and 'countryside education'. Members of staff who worked at Turners Court as instructors, in one case from 1971 to closure in 1991, remember that much time had to be spent on basic literacy and numeracy because many of the boys had little previous schooling. Some boys went on day release to Henley Technical College where they could obtain City and Guilds qualifications, following which the Turners Court instructors would help them prepare for job interviews.[6]

In the early 1970s, total staff numbered between 70 – 80. Turnover of staff – there were several changes of farm manager in this period – seemed to be a continual problem and, with staff illness, represented 'an unsettling factor for the trainees.' Relations with the new, more professional and perhaps better organised, training staff were not always harmonious; at the end of the decade the residential social workers met to formulate a 'report on grievances' (they claimed that Turners Court was falling behind comparable local authority establishments) which was presented to Howells. Like Menday, Howells also inherited a few long-serving staff members whose history of relatively poor salaries, and hence small savings made it difficult for them to organise their retirement. In 1976 the 'houseparents' Mr and Mrs Oscroft were due for retirement and were asked to vacate their house; having nowhere else to go, they applied for local authority housing without success

---

6. Telephone conversations, J. Glavey, P. Honeybone, 2006, 2007; the Honeybone family ran a sadlery business in Wallingford and at one time provided harness for up to 35 draught horses at Turners Court. A partial list of instructors, house staff and others around this time is at Appendix I.

and, as a last resort, Turners Court had to evict them to improve their chances of re-housing.[7]

The 1970 article already quoted explained that although around half of the boys had been before the courts, they were not selected for this reason but because they were thought capable of benefiting from vocational training. Each boy was judged against this criterion at an interview, accompanied by his child care officer, with input from a consultant psychiatrist. Turners Court was, the article said, 'unique in its emphasis on remedial work with the trainees.' The article also judged that many of the boys were 'casualties of the education system', with low levels of basic literacy and numeracy: hence Howells' emphasis on resources for further and remedial education.

In 1986, Howells set out his further thoughts about the role of Turners Court in the promotional video.[8] Interviewed by Clare Francis, he emphasised the need for co-education and for preparing both boys and girls for independent living. Turners Court, he says in the video, was 'building an independent living unit [and] developing social skills.' As Principal, he saw his job as 'getting young people to become good husbands and fathers.' Although this sounds a considerable way from the kind of objective set by the NUCSS back in 1912, Howells also mentions his wish to preserve 'continuity' with Turners Court's history, by offering a 'fairly steady, well-programmed formula.' Without the voluntary sector being 'prepared to innovate', Howells argued, the provision of this kind of help for young people would not exist, since the public sector was not

---
[7]. Menday, *Turners Court*, 1998, p.120, 151, 129.
[8]. OCRO, TCYT Box H08: VHS tape, *Turners Court*, 1986 (BUFS). This and other film/video matter have been digitised and transferred to disc by Wessex Sound & Film Archive, Winchester.

The End of Turners Court: 1968-1991

flexible enough. Elsewhere in the same video, Francis toured the Turners Court farm, greenhouse and other buildings, to illustrate the 'unique' nature of the institution.

Writing, in 1998, about Turners Court's final two decades, Menday noted, almost superfluously, that 'throughout its life Turners Court seemed to be in urgent need of more money, and 1971 was no exception.' In the early 1970s, the annual accounts showed a deficit of £800, a relatively small amount, although a surplus of £3,000 had been anticipated; steadily increasing salary costs were said to be mainly responsible. In October 1973, the management committee, although noting that there was great enthusiasm for the educational programme, expressed concern at the bad state of the premises, and insufficient classroom accommodation (in Sturge House). A 1968 plan for a new hostel for those boys about to leave Turners Court, estimated to cost £30,000, had already been abandoned (Home Office officials had told Howells that finance could only be provided if Turners Court became a Community Home).

A working party headed by the Principal prepared a discussion document under the title 'Turners Court – What Next?': it thought that outsiders would find the former 'colony' old fashioned - 'a one off' - and that staff-management relations appeared poor. Around the same time an application was considered to the Department of Education and Science (DES) for Turners Court to be registered as an 'Independent School', subject to inspection by DES rather than DHSS, and ceasing to be officially a 'care' establishment. In theory this could have opened the way for capital grants from DES for the replacement or refurbishment of the 'old-fashioned' buildings; however, they felt this would be inappropriate, ending Turners Court's tradition of providing care, training and a degree of hope for the disadvantaged. [9]

Early in 1974 a meeting took place between Turners Court senior staff, officials of DES and DHSS and local authority officers at which various suggestions were put forward for future training: numbers of boys needed to be cut; more varied trade training provided; perhaps a link instituted between farm and horticulture. It was thought that immediate capital expenditure might amount to £37,000 which would imply an increase in fees of about £300 per boy each year; the local authorities would need ample advance warning of this. Having failed to secure money from DHSS (or other Departments) for new house-building, it was suggested that local houses might be bought, for staff use, in the hope that such purchases *would* qualify for government grant aid.[10]

In March 1976, plans were presented to the committee for a substantial rebuilding of the 'campus' surrounding Carr's Meadow; Menday's history calls these plans 'ambitious', perhaps an understatement in view of the already existing financial problems. In 1977-78 the possibility of finance from one or more European Community fund towards rebuilding costs was discussed, but apparently never realised, and another appeal was launched to raise – according to a local press report – £400,000. By 1978 the accumulated deficit had risen to £29,000. In November 1980, a negative cash flow of £33,000 was reported and in the next few years the deficit was around

9. Menday, *Turners Court*, 1998, p.107; OCRO, TCYT Box H12, H13: Committee minutes.
10. Menday, *Turners Court*, 1998, p. 109. Menday is less than helpful on the precise proposals of the January 1974 meeting; one idea, he claims, was to appoint a teacher 'with an educational bias'.

£50,000. By the end of 1986 it was estimated cash flow would show a deficit of £92,000 on the school account (excluding any profit from the commercial operations of the farm).[11]

The fees paid by local authorities were just sufficient to pay running costs. New building work was halted. An appeal (it is not clear whether this was the same one referred to in the local press) was said to have raised only about £6,000. Proposals were put forward for saving money by, for example, again reducing the number of boys, closing one of the houses, abolishing senior posts.[12] Howells, while expressing his confidence that Turners Court filled a real need in the provision of child care and special needs education, admitted that constant fluctuations in numbers, changes of staff and worries about salary levels produced an unsatisfactory 'stop-start' policy.[13] The farm was finding it difficult to turn a profit. In 1974 the committee thought it was being 'run against all the principles of general farming'. It was hoped that the appointment of a new farm manager (Mr P. Hall) would put things right; there was some suggestion that more land might be sold for gravel extraction.

Throughout this difficult period, despite the financial constraints and concerns about the future of the institution, boys continued to be referred to Turners Court to be trained, and in many cases thrived and moved on to successful careers. Former residents from this time pay tribute to that training and recall the individual instructors with some affection. Several mention, approvingly, the horticultural training; one,

---

11. Menday, 1998, pp.119, 128, 143. In 1979 land at Oakley Little Wood was sold for £38,250 (OCRO TCYT Box H13, management minutes)
12. Menday, *Turners Court*, 1998, pp. 128-129, 143.
13. Ibid, p.162.

who was among the first to get City and Guilds (at Henley) as well as internal qualifications, writes about the 'really lovely gentleman' (possibly Peter Smith, see Appendix I) in charge; that particular trainee was one of several who found careers in horticulture, going on to manage a garden centre, until pressure from the firm's directors induced an ulcer (he is now one of several ex-Turners Court residents to work as an HGV driver). Another, having served six months on the farm, eventually settling into engineering, where he learned welding and basic machine crafts; he too graduated at Henley Technical College. The painting and decorating course gets a commendation from one who took it up as a trade before realising, he writes, that there was more money in the thermal insulation industry. The tutor of the catering course, whose name is given as Greenslade, sounds, according to another former student, a natural for TV:

> 'one of the best teachers I ever had. Unusual reaching method: he would sit you down, give you the recipe and explain [it]. When you said "OK" you went and did it. Get it wrong, he . . .went nuts at you, then undid [your] errors, explained where you went wrong and how to fix it.'

Some informants also recall those tutors (see Appendix I) including Ms Jo Elvin and a 'smashing bloke called Dave Edgar', responsible for the literary and numeracy classes which occupied around four hours each per week; Edgar also offered guitar lessons.[14]

The athletic and social life of the 'colony', so important to Menday and others in terms of character-building and

14. Private e.mails, Jun-Oct 2008, 'GB', 'PG', 'FP', 'MW'.

the instillation of self-esteem in the boys, flourished and also features in those personal recollections of former residents which are available. The Sports and Social Club (as the Boys Club now became known) must have been the most appreciated legacy of the Menday years. Certainly the Club, along with the name of its leader, Mike Dornan, feature most commonly in the recollections of former residents. One writes neutrally, 'the clubhouse was run fairly well' but most are more enthusiastic. The Club featured water polo and other sports against local teams, pottery and other crafts, and social events. Inter-house competitions continued, and the swimming pool, which featured strongly in the 1986 video, saw constant use both by the Turners Court boys and local schools although during Turners Court's last decade these outsiders grew less frequent as other modern pools became available locally. Despite the tentative proposals of both Manley and Menday in this respect, Turners Court never did became co-educational but some girls – including daughters of staff members - took part in Club activities, including the regular 'Action Weeks' which involved outdoor activities like orienteering, hiking and camping expeditions for which, on some occasions at least, food would be brought each day from the Turners Court kitchens.

Less formal weekend expeditions for smaller groups of boys were organised by Olaf 'Pop' Hansen, the 'tuck shop' manager, whose unique contribution to Turners Court's social life, already noted (Chapter 5) is again recalled by members of staff and boys from this period. 'Pop' clearly had an entrepreneurial streak (one correspondent thinks he had a family link with the Danish bacon company). With the relaxed attitude to smoking prevailing in the 1960s and 1970s, 'Pop' sold half-ounces of 'Old Holborn' rolling tobacco ('we made the thinnest hand-rolled cigarettes ever') and for less sophisticated tastes sold home-made iced lollies for one penny (0.5p). Hansen's weekend expeditions with car loads of boys, to locations ranging from Portsmouth dockyard to the Tyseley railway locomotive depot, were viewed with concern by the professional staff, not least because of his uncertain driving skills. One former resident also recalls Hansen's 'addictive' home-made ginger wine.[15]

One correspondent remembers most vividly the time he spent in the late 1960s on the Sail Training Association's 'Tall Ships' training course on the schooner, *Sir Winston Churchill*, after which he completed the painting of a schooner which was said to be much admired by the staff when hung in the school office. More prosaically, he recalls the quality of training on the painting and decorating course – despite being severely reprimanded when he 'accidentally' sat in a bowl of turps.[16] Sail training would also feature in two articles written by another former resident for the *Turners Court Magazine* (of which more shortly), the first of which was an account of the Whitbread Round the World Race in which he had taken part in the 1970s.

By the 1980s, some boys were able to experiment with still and ciné photography. This is apparent from an interview with a boy recorded on tape for the 1986 video. Speaking to camera, the un-named boy exudes confidence about his own life and

15. Telephone conversation J. Glavey, June 2006. Private e.mails, Jun-Oct 2008, 'AP', 'KC', MH'. Several informants mention Hansen as having lost one or more finger, but his connection with the Danish Bacon Company has not been authenticated.
16. Private e.mail, Jun 2008, 'MH'.

film-making. Reclining on top of a low wall somewhere in the grounds, he admonishes the (unseen) interviewer, 'don't keep asking me stupid questions,' then, winking at the camera, he adds 'autographs later.' Asked how Turners Court came by its up-to-date dark-room equipment, he first quips, 'it just fell off a lorry'; then, perhaps more plausibly, he boasts that if new equipment is needed, the boys first try to 'con Graham Kelly' then 'go and moan to [Howells], then smash the whole place up, then they listen to you.' Perhaps not surprisingly, that sequence was not used on the final tape, although the same boy goes on to describe more soberly the training he is getting in the metal workshop, turning out decorative ironwork and other products.[17]

Some boys earned extra cash taking on weekend jobs in Wallingford or elsewhere. One worked in the kitchens of a Wallingford hotel (his course at Turners Court was horticulture rather than catering) then at the Sue Ryder home in Nuffield (just up the road from Turners Court) where he had the unpleasant task of moving deceased residents by trolley to the mortuary.[18]

In the mid-1980s, Turners Court staff had another shot at a house journal, a few issues of which survive in the archive, now in the Oxfordshire County Record Office. The *Turners Court Magazine* carried the same sub-heading – 'Being the magazine of the Wallingford Farm Training School' – as the short-lived *School Review* of 40 years earlier (see Chapter 3) and used the same (unattributed) line drawing on the front cover: the December 1987 issue saw a Father Christmas skilfully

---

17. OCRO, VHS tape, *Turners Court*, 1986; the reference to 'Graham Kelly' is obscure.
18. Private e.mail, Oct 2008, 'AP'.

added to the rural scene. The school's office technology now included electric typewriter and photo-copier; each 20-page A4 issue carried a number of roughly reproduced photographs, line-drawings and cartoons with hand-written balloons. Far more informal than the 1940s *School Review* (and miles away from the staid columns of *Social Service* as edited by William Hunt) the *Magazine* reads as if it was mainly, if not entirely, written by and for staff members, rather than boys – although the exploits of some of these, in training, sport and so on – feature in surviving issues.

Much of each issue is taken up by previews of or reports on events organised by the 'Staff Social Club', an entity quite distinct from the well-established 'Boys Club.' One of the later editions (December 1988) carries a restaurant review, commending the Italian bistro 'La Capannina' in Oxford's Cowley Road – 'seek out this little jewel of a place' - which seems unlikely to have been aimed at the boys ('La Capannina' survived into the 21st century but faced closure in 2008). A regular feature was 'Ianto's Diary', which purported to reflect the thoughts of John Howell's Labrador, and commented in a mildly subversive fashion on the 'comings and goings' of staff and their families, supposedly revealing the inner thoughts of 'the old man' himself. Thus, in the 8th edition (July 1987) 'Ianto' writes roguishly about a recent 'Staff/Adolescent Party': ' . . . oh boy, were there some goings on there . . .The old man [Howells] danced with the noisy woman in the office upstairs and had such a good time people actually left before he did.' In the 10th edition (Autumn 1988) 'Ianto' records the recent landing of a hot air balloon on Carr's Meadow which, the dog points out, 'could only have happened in the holiday with all the hot air given off by the staff here.'

There were occasional pieces about social work in general, for example on health and safety at work, and an editorial item in the 7th edition compared Turners Court's constant search for funds with the state child-care sector where 'controls on spending have often been lax.' Another issue reproduced a DHSS leaflet on the 1988 social security payments system, aimed at 'Reducing the sullen apathy of dependence.' The *Magazine* was also used to alert the Turners Court professionals to forthcoming staff conferences on such topics as 'Thinking Skills' and 'Handling Aggression and Violence.' On occasion professional concerns could be leavened with schoolboy humour: the 9th edition (December 1987) carries the announcement of a regular staff committee on health and safety at work, immediately followed by the reproduction of a hand-written note from Cory House to the school maintenance team, marked 'Urgent' and reading: 'Please could we have live wire in bed made safe.'

Drugs and other misbehaviour

The threat made by the boy in the off-cut from the 1986 promotional video, of 'smashing the whole place up' to squeeze money for more photographic equipment out of the management, may have been no more than teenage bravado for the cameraman's benefit. Menday's 1998 history, however, and other records include examples of more genuine misbehaviour from this period. They include the case of boys attacking a housemaster; on another occasion the 19 year old daughter of a staff member had been assaulted (she defended herself with an umbrella); in a separate incident (undated) a boy assaulted a female staff member at night: bizarrely (according to Menday) *she* was then asked to resign. In February 1983 the committee minutes record an incident where boys were said to have painted walls, ceiling, carpets and furniture in one of the residential blocks chocolate brown and then either been handled 'robustly' (according to the house staff) or 'had the pulp beaten out of them'; clearly unable to establish all the facts, the committee comment, 'There was a great degree of variance in the statements.'

Cases of drug-handling and abuse, shop-lifting and more vehicle thefts involved the police. Four different Turners Court boys involved in various crimes were sent to Detention Centres. In 1978 five boys were charged at the Didcot magistrate's court with stealing cars; a former resident, back on a visit, took a group of boys out for a drive and was involved in a serious accident; earlier accidents, such as one recorded in 1956, had generally involved tractors either within the 'colony' or on the surrounding roads.

The staff member responsible for producing the Christmas pantomime in the late 1970s recalls the embarrassment caused when the slightly built boy who had been cast as Cinderella vanished just before opening night; a telephone call from Rickmansworth police station revealed that the boy was being held there, charged with driving and taking away a car. A replacement 'principal boy' was found in time for the curtain to go up, but sadly his size 11 feet ruled out the previously rehearsed 'glass slipper' routine.[19]

Another former staff member thinks that in general, in the 1970s relations between the boys and local residents were reasonably friendly – groups of boys still regularly visited the Regal cinema in Wallingford without incident – but that things got rather worse through the 1980s, with Crowmarsh, as the nearest village, suffering most; on the other hand he believes that what then went on was no more than 'kids' play' compared with the worst of juvenile behaviour today. From the mid-1980s, Menday records one occasion when, following 'a long standing disagreement' between boys from Turners Court and from Wallingford 20 of the former walked into the town 'determined to give battle.' The police apparently arrested six boys and the rest returned unharmed to Turners Court. Such aggressive behaviour, Menday points out, was often linked to solvent and/or drug abuse.[20]

If Menday's 1998 history and the surviving management files tell us little about relations between 'colonists' and local residents, they are even less revealing on the subject of bullying and internal violence. For the most recent decades of Turners Court's existence, however, it is possible to obtain an admittedly small selection of anecdotes from former residents – always remembering that those who were generally content with their lot are less likely to come forward with contributions.

---

19. Menday, Turners Court, 1998, pp. 93, 101, 109, 126, 140, 148; OCRO, TCYT Box H12; telephone conversations, J. Glavey, June 2006, P Honeybone Apr 2007.
20. Menday, *Turners Court*, 1998, p.152; telephone conversation Apr 2007, P. Honeybone.

One Turners Court resident from the years 1973-1976 writes thus about what he claims was 'one of many bad episodes':

> 'I shared a room [with] two lads [who] were gay. When I asked to be moved I was asked why. Word got round. The two lads denied the fact. I was confronted with five east end hardliners . . . accusing me of telling lies. [A] bottle was smashed against the wall. Then some idiot turned off the light. I was . . lucky. . . managed to fight my way out. I ran [away]. I returned a hero to [Cory] house. It seemed that I had decked these lads and got away. They questioned the boys and got the truth TC [sic] style. People commented they did not know I could hit so hard.'

During his time at the School, he goes on to allege, 'there was nasty lads, mean; they made the Krays look like boy scouts,' and, 'the judgements handed out were tough [administered] by the other boys; there was a bullying . . hierarchy; the houseparents had their favourites.' As a throwaway line he adds 'the locals hated us', perhaps supporting his other memory of a sort of solidarity among the boys which helped the less confident ones mature: 'TC gave them support through each other.'[21]

Another respondent, who lived in Albright House in 1981-82, claims that the Housemaster was, ' . . . very volatile and most [boys] feared him a bit, he wasn't a bloke you messed about, he wasn't worried about giving anyone a backhander. The man was a fucking loony really,' going on to detail a couple of alleged incidents:

---

21. Private e.mail, June 2008, 'PG'.

'One night me and my mate had been to see a couple of birds in Wallingford. I done over half a bottle of whisky, we got a cab back. As I staggered in, bouncing off the walls, [the Housemaster] gave me a whack. I hit the floor. He shouted to [staff member] 'Miss T' to run the bath. He dragged me in the cloakroom by the hair, slapping and punching me. . .When the bath was run he held me under the water for what seemed like forever. All I remember of the rest of the night is laying in the cloakroom throwing up.'

The second story he tells is perhaps mainly interesting for the way that the passage of time allows one to form more mature, perhaps more kindly, judgements about people. After again disparaging 'Miss T', he writes about another junior member of the house-staff, 'John', who lived with his wife and children in a flat next to Albright House; 'John' was, he writes, 'one of those types who was always trying to be your friend, soft as shite, people used to tell him to fuck off, call him a cunt and all that. I used to think to myself, years later, god there was a nice bloke. . who'd really try and help you, and was treated like shit by most of us.' After the outing to Wallingford the 'mate' had been 'gated' for two weeks, but insisted he was going out anyway, with a volley of abuse at 'John'. Some pushing and shoving ensues, with six other boys joining in to support the 'mate' and attack the member of staff. 'Miss T', who seems not to have been attacked (perhaps that would have been thought unchivalrous?) appeared and said she was going to inform the Housemaster when he returned later in the evening. About 10.30 p.m,

'... I went to bed, put my headphones on and listened to John Peel. After about 15 minutes I heard a bit of a rumble, looked out of the window... it was [the Housemaster]. I jumped under the bed clothes and was terrified. I heard him flying up the stairs, my room was the first one you came to, he pushed open the door, threw the light on, and was shouting "You want a fight, lad, I'll give you a fucking fight (he had a deep Yorkshire accent), the blows rained down on me, but lucky for me the onslaught was short lived; I think he was so keen to deal with all the others involved.'[22]

In the absence of evidence from the other boys, Housemaster and other staff members there is, of course, no way of telling just how highly coloured by memory these accounts may be. The first of the two boys, who regards Turners Court as one episode in an early life in care which left him, he says, 'very bitter and damaged', signs off 'good luck: you never know you've missed it till its gone', presumably a reference to what he feels is his lost youth. The second, however, victim of the 'volatile' Housemaster, nevertheless considers Turners Court to have been 'a beautiful place', and regularly cycles there from his present home near Oxford.

Rather peripheral to this catalogue of misdeeds, but included by Menday in his 1998 history, perhaps to illustrate what he saw as a general decline of standards in the years before Turners Court closed, is an alleged comment by the management committee that the quality of food served to the boys appeared to be slightly lower than that served in Reading

---

22. Private e.mail, June 2008, 'MW'. He apologises for some of the graphic detail: 'all this has got me a bit hot under the collar.' The 'mate' and the Wallingford 'birds' are named, along with the Housemaster and junior staff member; 'Miss T' was subsequently identified, last seen living in a mobile home a few miles from Turners Court (private e.mail, Sep 2008, 'DW').

gaol. But the former resident of Cory House, in the midst of writing about his traumatic experiences, says he found the food 'good – off the farm, fresh milk daily, and the orange [sic] bread loaded with the stuff to stop erections.'

More positively, Menday's narrative for this period interleaves the reports of misbehaviour with up-beat anecdotes - boys, for example, raising money by sponsored walks and other means for medical research and local charities. And a typewritten note, undated but probably of 1988/89 and seemingly written by a former Hedges House resident ('HEDGES BEST HOUSE ON SITE!') acknowledges the hard work of the house staff in 'turning round' difficult boys: 'Always remember . . . your work is not a waste of time, look at me, the mess I was in, it just shows when a person grows up and understands and realizes what people have done for you.'[23]

Although the effect of 'Small Group Living', as opposed to life in the old barrack-like dormitories, was generally felt to be 'very positive', it was thought to create its own problems of behaviour, since boys might be more inclined to act up, and to need a much more flexible approach by staff. Under Cornfield's leadership it was also decided to move the oldest boys, those soon to leave Turners Court, into almost fully independent quarters, where they would be expected to fend for themselves. It was noted that the 'independent living experience was useful for some boys, but loneliness [also]

---

23. Menday, Turners Court, 1998, p. 155; OCRO, TCYT H.06. The boy's name is not given. Hedges House (named for the former committee chairman) and Grove House look to have been names given to parts of the original larger residential blocks in the later days of Turners Court.

posed problems.'[24] With the national change in the approach to children and others in care, from residential care, to 'care in the community', it was perhaps inevitable that only the more 'difficult' boys were sent to Turners Court. Menday writes that during this period over 50 per cent of the boys had (undifferentiated) medical problems, and 20 per cent were receiving psychiatric treatment or supervision. By the 1970s, too, the professionally trained staff sometimes doubted – as Hunt and his contemporaries almost certainly did not – that taking unruly and disturbed boys from the inner cities to the remote countryside might not necessarily be in the best interests of the boys, the social services, and the taxpayer. Of course it may also be true that the apparent increase in serious misbehaviour inside Turners Court, and on the mean streets of Wallingford, could be due, partly, at least, to better record keeping than in the past.

'not the final chapter'

In June 1989 Mike Cornfield replaced John Howells as Principal. With hindsight, it now begins to look inevitable that the 'colony' could no longer survive as a separate training establishment, and it is hardly surprising that the bulk of the surviving papers for these last years concern Turners Court's financial problems and possible solutions. The new Principal inherited a steadily declining intake of boys; three years earlier, on the occasion of one of many reviews of the finances and staff, it had been suggested that the school could turn a profit

---

24. OCRO, TCYT Box H. At least initially, the 'independent living unit' seems to have consisted of a caravan, for two boys, parked in a remote part of the site (Private e.mail, Sep 2008, 'AP').

with 56 boys, but a loss with 47; by 1988 numbers were down to 35. By the end of the decade, the accountants reckoned that 'break even' could be achieved with 43.5 full time equivalent students, later revised downwards to 35, but by 1990 even this number proved out of reach. The expected deficit had reached £0.5 million, unless some land were sold, and fees were set to increase from £9,500 to £10,400 per 4 month 'term.' By this stage it was said that too many boys were leaving within a year of admission (42% did so in 1987).

The legislative background, too, had once more shifted, and was now even less conducive to residential institutions like Turners Court. The Children Act 1989, based on a short DHSS report of 1984, represented, one commentator argues, 'a change in attitude towards children and their families'. The wording of the Act deals in terms such as 'parental responsibilities', 'support for children and families' and the importance of 'partnerships' between social services and families, all of which sound a long way from the 'colony' tradition of institutionalism (not to mention emigration).[25]

For some years the school had not broken even. The farm, separately accounted for, showed a profit in some years, but, as always, a poor harvest could be disastrous: in 1986 it was estimated that bad weather would cause the farm to show a deficit of £30,000. Four years later heavy storm damage was caused to several of the Turners Court buildings, seemingly not covered by insurance and the committee of management found 'much shabbiness and an uninviting atmosphere' when they visited the Boys Club, although the staff were seen to be interested in their work. New technology called for further

---

25. Hendrick, *Child Welfare*, 1994, p.276.

capital investment; in 1988 a computer (a Nimbus, costing £7,500) was eventually purchased for education and training purposes. The Charity Commission was asked to sanction an extended overdraft of £180,000; even this, it had been acknowledged, would only offer a 'temporary breathing space.'[26]

The financial instability and some feeling that the establishment was already running down, resulted in poor motivation and further staff changes; in one month, May 1988, four members of staff resigned, and three new members were recruited. In 1988-89 the farm manager reported to the committee that boys were 'no longer interested' in dairy work, and it was agreed that the dairy herd should be sold. No DHSS grant aid (under the 1989 Act) could be claimed in this financial year, although the Department advised the committee to apply again next year. The committee noted a 'lack of motivation by teachers . . . and a very light work load.'

Even at this stage it is important to realise that the day-to-day routine continued and perhaps the gloomy atmosphere was not always evident to the few boys still in residence. A typewritten account headed 'Life at Turners Court' which must date either from 1990 or 1991, unsigned but known to have been written by a boy from Grays, Essex, paints a cheery picture:

> 'I enjoy life at Turners Court. I am in painting and decorating trade. . we are learning about sign writing and . . . we are learning to paint cartoon pictures. I get on well with everyone and am learning a

---

26. Menday, *Turners Court*, 1998, p.152. 156-157, 167.

The End of Turners Court: 1968-1991

lot in my trade. At Turners Court you can do all different things . . . you can go abseiling off the tops of big cliffs. It can get boring at times. I am in Basden House with six other boys. A new cook has just started work and the dinners are getting better. . . Two days ago for tea we had prawn cocktail, minced beef pie and chips . . . and chocolate gateau.'[27]

Meanwhile, the Staffing, Welfare and Housing Sub-Committee had no shortage of concerns, ranging from the perennial problem of boys smoking (although no longer with the encouragement of 'Pop' Hansen) to the urgent need for staff quarters redecoration and improved toilet facilities, extra allowances for staff 'sleeping in' over Christmas and New year and a proposed recycling campaign. By spring 1991, with closure imminent, the main concerns of staff were, not surprisingly, what help they might expect to get in seeking new employment, and the staff pension scheme.[28]

By this time Principal and management committee were effectively committed to closure of Turners Court, acknowledging that the maximum number of boys expected on 1 April that year was 23, well under the most optimistic break even point of 35. Staff sickness and continued uncertainty about the future were severely affecting efficiency. The overdraft was expected to reach £152,000 by the end of March, £550,000 by the end of December; redundancy payments to 23 members of staff were expected to reach £33,000, but this figure did not include 'principal members of staff' or those such as maintenance and farm workers who would be expected to stay on. Grants from DHSS for building

27. OCRO, TCYT Box H06.
28. OCRO, TCYT Box H03.

staff houses might have to be repaid if there was change of use. The Principal had prepared a feasibility study outlining options for closure; on 29 January 1991 the managers agreed to close Turners Court 'in the most humane way and to the best financial advantage . . . possible' and on 30 April, the last two boys left. A 'Farewell Do and Reunion' was planned for 4 May: 'there could very well be over 250 current and past staff and families present' according to sub-committee minutes: sadly, no account of the event itself seems to have survived.

Negotiations began with local estate agents; the management committee also made contact with possible interested parties, including a local Housing Association and possible temporary use of some of the buildings for conferences. One or two small parcels of land were sold off separately, and in 1993 all of the remaining land and buildings, including 9 staff houses or flats and about 50,000 sq. ft. (4,640 m^2) of the former living blocks and workshops were sold to Rock Investment Trust for £1.85 million. A proposal by the eventual owners, Berkeley Homes, to build around 150 houses on the site did not succeed. Instead, a much smaller number of large detached houses now encircles Carr's Meadow, which remains open grassed space, although now more enclosed by hedges than in the time of the 'colony'. The name 'Turners Court' perhaps being judged to have too many unsavoury echoes, the site was rebranded as 'Oakley Court', after Oakley Wood, the long-standing name for one part of the original Turners Court estate.

The big 3-storey accommodation blocks were all demolished, along with most of the workshops, offices and farm buildings, swimming pool and boiler house. The surviving buildings include Hunt House, the last and smallest living unit to be built, and several of the staff houses and cottages. Ogilvie Hall, home to the Club and 'Pop' Hansen's shop, with the double doors and clock tower which Menday described as having 'something of the village church about it', was left to become derelict, but the planning authority did not, it seems, wish it to be demolished. Eventually it was bought and skilfully converted into two stylish dwellings; the clock face still looks out over the Meadow but, shorn of the weights that drove its mechanism, its hands remain stuck - one hour later than those of its Grantchester counterpart - at 3.45.[29]

One correspondent to a local newspaper found the closure of Turners Court both sad and ironic, noting that it coincided with publication of a Home Office consultative document recommending that 15 and 16-year olds should no longer be remanded in prison, but should be held in secure accommodation provided by local authorities; money, the letter argued, would have to be found for this 'tardy initiative' while at the same time 'no cash is seemingly available to pay for boys to be given a home and help at Turners Court .. to enable them to build towards a stable adult life.' 'Thus came to an end', writes Menday, '. . . the dream of Pioneers . . . an establishment where hundreds of disadvantaged young people were given the opportunity to "find themselves".[30]

The history of 'Turners Court' as a collection of buildings, people, farm animals and machinery ends here but it would be wrong not to mention, however briefly, the post-closure

---

29. Brian Basden, former member of the Turners Court management committee, writes (Jan 2009) that a plan to get the major buildings listed, and hence preserved, was thwarted by the developers.
30. *Henley Standard*, 8 Feb 1991; Menday, *Turners Court*, 1998, p.179..

formation of the charitable foundation which perpetuates the name, arising, as Menday's history inevitably puts it, like a 'Phoenix from the ashes' and ensuring that the sale of the land was *not* the final chapter in this narrative. Between closure and final sale, a core staff of maintenance and other workers remained on the site and Mike Cornfield became Director of the newly formed Turners Court Youth Trust, some of whose Trustees provided continuity with the former institution. The Trust's objectives were summarised as 'to identify and meet, directly or in partnership with others, the needs of children and young adults with emotional and behavioural difficulties in order that they may acquire social stablility and prepare for independent adult life.' The Trust's publicity material cites its pre-history, back to the 1911 foundation of the 'colony', and sets out the success of its current role in offering grants to charities and other groups providing services to disadvantaged children and young adults.[31]

The final chapter of this book will try to draw together some of the underlying themes of Turners Court's history and compare the fate of the Christian Service Union's Wallingford 'colony' with that of the Salvation Army establishment at Hadleigh, whose origins were covered in Chapter 1.

---

31. See www.turnerscourt.org.uk

CHAPTER 7
Reflections, conclusions

Those who hope, by retiring from the world, to earn a holiday from human frailty, in themselves and others, are usually disappointed
- Iris Murdoch, 'The Bell', 1958

Forsan et haec olim meminisse juvabit – Virgil, 'Aeneid' Book I

Ron Menday's privately published 1998 history of Turners Court, based on committee minutes and other papers of the Christian Service Union supplemented by the author's memories of his own time as Warden, identified three 'themes' that the author saw as having run through the 80 year history of the 'Colony':

- An ecumenical interest, among British churchmen, in helping the unemployed and unemployables.

- The origins and growth of 'colonies' in Britain.

- Increasing involvement of national and local authorities, including Boards of Guardians, Local Government Board, Ministry of Education, Home Office, although, Menday added, 'overall the voluntary and the Christian ethic was insisted upon by the pioneers.'[1]

---
1. Menday, *Turners Court*, 1998, p.4.

Of these, the second was treated only briefly in Menday's book and has been somewhat expanded upon in the first two chapters of the present work. Although the Christian Service Union liked to emphasise the 'unique' character, first of the Lingfield colony, then of Wallingford ignoring or writing down the efforts of rival philanthropists, we have seen that, by the end of the 19th century, there were plenty of broadly similar institutions in Britain; the CSU's ventures may indeed be thought of as having been in the mainstream of social work at the time. Only its comparatively late survival into the 1990s distinguishes Turners Court from other 'colonies'; even in this it was not quite unique: the 'post-history' of the Salvation Army colony at Hadleigh gives it a plausible claim to having kept alive at least part of its original activity from 1891 into the present century.[2]

The German origins of the Wallingford Colony, much cited by pre-1914 CSU apologists, were also characteristic of the social and economic background of the late 19th and early 20th centuries. German examples were followed, although not necessarily always acknowledged, in many aspects of British social legislation and practice, including the state education system and the 'Lloyd George' schemes of sickness insurance and old age pensions. Industrially, too, Britain's chemical and electrical sectors developed both as spin off from, and in competition with, German originals. And the drive to improve 'efficiency' and 'backbone' among the British working population, and the parallel drive to people the Dominions with healthy, trained and British-oriented men, was largely inspired by fear of German military and industrial power

---

2. The CSU's work with epileptics, as we have seen, continues today at Lingfield.

once the folk memory of the French as Britain's natural foes had started to fade.

This drive for able-bodied emigration which, as has been argued in Chapter 1, appeared to provide such a powerful argument for institutions like Turners Court, effectively overshadowed the original philanthropic ethos, so that today it is not easy to determine which was the more important motivation for those who subscribed to the CSU's colonies: helping the (deserving) disadvantaged, or bolstering Britain's industrial and military potential. At the time no doubts were raised as to whether the two were perfectly compatible. The German colonies of von Bodelschwingh and others, which had so enthused Julie Sutter and the Earl of Meath, generally lacked this 'emigration' purpose; even at the end of the 19th century, Germany still had comparatively few overseas dependencies to which 'colonists' might emigrate. The wave of 'social imperialism' that swept British politics at that time, however, ensured that emigration was firmly on the CSU's agenda. In terms of numbers, colonist emigrants were an important factor for the first two decades of the CSU's existence.

Wallingford was set up towards the tail end of the 'social imperialist' enthusiasm; after the First World War, although visiting politicians and retired generals might continue to talk about it as a central part of the Colony's objectives, the policy of mass emigration would never again be so enthusiastically pursued, either in Britain or in the recipient Dominions, although individual 'old boys' continued to leave Turners Court for Australia and New Zealand until well after the World War II.

In other ways, too, Wallingford would diverge from the Bielefeld example, side-tracked first by the need to cater for epileptics at Lingfield, then by realisation that the colonists they could expect to see moving into Wallingford and the rest were not the 'able bodied unemployed', temporarily looking for re-training, ready to step into new jobs, but the despised 'unemployables'. What were portrayed at the time as substantial differences between CSU and other charitable organisations, especially the Charity Organisation Society (COS) now look less fundamental. Although COS officials wrote scathingly about how little could be expected from the futile efforts of CSU and other colonies, their philosophies now seem less sharply differentiated: if the CSO constantly nagged charities and their members not to support 'undeserving' cases, CSU publications too refer to the need to concentrate on 'the most deserving' cases.

In the longer term this handy taxonomy (handy for the philanthropist that is, not for the indigent client) of more or less 'deserving' cases for treatment, whether in a colony or elsewhere, would be overtaken by the supplier-customer relationship of training school and local authority children's or social department. The high-flown Christian rhetoric of annual reports and Open Day speeches was augmented, and eventually succeeded, by the requirements of secular bodies – Government and local authority departments, inspectors and welfare officers. By the last quarter of the 20th century, Turners Court looked more to the tenets of social science and management studies than to those of Christian dogma.

Changes in the organisation, work, staffing etc at the Wallingford Colony over the 80 years of its existence, its increasing secularism and professionalism, and the growth of Government oversight, illustrate on a small scale more general changes in British legislation and economy. When the CSU was founded, after the meeting in Christ Church in February 1894, efforts to help the sick, aged, infirm, unemployed and indigent had for centuries been financed from local, unpredictable and often inefficient parish funds, supplemented by voluntary donation. Voluntary money was also largely responsible for health care – with strings attached: voluntarily funded hospitals would, for example, not treat sexually transmitted diseases. The idea that national taxation should pay for most, if not all, of these services was scarcely debated. Other services which we now think of as naturally benefiting from taxation, such as fire prevention, were still largely voluntarily funded until the World War II (as saving lives at sea still is). Centrally-funded and universal health care only became a reality in 1948 – although the establishment, after the First World War, of a Ministry of Health may be seen as a portent of the future; as Chapter 4 has illustrated, the new Ministry quickly made an impression on the day to day operations at Turners Court.

Colonies and communities

Left-inclined historians argue that we cannot isolate the overt evangelical aims of 19th century philanthropists from political - essentially class-based - motives; doing the Lord's work, it is argued, went along with a wish to stave off the perceived threat to comfortable society from disaffected urban masses. Harry Hendrick offers such an analysis of the various plans to 'save' the inner city child or young man from the immorality of his environment: 'Children with irreligious parents would "grow in evil"'; saving their souls could only be accomplished by 'rescuing them from the damnation in which they were cast by economic, social and moral circumstance'. Onto this foundation was added the Imperial dimension: children as the investment in Empire, part of a shield against the various hordes of Germans, Bolsheviks or Asians. Hendrick concludes that 'it would be a mistake to imagine that [philanthropic societies] were simply Christian . . . institutions, innocent of wily political ambitions with respect to instilling social discipline in their charges.' Especially after the unsettling social unrest in London of the 1880s, it is not fanciful to detect a class element in the move to take as many as possible of the indigent, rootless children out of the inner cities; this met both a 'social and political necessity', an arrangement which neatly satisfied doctrinal conscience and cleared the towns of unreliable elements.[3]

Of course it is hard, whatever period of time one is studying, to find people, politicians, philanthropists or others, whose motives are strictly one-dimensional. Those like William Booth and Julie Sutter who planned the 19th century 'colonies' had mixed motives, conditioned by their own upbringing, surroundings and preferences. Further, within an organisation like the CSU there would always be differences of opinion or philosophy between supporters: apart from their shared interest in making a success of the Colony, the Quaker Edward Sturge and the imperialist Earl of Meath would seem to have had little in common. The similarity in names and

---

3. H. Hendrick, *Child Welfare in England 1872-1989*, 1994 (London:RKP) p.82.

(as we have seen) the consequent possibility of confusion, between Christian *Service* and Christian *Social* Unions, is covered in more detail in an Appendix. In brief, however, although Christian Socialist writers would occasionally support emigration as part of a wider and more radical political response to unemployment, the more general flavour of Christian Socialist dogma would have been unappetising to those who founded the Lingfield and Wallingford colonies. The rough reception accorded to Meath by the SDF hecklers (Chapter 3) show just what such an audience would have thought of 'social imperialism'.

Certainly in the first 40 or 50 years of the Wallingford Colony's existence it is hard to detect left-of-centre sympathy within the CSU. Leaders of the Wallingford project, including William Hunt, went out of their way to advertise their antipathy towards any hint of 'socialism'. In 1922, writing in *Social Service* about the supposed attempt to found a colony at Starnthwaite before the CSU eventually succeeded in doing so, Hunt calls it a 'hopeful experiment' which had, however, been 'destroyed by Socialists' who were – ironically – 'too individualistic'. 'Communists,' Hunt concluded triumphantly, 'are the last people likely to live successfully in communities!' The odd episode of the reaction to Dr. Tioli's alleged attempt to recruit communists, perhaps as volunteers to fight Franco's reactionaries in Spain, outlined in Chapter 4, shows how keen the Wallingford Colony management was to distance itself from any taint of 'leftism'. The establishment-heavy membership of CSU committees, and the choice of retired generals, diplomats and other right-of-centre dignitaries to preside at Open Days and other events, carry the same message.

By contrast, over the years the Colony's leaders did like to represent it as a 'community'. In his first description, published in 1959, of what had by then become the Wallingford Training School, Menday writes: 'To arrive at Turners Court is to arrive at a community . . . a body of people having common rights, interests and occupations . . . [and] where all the inhabitants are engaged upon a common task.'[4] Menday (or perhaps his collaborator, John Wiles) then writes lyrically of the 'Houses' and farm buildings, especially the Ogilvie Hall, home to the Boys Club, which, with its double doors and clock tower had,

> ' . . . something of the village church about it. On a summer evening the sun broods in peace over Carr's Meadow, and as the clock strikes the hours the notes seem to hover for a moment before fading into the general quiet of the country which lies about it. To stand for a moment at sunset . . . to hear the birdsong, the lowing of the cattle, the chink of milk cans, the distant shout of a boy on the playing field, is to discover .. the real peace of Turners Court. It is this serenity of nature, this proof that here is a place to be loved, that lends most balm to the heart of the boy.'[5]

Only warm beer (which Menday was perhaps not likely to include on any list of desiderata) the sound of leather on willow, and spinsters cycling to evensong are missing from this evocation of mythic middle England. Just how much 'balm' was sensed by the average boy exiled to the rim of the

4. Menday & Wiles, *Everlasting Childhood*, 1959, p.104-105.
5. Ibid, p.116.

Reflections, conclusions

Chilterns, is impossible to calculate, although several of the published letters 'home' to Turners Court already quoted in this book, and the unpublished recollections of more recent residents, referred to later in this Chapter, include an element of nostalgia which Menday and his fellow Wardens/Superintendents would have taken as supportive of their regimes. The romantic, generally erroneous, view of what journalists like to call the 'close knit' village community at which Menday hinted is still alive, even when most genuine villages as depicted on postcards or in TV series are populated largely by well-heeled commuters or 'second home' tenants. The myth of that pre-industrial Eden when we all lived in peaceable, self-governing, collaborative communities, refuses to die, although severely wounded by a number of authors; 30 years ago an Open University project mischievously pointed out that authors continue to get away with the romantic myth mainly because the medieval village is so remote from the direct experience of people writing and reading history today that few feel equipped to contradict it.[6]

At no time, of course, could Turners Court claim to have been a *self-sufficient* community; although based on a sizeable and generally successful farm, the Wallingford Colony was always dependent upon local trades people for essentials like meat and slab cake, not to mention bread, the quality of which caused such resentment in the 1930s (Chapter 4). More seriously, the government of any 'community' visualised by Hunt, Menday or most CSU members, was almost inevitably going to exclude from decision-making the greater part of the Turners Court population, the 'colonists' themselves.

6   C. Phythian-Adams etc, *Fabric of the Traditional Community*, 1977 (Milton Keynes: OU) p.38.

Even allowing for that, Turners Court, certainly until the final decades of its existence, looks to have leaned towards the authoritarian, even militaristic, end of the management spectrum; one former 'colonist' from the late 1950s, after confirming that Menday, despite his avowed distaste for military rank was invariably known as 'The Colonel', said his recollection was that 'most of the staff were ex-military – perhaps that was needed to control us?'[7]

Promise and practice could differ radically. When the Wallingford Colony was launched, the NUCSS, in its publicity and in the columns of *Social Service*, explained that the lay 'Brothers' who volunteered to spend time there would work *with* the young 'colonists', teaching by example the rudiments of agriculture and the benefits of a Christian way of life. By contrast, a couple of examples from among the notes on individual 'Brothers', kept in William Hunt's own hand in a leather-bound register, show that his first priority was the imposition of firm discipline and exemplary punishment:

> 'war-resistance Brother, disbelieved in discipline; had to be detached from squad work'

> 'Useless as a Brother. Allowed boys to do as they liked. Did not believe in discipline or punishment.'[8]

Hunt, whether knowingly or not, was carrying on what we have seen (Chapter 1) to be the distinctly unilateral management style of Pastor von Bodelschwingh. In her book *Colony of Mercy*, Julie Sutter, too, wrote movingly about how

7. Private e.mail, June 2008, 'KC'.
8. OCRO TCYT Box H02: Register of Brothers.

each group of workers at the Bethel colony went about its daily task alongside a 'Brother' who was 'not a slave-driver but a man to keep them to their work by *just working with them* . . . He keeps up the cheerful tone, and shows them the beauty of work'. But a few pages earlier, a drawing captioned 'Colonists reclaiming the soil' shows a man in what look like riding-breeches and boots, carrying a cane, obviously directing the work of smock-clad labourers from the top of a small mound.[9]

The military tinge of Turners Court's senior staff and committee members was not exceptional for its time: Oxfordshire County Council, for example, usually had a substantial phalanx of Lt. Cols.and Majors among its elected members and aldermen (as well as heavyweight aristocrats like the Duke of Marlborough and the Earl of Macclesfield, the latter a long-serving Council chairman). Although Hunt and his CSU contemporaries did not choose to take on 'military' rankings, as did the Salvation Army, Hunt's position at Wallingford looks to have been not much different from that of the 'Colonel' in charge of the Hadleigh colony who, having been appointed by 'The General' (Booth) was said to have enjoyed 'absolute control'.[10]

Hunt's individual and non-negotiable way of hiring and firing 'Brothers', and Menday's insistence on keeping all casework in his own hands, exemplify the same authoritarian model. Hunt, that 'great man', would have been surprised and perhaps outraged at any suggestion that the Colony might be run with a modicum of consensus. The contrast

9. Sutter, *Colony of Mercy*, 1893 pp 159, 151 (original emphasis).
10. Anon, *Hadleigh, the story of a great endeavour*, c. 1902 (London: Salvation Army) p.3.

comes in the post-Menday years, when staff shared common professional qualifications and background; by then Turners Court's internal magazines, too, give the impression of a more oligarchic structure, along with a distinct lack of deference to the Principal himself: hard to imagine Hunt or Menday permitting the kind of disrespectful badinage that enlivened 'Ianto's Diary' (see Chapter 6) in the 1980s.

Only in the last years of the 'Colony' are there substantial signs of the 'lads' themselves being involved in the running of the institution and, now supported by their personal advocates the Local Authority social workers, in deciding their own futures. The, no doubt carefully selected, case conference filmed for the 1986 video not only allows 'Bhutta', the boy whose progress is under discussion, to speak about his plans and preferences, but makes it seem that these would be taken into account by the Turners Court staff. And the way another, film-struck, boy then speaks to the interviewer, in the material taped for but never used in that video, conveys a sort of breezy assumption that it was actually the boys who were in charge.

From the 1930s through to the 1960s it is possible to compare what looks like the conventional, authoritarian regime which obtained at Turners Court with a couple of other well-documented 'experiments' in the handling and 'treatment' of wayward boys – although such comparisons should not be taken too far. One such 'experiment' was the first of the 'Q Camps', whose establishment was noted, with apparent approval, in *Social Service* (May 1936); the new Editor – presumably Grant, who had succeeded Hunt – referred to the involvement of David Wills, the former Wallingford

'Brother', whose mixed memories of Colony life in the 1920s were cited in Chapter 3. Wills himself described the 'Q Camp' venture in his 1941 book, *The Hawkspur Experiment*. It had originated, much as had the National Union for Christian Social Service, with a meeting, in May 1935, of a number of like-minded organisations and individuals. Although, like Wills himself, many of the 'Q Camp's' backers were Quakers,[11] they also included the Archbishop of York, the Humanist Julian Huxley, and Laurence Housman. It was originally intended that camps should be set up all over the country, for young men, between the ages of 17 and 25, who were 'having difficulty adjusting themselves to Society.' Some had been before the courts, others thought to be 'heading that way.'

At the 'Q Camp' they would be given 'a healthy outdoor life with plenty of adventure and the maximum of freedom.' The 1935 meeting drew up a memorandum outlining activities at the proposed camps: 'Gardening, elementary farm care of livestock and various handicrafts . . . games, folk dancing, drama, music, debates, reading and, when desired [by the inmates] instruction in academic subjects.' Initially housed in tents or 'rude block houses', the members and helpers were to proceed to build their own permanent accommodation. Each camp should be largely self-governing; the inmates were to be called 'members', all equal in domestic matters with the staff; the CSU's 'Brothers' would re-appear as 'Student helpers', young men who intended to take up work among delinquents, and perhaps had a certain academic knowledge of their problems, but who lacked experience. Early 'helpers' from Saffron Walden School recall sharing mugs of tea with

11. Hawkspur, a village in NW Essex, is a cycle ride from the Society of Friends' school at Saffron Walden.

Wills in the original wooden hut in summer 1937, after days spent hoeing vegetables.[12]

All this is reminiscent of the early years of the Lingfield and Wallingford Colonies, although neither Hunt nor Menday would have written about Turners Court as Wills does about Hawkspur, ' . . . the work which was done [there] was a co-operative effort [although] . . . as Camp Chief [Wills] was necessarily the pivot around which the work . . . revolved,' going on to explain that,

> 'we don't call it self-government because so many people seem to think that . . .   means giving the inmates [sic] the whole responsibility for running things which they can only   imperfectly understand [so] we have adopted [the] phrase "shared responsibility." The "members" share with the staff the job of running the camp, and the staff accept the jurisdiction of the Camp Council on those matters with which the Council is concerned.'

Meetings of the Council were summoned by the Chairman (a senior staff member) calling out, after supper: ' . . . will you chaps round the fire come to the table please': one of the (few) rules was that only those seated could speak during meetings, a protocol that today invites comparison with Golding's *Lord of the Flies,* or the less than satisfactory council meeting in *The Bell*, Iris Murdoch's satirical novel from which an unenthusiastic view of rural community life heads this chapter. At Hawkspur, matters governed by the council included allegations of bullying, theft, waste of money on provisions, waste of food and so on. Whereas, at Turners Court, the quality of bread in was, in the 1930s, as we have seen, a

12. Private letters/e.mails, 2006, D. Mitchell, T. Evens.

management matter not up for discussion, at Hawkspur it was open to debate by the Council: the quartermaster (hard, even for Quakers, to avoid those military ranks) having claimed that one of the boys had been cutting crusts off new (home baked) loaves, not only at each end but down the sides as well 'so that practically the whole of the inside gets wasted', the alleged culprit claims that it is common practice; unable to apportion blame the Council agrees not to fine anyone on this occasion and to meet the cost of extra bread, but 'members' must not let it happen again.[13]

Some supporting evidence of the 'shared responsibility' system comes from a later short-term 'student helper,' recalling a 1945 visit to Hawkspur, under the auspices of the International Voluntary Service for Peace (IVSP). She and other volunteers were there to help dig foundations for a brick common-room which would replace one of the wooden huts which had outlived its usefulness,

> ' . . . they had meetings at which the boys decided on rules and penalties. Their system was that a boy would do as he pleased, but he must be responsible for paying from his allowance of pocket money for any damage done. One lad demonstrated his anger and frustration by going round the camp at night . . . breaking windows. We wondered how his pocket money would cope. We asked where [David Wills]

---

13. Wills, *Hawkspur Experiment*, 1941, pp.10, 59, 81. More detail about the aims and working of 'Q Camps' is in M. E. Franklin & others, *Q Camp: an epitome of experiences at Hawkspur camp*, c.1942/3 (Howard League for Penal Reform) and www.utopia-britannnica.org.uk/pages/Qcamps.htm. Wills was apparently known as 'Duke' at Hawkspur; at Wallingford he had been derisively nicknamed 'Woodbine' (an enormously popular brand of cigarette manufactured by the Bristol firm W.D. & H.O. Wills).

was, feeling the need for support or advice, but were told that he rarely visited. We never met him.[14]

By this time Wills was in fact running another 'community', which he also described in print. This was Barns House, near Edinburgh, essentially a wartime expedient known as an 'evacuation hostel' financed by Edinburgh City and Peeblesshire County Councils who delegated oversight to a Quaker-dominated committee of management; their underlying philosophy, Wills writes in Quakerly terms, was that of 'liberating a man [or boy] to do a piece of work for which he is "under concern".' While Barns House afforded sturdier and more permanent accommodation for the 30 or so 'difficult' boys who were in residence at any one time, the self-government was, if anything, even more outstanding. After Wills himself imposes a period of top-down control – mainly, it appears, to goad the boys into rebellion – the boys call a meeting 'to end the dictatorship' and elect a 12-year old 'Minister of Justice' to chair 'House' meetings and lay down rules regarding, for example, times of meals and bedtimes. The boys made themselves responsible for 'charging' others with offences such as bullying. On one occasion Wills describes a 13-year old as making 'a very good President, though inclined to be a little self-righteous.'[15]

What sounds, from another published account, to have been an equally forthright example of a quasi self-governing (anarchistic, ill-wishers would have said) institution for bad boys, was Finchden Manor, which occupied the Jacobean/

---

14. Private letter, 2006, M.Slee.
15. D.W. Wills, *The Barns Experiment,* 1945 (London: George Allen & Unwin) pp.9, 52.

Reflections, conclusions

Victorian house of that name near Tenterden in Kent from the 1930s through to the 1960s. The rewards and dangers of working in this off-beat educational establishment are described in a memoir by a one-time member of the teaching staff, entitled *Mr Lyward's Answer*,[16] G.A. Lyward being the founder and head of the establishment. As Hunt had done earlier, Lyward combined this job with editing a monthly journal: *Home and School*, which first appeared in 1936, was largely devoted to promoting the spread of parent-teacher associations in England, with articles by educationalists, child psychologists, dieticians and nurses. Strictly speaking Lyward was not editor, but 'chairman of the magazine committee', which, apart from him, was largely female and from the medical and nursing professions. Like *Social Service*, Lyward's journal shrank in wartime; the last issue appeared in 1944.

Michael Burn, author of the semi-fictionalised account of Finchden - like Wills, he refers to boys and most staff members by pseudonym - had been a temporary and seemingly unqualified teacher. The book never quite pins down the status of the establishment, loosely termed a 'special school'; Burn concludes lamely that it 'evaded categories,' being neither school nor clinic. Lyward, with six ever-changing staff members, catered for around 40 boys at any one time. A few (perhaps 30 out of 270 between 1930-1956) stayed at the school for less than six months; the rest were there for anything up to 6 years. In the early days, most boys were placed and paid for by relatively affluent parents, many of whom lived

16. 1956, (London: Hamish Hamilton). There must be something in the water in that part of Kent: Michael Holroyd's collective biography (*A Strange Eventful History*, 2008, Chatto & Windus) of Ellen Terry, Henry Irving and their circle reveals that Terry's daughter Edy set up an avant-garde theatre group and lesbian community at her mother's house near Tenterden.

outside Britain, for example in the armed forces. After the World War II some boys were paid for from public funds; in 1946, 'enthusiastic' education officers, probation officers and social workers, says Burn, were applying for vacancies at the rate of four a week: ' . . .doctors far beyond Harley Street, Councils far . . . from London, had begun to make use of Mr Lyward's gifts and experience.'

In terms of style and possessions the contrast with the inner-city residents of Turners Court could be considerable: one boy arrived at Finchden Manor with several suitcases containing, among other things, four dozen butterfly collars and 100 ties; another came by Rolls-Royce, wearing dark glasses, floral shirt and sombrero and speaking fluent French, German and Italian. On the other hand, many of these boys also suffered from more or less severe behavioural problems. 'A very great number,' writes Burn, 'had stolen . . . more often than not from their parents. Many had been bed-wetters. Some had been violent . . . Some were merely called backward . . . One had been sending anonymous insults to his head-master. Two or three had threatened suicide.' The violence was not always life-threatening: one boy, told, by a psychiatrist, that he was 'something like incurable,' later told Burn 'I wasn't going to have that, so to prove he was wrong, I went and spat in his letter-box.'[17]

Rather than the vocational training on offer at Turners Court, Finchden's curriculum mimicked that of a traditional public or preparatory school – at least as regards content; there were, however, no fixed hours for tuition or anything else, apart from meals, which the boys cooked and served

---

17. Burn, *Mr Lyward's Answer,* 1956, pp.17, 27, 49, 124.

themselves. Discipline was not so much self-administered, as at Hawkspur, as non-existent. Its success, Burn claims, came from,

> 'The suspending . . . of moral judgements, and refusal to plant premature ideals and standards . . . in the boys' paths, gave them the opportunity to feel their own way through unhindered. Respite came first, from the world in which they had been asked to lead the lives of others; then re-birth into their own.'[18]

Lyward's 'answer' to deviant behaviour appears to have been to allow boys to commit their follies and then let themselves be argued into a realisation of their errors, 'recreating', for the boys, Burn writes, 'a lost family, welcoming . . . boys whose roots were shrivelled by striking them afresh and nourishing their natural growth.' Lyward insisted on two basic conditions, the first of which was, paradoxically, 'unfairness' – not trying to relate one case to the outcome of another: the response to boys' requests and activities must never be allowed 'to harden into a rule or habit or tradition.' The second, simpler, condition was a 'ruthless quarantine': parents must be kept at arms length (a stance which it seems most of them were only too happy to adopt) and never be allowed to interfere. Despite the 'happy family' atmosphere at Finchden Manor, some boys, as at Turners Court, simply refused to accept the regime – or lack of one – and ran off. With self-confidence less common among Turners Court boys, they would then telephone the school – reversing the charges – and wait to be picked up by Lyward himself.

---

18. Ibid, p.69

Burn (like Menday) used 'community' to describe Finchden, one which 'had the hospitality of a happy family', citing the way that - as at Turners Court - former inmates and staff would turn up for meals, meet the new boys and introduce new girl friends. Burn also writes (but without supporting evidence), that the Finchden Manor boys,

> 'had many friends in the neighbourhood, and no irreconcilable enemies. Any tradesman who saw them week in week out was bound to observe the alterations in them. Mr. Bolton, who ran the sweet-shop, would keep an eye on certain boys . . . but a time came when – except with a few – he could take his eye away'.[19]

Sex and violence

It would be wrong to make too much of comparisons between the Wallingford Colony/School and the seemingly more free and easy institutions such as Hawkspur, Barns and Finchden Manor: all three were much smaller establishments than Turners Court; Hawkspur, in particular, had boys for shorter periods of time. Importantly, Finchden and Hawkspur enjoyed what was denied to Turners Court, the luxury of picking and choosing which boys they would take – even though, as we have seen, some at least of their inmates could seem at least as disruptive as those despatched to Wallingford by local authority children's departments. The Barns school did have to accept the 'difficult' boys picked up from Edinburgh by the local authority; Wills was strongly advised by one of its elected members to 'keep a strap behind the door', but resisted

---
19. Ibid, pp.70, 97.

this suggestion. The other side of this coin was that Barns was more certain of financial support than was the case at Turners Court.

In terms of perceived changes in the behaviour and attitude of boys at Turners Court over different periods, the evidence is far from conclusive. Menday's (1998) narrative of the later decades – 1970 onwards – appears to feature more by way of serious incidents such as assaults on staff and their families, violent clashes between Turners Court boys and locals, and so on than in earlier years. One needs to be cautious about attributing reasons for this. As has already been pointed out (Chapter 6) the threat of 'smashing the whole place up' to squeeze money for new equipment out of the management, may have been mere bravado for the 1986 cameraman's benefit. It might also be the case that a higher proportion of violent or misbehaving boys were referred to Turners Court in later decades; the disciplinary and management regime may have been less efficient; or the apparent increase might be, partly at least, the result of better record keeping.

That last possibility applies most strongly when comparing the final decades with the earliest, when Hunt was in charge. While not suggesting that evidence of violence by the boys or undue punishment by staff was necessarily suppressed on purpose, *Social Service*, NUCSS annual reports and other published accounts from the first couple of decades have little to say about serious crime or misdemeanour; it seems improbable, however, that in an institution of this kind there simply wasn't any. The 'punishment book' which Hunt assured Ministry officials was carefully kept (Chapter 3) no longer exists. In the earliest years, of course, boys who misbehaved or felt they had been mistreated could well just have walked off, to be recorded without much further comment, in the 'absconsions' column of Hunt's register; the option of communicating to outside authorities or friends in high places would only be available to the minority of more literate, privately-funded, 'colonists' like the aggrieved J. H. Mackie, whose letter of complaint triggered the visit by officials in 1924 described in Chapter 3.

In those early years, the effort made to search out and reclaim boys who absconded might vary as between Boards of Guardians. From the 1930s onwards, however, local authority Children's or Social Service officers would be under increasing pressure from elected members, the press and the public at large not to 'lose' their charges in this way. The most that can be deduced with any safety is that in any decade a minority of boys, a minority of staff members, might occasionally resort to violence; for the later decades voices of the boys themselves helps to colour in such episodes – as illustrated in the previous chapter.

One facet of life in the 'colony' which is largely missing from the available records is that of race, or what would, in Hunt's day, have been called 'colour'. As all personal records of the boys have now been destroyed, it is not possible to see whether they included evidence of ethnicity, although surely they must have done so in the later years. Menday has little to say on the subject: the autobiographical work he produced, with John Hartley, in 1995 identifies 'one coloured boy from Liverpool' from Menday's own time as Warden, but then tells the reader nothing about the boy.[20]

---

20. Menday & Hartley, 1995, *To a peak and beyond*, 1995 (private) p.171.

Reflections, conclusions

Surviving papers are silent as to whether racial tension was ever considered by the Turners Court authorities to have contributed to problems of discipline. Asked about this, former residents contacted through the 'Friends Reunited' website vary in their accounts: one, from the late 1950s, remembers quite a few 'coloured' boys in his day, 'both black kids and Pakistani [sic]. There was never any animosity of any kind that I can remember. Colour was never an issue.' Another, (at Turners Court in the 1970s) writes that he does not recall any black or Asian residents but then produces a photograph from a few years earlier, showing a black lad. A third, again from the 1970s is more positive, writing that there was 'a good mix of colours;' he can't remember any boys of ethnic Asian origin, but there were 'a couple of Caribbean – some hard workers' with one of whom he shared a room: 'listened to reggae for six months; never had any problem.' From the end of that same decade, the boy whom we have already met, putting his horticultural training to good use as manager of a garden centre refers in passing to what he terms 'first term treatment' from the other boys, which in his case involved dyeing his (black) hair bright orange, but claims he found such treatment neither overly malicious nor racist and goes on to commend Turners Court for having given him 'a good grounding in life.' Finally, in the 1980s, there is firm visual evidence in the shape of the boy named as 'Bhutta' who takes centre stage in the case-conference sequence of the video.[21]

Bullying, whether racially slanted or not, may well have been no worse than that on offer at many public schools; the likelihood that 'intimidation' was endemic in Turners

---

21. Private e.mails, August 2008, 'AP', 'GB', 'PG', 'KC'. '

Court's residential blocks is implied in a record of 1965 where Menday, as warden, had to talk to the House master and three boys in Stapleton House where a 'Case of bullying [was] rather more than usual run.' Five years later one boy in another house had to be removed by his local authority for 'intimidation' of others.[22]

Turners Court was always a predominantly male institution – as were Hawkspur, Barns and Finchden Manor. Although it was a woman author, Julie Sutter, who played a pivotal role in establishing the Christian Service Union and its colonies, all of the executive decisions and posts were taken and held by men; there seems to be no record of Sutter actually ever visiting Wallingford. Although Von Bodelschwingh's Bethel colonies included the training home for deaconesses, the idea of copying that part of the plan never seems to have been discussed; presumably, for the Congregationalists that would have been a step too far.

It was the dream of 'male bonding' between volunteer Brothers and involuntary colonists that informed the early years of Lingfield and Wallingford. Women *were* soon in evidence at the 'Colony', but in subordinate roles, as laundresses, seamstresses, cooks and so on; the contribution they made to the running of the establishment gets short shrift in annual reports and *Social Service*. Mrs Hunt may well have had some influence but her voice is never heard – although Hunt's son, leader of the colony's Boy Scout troop, is named several times in the journal. The introduction, from the 1920s onwards, of more married staff and their children, and female office workers, helped to dissipate the original

---

22. OCRO, TCYT Box H13 'Events of importance'.

quasi-monastic ambience. The development of the 'house' system, in particular, gave a key role both to 'house fathers' and 'house mothers', some of whom are fondly remembered by former residents, some not (not to mention the probably maligned 'Miss T' who featured in the previous chapter as Turners Court's answer to the Gestapo).

Inga Menday, Scandinavian, educated, a professional woman who had enjoyed considerable responsibility while working in occupied Europe after 1945, not only cooks meals to charm potential supporters, but gets to direct plays that win prizes. Even Inga Menday's words, however, only get recorded at second-hand, through the writings of her husband. The other staff wives of the time still mainly fulfil traditional roles – making costumes, providing refreshments for the 'Arenascope' productions and other events.

Despite being floated both by Manley and Howells, co-education never became a reality for the training school, but in its final three decades there is, unsurprisingly, more evidence of the contribution of professional women – social workers, administrators, teachers and the rest; the 1980s house magazine had a female editor, and other female members of staff now join the staff wives in the pages of the journal. The 1986 promotional video is fronted by the woman 'celebrity' Clare Francis (sister of Ann Boyd, a member of Turners Court management committee), while the social worker featured in the case conference is both female and from an ethnic minority.

In the 1950s, as we have seen, Menday intended the introduction of girls to social events in the Club to be part of his over-arching strategy of equipping boys to live life to the full on leaving; this kind of controlled social encounter finds some evidence in the official records and the contributions of former 'colonists,' who confirm, but without much by way of comment, the presence of girls at dancing classes and some outdoor events; Chapter 6, however, also gives us the distinctly more colourful anecdote about visiting the friendly 'birds' of Wallingford.

Menday and Wiles' book, *Everlasting Childhood*, includes case-studies emphasising the need to understand the sexual problems of boys who have been taken into local authority care: one such, having arrived at Turners Court, is said to have been steered away from an early leaning towards homosexuality by joining the Boys Club; having overcome his 'shyness of girls' by attending the dancing classes he was 'full of confidence' on leaving, and employed as a shepherd in Hampshire.[23] The authors write about sex in what now seems a breezy or even off-hand fashion. Some boys are described as arriving at Wallingford having had unfortunate or ill-advised sexual encounters, or having suffered from the sexual misdeeds of parents, including mothers who worked as prostitutes. What were, in the fashion of the time, seen as homosexual aberrations of boys before they arrived at Turners Court are also cited, but Menday tells us nothing about such activity at the 'colony' itself; in a passage that now reads somewhat quaintly, he (or Wiles) writes about sex education as a by-product of Wallingford's agricultural training:

---

23. Menday & Wiles, *Everlasting Childhood*, 1959, p.140-141. Menday's own early sex education may have been scanty: his mother was, he writes, repelled by sex, 'a matter never to be talked about or referred to'; he also alleges that she strongly disapproved of Inga.(Menday & Hartley, *To a Peak* . .1995, p.3-4).

'...sex is not the furtive thing it was in the tenement, and by the time boys have learned to take the cows to the bull, they have usually come to accept the complete normality of procreation and birth. One cannot snigger indefinitely at the fecundity of nature, and there is little to laugh at when one has to watch a caesarean or assist at a castration.'[24]

All of which may be true, but takes us little further in deducing what the boys themselves may have done. Menday's 1998 history of Turners Court also has little to say about problems that might have arisen out of overt or covert gay behaviour. The colourful episode from the 1970s, quoted in the previous chapter, however, seem to show that it was not unknown. From an earlier decade, another correspondent, a resident of Cory House and chair of the Boys Club in 1960, writes that '... some of the staff you had to be wary of, they liked boys, if you know what I mean.' Unlike the two boys with the obliging 'birds' in Wallingford, he also writes that 'we did not mix much with the locals.'[25]

David Wills, by contrast, writes about sex maybe a little mawkishly for 21st century tastes, but also more openly and sympathetically than does Menday. He describes the way boys at Hawkspur Camp tell him they want to meet girls and kiss them, writes about boys imitating contemporary film stars, singing cowboy songs to girls, and about Wills himself taking a boy in his car up to London to meet the boy's girl friend, so that this became an open, rather than covert and

---

24. Menday & Wiles, *Everlasting Childhood*, 1959, p.162.
25. Private e.mail, June 2008, 'JS'. Significantly, perhaps, this correspondent's first memory is of the Turners Court food which was, he says, 'average.'

embarrassing, activity: 'So we had a very nice party, and then we all went home'.[26]

Did it 'work'?

Having looked at surviving documentary evidence, heard a few accounts from former 'colonists' and staff, and made some brief comparisons with a couple of contemporary institutions with roughly similar aims, how close may the Wallingford 'Colony' come to fulfilling the dreams of its founders? Some hostile comments on the concept of the farm colony have been quoted in earlier chapters; others came not only from competitive philanthropic bodies like the Charities Organisation Society, but from supposedly neutral officials. The 1899-1900 Annual Report of the Local Government Board quotes Mr M. Lockwood, one of its inspectors, writing that some Metropolitan Boards of Guardians were sending 'likely cases' to the Salvation Army and CSU colonies at Hadleigh and Lingfield, with,

> 'so far as I have been able to learn, but moderate results in rehabilitation; it would be unfair to regard the small percentage of success as reflecting on the methods adopted . . it is due rather to the, for the most part, hopeless character of the material My experience leads me to believe that nine-tenths of workhouse inmates under 50 have drifted into chargeability owing to mental or physical flabbiness (often congenital) of which a complete and lasting cure [sic] is in the great majority of cases impossible.'[27]

---
26. Wills, *Hawkspur Experiment*, 1941, p. 76.
27. 29th Report of the Local Government Board, 1899-1900.

If that estimate were taken at face value it would seem to imply that Wallingford could be considered to have done well if anything much more than ten per cent of 'colonists' turned out to be sober hard-working citizens, whether at home or abroad. But there is probably little value in pursuing any quantified comparison of this kind: the statistical evidence is simply not available and in any case, as the earlier chapters show, after its earliest years the nature of the 'Colony' was several times transformed. The establishment that closed in 1991 was quite different in size, organisation, financing and 'output' from the original. Over its 80 year history it had adapted, perhaps sometimes too slowly, to the changing legislative, economic and social background. Whether it might have changed yet again and hence might exist today in yet another manifestation, is something we can look at in a moment.

Looking at shorter time-frames and more specific aims, the answer is probably a qualified 'Yes'. The main intention of the Christian Service Union's founding fathers, like that of 'General' Booth and other enthusiasts for 'colonies', was that the detritus of London's streets should be swept up, trained and packed off to the Dominions; the Wallingford 'colony' fulfilled that intent over the first two decades of its existence during which perhaps parties of 20 or more 'lads' set off several times a year from Wallingford station, to Australia, New Zealand and other 'imperial' destinations. How they fared when they got there is another matter, and one which the records leave largely unanswered. Some wrote the kind of appreciative letter already quoted, saying how they missed Turners Court and how well they were doing on their respective farms; most never wrote at all. Only towards the end of Hunt's reign was there much suggestion that the CSU ought to interest itself in the after-care of the boys and there were plainly practical difficulties of doing so in the case of those who had already emigrated.

Substantial studies like those of Gillian Wagner, in 1982, and Eric Richards in 2004 show (something that Hunt and his contemporaries may have guessed at, but fail to mention) that not all young emigrants, from whichever source, would find any sort of success or happiness in their involuntary exile. On the other hand there is no reason to think that those from Wallingford were any less well trained or less well prepared for a colonial life than 'lads' (girls too, of course, in some cases) shipped out by other emigration-funding bodies. Of Turners Court 'old boys' traceable today, only a small handful live overseas; they sound happy enough, but so far as we know they went by their own choice, long after the days of the cardboard-suitcase carrying parties of Hunt's years, or even the £10 passage schemes of the 1940s.

Apart, therefore, from its relatively short-lived success as a machine for turning out young emigrants, how did Turners Court fare in the longer term as an establishment for dealing with 'difficult' boys? Between, say, the 1930s and the 1990s, did it match up to the ideal set out by Menday and Wiles in *The Everlasting Childhood*, of providing not only useful vocational training, but a rounded preparation for life 'outside'? Again, the answer is probably a qualified 'yes.' Once the more formally regulated regime of inspection by civil servants and local authority Children's Departments became established in the 1930s, followed by more considerable changes later, the simplest test would be whether those Authorities would continue to send boys to Wallingford, and what sort of reports they and the civil servants produced. As we have seen, from Chapter 3 onwards, such reports were, by contrast to the pessimistic view of Mr Lockwood back in 1900, generally satisfactory. Most local authorities were prepared to pay Turners Court's ever-increasing weekly fees, together with extra charges for clothing and so on.

Of the successive superintendents/wardens/principals, Menday was certainly more adroit than his immediate predecessors in seizing the opportunity for central government funding of capital projects, and for pushing through a wider platform of vocational and academic training. His own history of Turners Court sometimes reads as though he considered his time there to have been a 'golden age' for the former Colony, when everything went right; although this may be unfair on both his predecessors and successors, it was a time when what Turners Court had to offer fitted pretty well with what local authorities were prepared to pay for. Menday's 1950s 'survey' of ex-Wallingford residents, now lost, showed, according to his account, that Wallingford's record compared well those of Approved Schools in terms of likelihood to re-offend. The ideas that he and Wiles put forward for reforming Approved Schools still read well today:

> 'their very name and nature should be radically altered . . . they should be [ad]ministered in future as graded vocational training centres, providing for treatment of all kinds and carrying no social stigma whatsoever . . in fact *all* establishments providing specialised treatment and care, should be similarly graded; and . . . this vast accumulation of

facilities should be laid entirely at the services of the [Local Authority] children's officer, enabling him [sic] to place, where he thought best, any boy who had come into the occupational observation centre, either through the Courts or direct from his home.'[28]

The emphasis that Menday, his collaborator Wiles, and their successors put on all-round preparation for life, including fostering an interest in the performing arts and other skills, was also commendable for its time. Some of what was written, for instance in Wiles' own book on the subject, may have been unduly optimistic about the character- building properties of youth drama: 'With the present moral decline of adult values, it is now more necessary than ever that we give our young people a solid foundation on which to construct their lives.'[29] In practical terms, however, Turners Court's Boys Club and the increase in leisure time activities instituted by Menday and continued by his successors now look like winning ideas. The grand scale drama productions of the Menday era and the Club are among the features of Turners Court life most likely to be spontaneously and approvingly recalled by former residents. Today drama is again reportedly approved as a way of integrating 'difficult' teenagers into society: since the mid-1990s, for example, we are told that the Grassmarket Project has been producing theatre with 'marginalised and socially excluded young people', creating drama based on their life experiences; among the 'converts' claimed for this project are

---

28. Menday & Wiles, *Everlasting Childhood*, 1959, p.226.
29. J. Wiles, *Leap to Life*, 1957 (London: Chatto & Windus) p.13. 21st century commentators who look back to a mid-20th century golden age of stability and conformity may like to note Wiles' reference to 'decline'.

Reflections, conclusions

many teenagers whose previous method of self-expression commonly involved knives and other weapons.[30]

It is, of course, impossible to transfer the kind of 'feel good' memory received from former residents into success rates for 'constructing' better lives for young people. Counterbalancing their generally positive contributions, comes a more downbeat verdict from the wife of one of the instructors who worked at Turners Court from 1969 to1989:

> 'Some of the boys did benefit from being at Turners Court; most went back to the lives that they had before. Many of them did return to visit the staff. . and some stayed and lived and worked in the area. . . It was a wonderful opportunity for any boy to spend time there and take advantage of all that was on offer, swimming pool, sports centre, a chance to learn a trade and be set up for life, but alas most saw it as a cushy meal ticket for 18 months and while they were there they would continue their life of crime.'[31]

Whether in fact 'most' of the boys continued to offend in some way during or after their spell at Turners Court now looks impossible of proof, although intuitively it sounds pessimistic. A former engineering instructor from the 1970s confirms that some boys went on to serve time in Borstal or prison after leaving Wallingford but thinks that the overall 'Turners Court experience' helped most boys sort themselves

---

30. *The Independent*, 11 Sept 2008. Iris Murdoch's communal livers also considered 'arts and crafts' to be 'so important', but with perhaps less happy results. (*The Bell*, 1962, p.20).
31. Private e.mail, October 2006, Mrs J. Busby; her busband was a motor vehicle instructor 1969-1989 (see Appendix I).

out: 'stability, continuity and order ... made a big difference' to many of them.[32]

As access to personal records over different periods is denied, it is impossible to resolve this argument by statistical means. A small – and self-selecting - snapshot of former residents is now offered by the 50 or so names on the 'Friends Reunited' website; a few others were identified through local newspapers and other sources. Their time at Turners Court ranges from the late 1950s to the 1990s. The mere fact of presence on the website, of course, implies that time at Wallingford cannot have been so bad for these individuals that they never wish to be reminded of it. Although the boys recorded as coming back to visit Turners Court, planning to do so, or just wanting to record their memories of time there may still only be a minority – we can never know – it is a consistent feature throughout the existence of the 'colony'. Given what must have looked, to inner city teenagers, distinctly strange and quite possibly inhospitable surroundings, the sometimes poor food, hard graft and – occasionally – actual maltreatment, this may seem surprising, but Turners Court is not unique: nine Approved Schools have pages on the 'Friends Reunited' site, one of them listing about the same number of former residents as at Wallingford; Finchden Manor, too, is listed, but (unsurprisingly) with fewer names.

Similar patterns can be found in the published memoirs of those who suffered under less friendly regimes than Turners Court. To take a local, Oxfordshire, example, *Hostilities Only*, autobiography of the auto-didact David Buckle, paints a grim picture of an orphan, abandoned or sold (he never

---

32. Telephone conversation, Apr 2007, John Glavey.

Reflections, conclusions

finds out which), brought up in the 1920s by 'Miss B', a semi-professional children's home mother, with regular beatings, unending housework, poor food and the invidious example of the 'nephew' (perhaps son) of the proprietress enjoying such luxuries as breakfast in bed. Yet, 20 years on, Buckle takes his young wife and children to visit 'Miss B' at Margate, and writes warmly about her wartime service as an ambulance driver. Apart from illustrating the healing effect of time, Buckle's story, like many others, also reveals the shadowy and seemingly ill-regulated world of voluntary children's homes that survived well into the 20th century, a system alongside which the organisation and accountability of Turners Court, with all of the shortcomings we have noted, look relatively benign and efficient.[33]

All of Turners Court's former residents on the 'Friends Reunited' website were asked if they would provide – anonymously - further detail for this book: most did not reply; those who did have had their comments interwoven, anonymously, into this and earlier chapters. It is also possible to get at least a faint idea as to how the majority of non-respondents have fared. Out of the 50 on the website, about a dozen give no information about themselves save the names of other schools they attended before or after Turners Court.

33. D. Buckle, *Hostilities Only*, 1999 (Oxford: Robert Dugdale) passim. I am indebted to Dr. Elizabeth Tonkin for drawing my attention to this work. After escaping from 'Miss B', Buckle was taken, in 1940, to live with about 40 other boys in a hutted camp near Radley, where they formed a pool of cheap untrained labour for local farmers, presumably under-cutting the output from Turners Court at that time. The farm where he ended the war was run by Stephen Dockar-Drysdale who went on to found, with his wife, the Mulberry Bush School at Standlake, Oxon, which pioneered work with 'difficult and disturbed' children and continues today; in April 2008 a report in *The Times* claimed the cost per child per year was now £123,000, paid by local authorities.

Like other 'old boys' traced independently, most of the 'Friends Reunited' names seem to have settled into family life, married (or enjoying a long term relationship) and with children; a veteran of 1967-69 may be writing (on the website) ironically when he claims he is 'Looking to settle down and find a life with a loving partner.' Many also provide some clue as to past and present occupation; those who might have opted for the life of crime would perhaps not choose to advertise it on the internet. Of current or previous jobs mentioned, some (as well as those already cited in earlier chapters) look to be related to Turners Court's vocational training: a handful of HGV drivers; smaller handfuls in agriculture (including horticulture, game keeping), engineering, construction, and catering. Several ex-residents worked for BR, a significant number served in the armed forces before taking civilian jobs (in some earlier decades, of course, many would have been conscripted unless claiming exemption through work on the land). Two or three look to have done well in material terms, running small firms, managing factories.

At least half a dozen out of the 50 mention university or professional qualifications, including MBAs. One, who left Turners Court in 1980, is (2005) 'trying to get into uni; got booted out last time.' About the same number are in local authority or other caring professions, working with young people and/or the homeless and have provided more detail. One works as a psychologist with a not-for-profit organisation in London. One, after leaving Turners Court in 1983, worked first as a cabinet maker (he recalls Mr Pomeroy, a Quaker, as carpentry instructor at Turners Court), then trained in social work; he would take fellow social workers to see Turners

Court, and in 2008 was planning to buy a farm in the USA and run it, with his girl friend, as a 'youth ranch' for abused children. Turners Court, he writes, helped him empathise with homeless and other socially deprived people; it was,

> ' a wonderful place. It is and will always remain one of the best experiences of my life. I would often visit years after I left. When I found it abandoned and sold off . . it broke my heart. . . I have no qualms about telling people I've been "in care" at Turners Court and elsewhere. . . .[Turners Court] was extraordinary . . . so little negativity. Self-expression was high on the agenda. I can't impress on you how fantastic it was.'[34]

On the whole, the website entries sound much what might be expected from former schoolmates anywhere. Among the information commonly provided – often where there is no reference to occupation or qualifications - is the make of car driven, or dreamed of: 'drive Jag – every man should have one'; 'drive Ford Maverick – still a punk at heart.' One who left Turners Court in 1963 and is shown on the website as 'retired', without specifying from what, is recovering from a quadruple heart bypass and living in Algeria; he gives his hobby as 'rebuilding old Land Rovers'. Up to 40 years since they were in the Turners Court Boys Club, many still enjoy the same sports; one, unable now to work through some unspecified disability, 'fishes and walks the dog.' A good number list music interests; the 1980 leaver still trying to get into university mentions attendance at 'free festivals – not your Glastonbury crap.'

---

34. Private e.mail, June 2008, 'IO'.

Oxfordshire Colony

Several others of those who replied offered general verdicts on their time at Wallingford. A couple echo the pessimistic view of the instructor's widow. The correspondent already quoted on the subject of race relations (he also writes warmly about the Boys Club and the drama productions) nevertheless concludes: 'I think my time at Turners Court was wasted, but of course it was very personal. If I was an observer instead of a participant, then I might feel that the place did do some good, but I'm damned if I can think what that might have been.' Another is ambivalent: 'Turners Court . . . was a good place in one way, but bad in the other', and condemns the local authority care system in general which, he says, left him bitter and damaged his self esteem. A third, from the 1950s, thinks the success he has made of his life owes nothing to Turners Court whose training was 'of little value.'[35]

Again, it must be emphasised that the 'Friends Reunited' and other contacts made in researching this book represent only a tiny minority of all Turners Court 'old boys'. With that caveat, most sum up their experience there positively rather than negatively:

'It was worth it; an experience I will not forget.'

'I loved my time there, on the whole.'

'Enjoyed my time there and learned a lot about horticulture.'

'Enjoyed life, and the Colony taught you a lesson.'

'It was a great place to be and I made a lot of friends ... I did not want to leave.'

'Turners Court was a wonderful place. It is and will always remain one of the best experiences of my life.'[36]

---

35. Private e.mails, Aug 2008, 'KC', 'PG', 'JS'.
36. Private e.mails, Jun-Aug 2008, 'RA', 'GB', 'MH', 'IOC', 'MW'; telephone conversation, Oct 2006, 'JCC'

In one of several conversations while this book was being written, Peter Honeybone, another former instructor, compared the 18 months which most boys spent at Turners Court (in the 1970s and 1980s) with the experience of National Service in an earlier decade: 'Boys didn't want to go at the time, but afterwards thought it hadn't been too bad.' Characteristically, the Turners Court 'community' may exist more strongly in our heads in later years than it ever did at the time. Or, in a rough translation of the lines by the Roman poet Virgil at the head of this chapter, 'Maybe one day even these times will be happily remembered.'

'Post-colonialism'

The vision that the Christian Service Union and its contemporary organisations had of taking delinquent, unruly, orphaned or unwanted teenagers off the streets and 'saving' them by setting them to work under close supervision on a farm, may now seem as remote from 21st century life as the music hall, horse-drawn cabs or Suffragettes. But the essential elements – country life, training, simple fare – are still around. Recent British administrations have toyed with the idea, familiar in North America, of the so-called 'boot camp', subjecting delinquent boys to rigid discipline in a militaristic environment - the 'short sharp shock' beloved of tabloid columnists. Separately, in 2008 press reports suggested that both private companies and charities (perhaps in the CSU mould) might be asked to bid for building and managing new prisons in London and on Merseyside.

Closer to the Turners Court model are charities involved in the running of specialist 'pupil referral units' (nicknamed 'sin bins') for teaching the most disruptive state school pupils. In 2006, an experiment was reported[37] under the title 'Learning to Listen' intended to offer a 'kind of last chance saloon' for children expelled from mainstream schools. The children were taken to a farm school near Ripon, North Yorkshire, taught rural skills such as welding, dry-stone walling milking, horse riding and animal husbandry, combined with formal lessons in mathematics, English and so on. 'I was a cheeky sod ... trying to show off,' one boy explained; 'I'd have ended up with a rubbish job if I hadn't come here.' The Alternative Learning Centre on the outskirts of Bradford, for example, run by avowedly Christian charity The Lighthouse Group, takes in some of the most badly behaved teenagers from comprehensives in the area.[38]

And a recent echo of the kind of communal decision making seen at Hawkspur and Finchden Manor comes from Reddish Vale Technology College in Greater Manchester which school is reported to be going into partnership with the Co-op to become the first where each of the 1,400 pupils will have a vote in the way it is run.[39] Even the public-school derived system of 'houses', initiated by Hunt and enthusiastically developed by Menday and others at Turners Court seems once again to be in favour in the public sector. In August 2008, a press report claimed that the Specialist Schools and Academies Trust (SSAT), representing most state secondary schools in England, endorsed the 'house' system as

---

37. *The Independent*, 29 August 2006.
38. *The Independent*, 21 May 2008.
39. *The Independent*, 26 May 2008.

a way of helping youngsters settle in during their first year of secondary schooling.[40] And most recently, the educationalist Sir Cyril Taylor suggested that children from 'broken homes' could be offered places at boarding schools as an alternative to mainstream local authority care; the author, in a phrase reminiscent of Ron Menday, is quoted as saying: 'If you identify these children at age 13 or 14 it is very difficult to turn them round.'[41]

Finally, and with a nod to symmetry, this book closes with the example of one of the 'training colonies' noted as preceding Wallingford in Chapter 1 – the Salvation Army establishment at Hadleigh, Essex. 'General' William Booth's aims and those of the CSU's founding fathers were much the same: to take unemployed (or 'unemployable') youths out of poverty, crime and vice, train them on suitable land, instil Christian virtues and ship them off to prosper in the Dominions. During the 20th century, both at Hadleigh and Turners Court, the agricultural emphasis changed. Hadleigh's clay deposits soon proved more than a profitable side-line. By the 1920s, as at Wallingford Hadleigh was training 14-19 year old boys not only in farming but - again, as at Turners Court - boot repairing, carpentry, laundry work and cooking. Hadleigh differed, however, in that many of its training courses lasted no longer than 6 weeks. In the 1930s, where Wallingford received Jewish refugees, Hadleigh gave temporary shelter to 1,400 Basque children before, during World War II, seeing much of the site requisitioned for military use and suffering extensive bomb damage.

---

40. *The Independent on Sunday,* 31 Aug 2008.
41. *The Independent,* 10 Feb 2009. Taylor's plans for state boarding schools are set out in *A Good School for Every Child,* 2009 (London; David Fulton).

Oxfordshire Colony

By the 1950s, the Hadleigh colony was - like Turners Court - described as 'in decline.' Although a handful of minor offenders still worked on its farm in the 1960s, the brickfields and other (non-commercial) activities were closed; some land was developed for housing and a rapidly increasing suburban population, plus increasing numbers of visitors to Hadleigh Castle were said to be adversely affecting relations between local residents and the colony. In the 1970s the training programme ceased; the remaining land continued to be farmed commercially, without any training element but contributing to Salvation Army funds; in 2007 the farm was reported to be aiming to go organic.

In the 1990s, however, the decade which saw both the centenary of Booth's *In Darkest England* and the closure of Turners Court, the Salvation Army re-opened the Hadleigh training centre, with the aim of helping local people with special needs to 'enhance their personal development and maximise their potential to enter mainstream education, training or employment.' The centre now acts as a contractor for Essex County Council, other neighbouring local authorities and Jobcentres. For a time funding was obtained from the European Social Fund. Skills taught at the centre include some familiar ones from the earlier 'colony', including carpentry, catering and horticulture, but with contemporary additions such as IT and graphics, office skills and retailing. The 30 or so retailing trainees benefit from practical experience in the on-site shop and tea rooms, which sell local produce and offer visitors to the farm and nearby Hadleigh Castle panoramic views over the Thames estuary. In 2008 a substantial refurbishment programme was completed, and the new training centre now bears little resemblance to the military camp-like appearance of the original colony.[42]

Geography and topography might have prevented that sort of solution being applied to Turners Court: its relative remoteness from large centres of population, which was originally seen as a positive feature, would make it less attractive as a 'day release' training centre whereas Hadleigh is now enfolded by Southend's housing estates. Although there seems no reason why the Turners Court farm might not have become a centre of organic cultivation, able to attract eco-tourists, there is no equivalent to the Hadleigh Castle site; the Thames may be only a mile or so away but sadly there is no view of it from Carr's Meadow. Organisationally, too, the cases differ: Hadleigh remains part of the global Salvation Army enterprise, potentially benefiting from some economies of scale when it comes to publicity and other services. From 1963 Turners Court, on the other hand, had no parent organisation.

In the 1950s, the committee and management of the Wallingford 'colony', led by Menday, showed themselves adept at seizing the opportunity of Home Office and Ministry of Agriculture capital grants. The physical structure and the training programme was up-dated; at that time, what Turners Court had to offer clearly fitted well with legislation and local authority budgets. But both of those would shortly change again. Menday's own understanding of the needs of young delinquents or maladjusted children (for example

---

42. M. Hancock & S. Harvey, *Hadleigh, an Essex Village*, 1986 (Chichester: Philimore) pp.27-28; Hadleigh Training Centre Annual Report 2006-2007. The Hadleigh site will feature mountain biking at the 2012 Olympic Games, suggesting perhaps that William Booth's purchase was not ideal farming land?

in substituting non-criminal procedures for criminal in the case of 14-year olds) is reasonably argued to have contributed to the next major piece of legislation – the Children and Young Persons Act 1969. The philosophy underlying that Act, however, and the 1968 White Paper *Children in Trouble* which preceded it, looks less sympathetic to the concept of large scale residential training institutions like Turners Court.

In future, the White Paper suggested, children taken into local authority care should live as near as possible to their original homes, whether with foster parents or in the newly envisaged 'community homes'. They should make use of the same educational, health and other services as other local children and enjoy 'much the same degree of freedom as children brought up in a well-regulated private household.' As was noted in Chapter 6, some thought was given to turning Turners Court into such a 'community home', possibly in collaboration with a local authority, but this proved unachievable. Later legislation (notably the Children Act 1989, based on a 1984 report) increased the apparent gap between what a 'colony' was perceived as offering, and what was now seen as good child-care practice: support for 'parental responsibilties' and 'partnership' between social services and parents sound a long way from big scale instutionalisation.

The Salvation Army's solution was to go for a relatively small-scale, non-residential training centre, physically and organisationally close to several large local authorities. It would be wrong, however, to conclude that the Salvation Army had somehow 'succeeded' at Hadleigh, where CSU and Turners Court had 'failed' in dealing with changing circumstances at the end of the 20th century. The Turners

Reflections, conclusions

Court Youth Trust, inheritors of the assets of the former 'colony' is now a major provider of finance for youth projects in the Thames Valley sub-region; the way that its money now supports a number of locally identified and locally provided needs, rather than one centrally-managed facility remote from many of its 'customers', is as much in tune with contemporary thinking about philanthropy and service delivery as was the rural training colony back in the 1890s.

Select Bibliography

Abbreviations

The following abbreviations are used throughout the book:

Bod.	Bodleian Library, Oxford
CSU:	Christian Service Union (formerly NUCSS)
NA:	National Archives (Public Record Office)
NCSS:	National Council for Social Service
OCRO:	Oxfordshire County Record Office
TCYT:	Turners Court Youth Trust
SA:	Salvation Army
SS:	*Social Service* journal

Unpublished sources:

Turners Court Youth Trust (TCYT) archive at OCRO (now fully catalogued). Family Welfare Association papers at London Metropolitan Archive. NA files, including those of Department of Health and Social Service (DHSS), Home Office, Ministry of Health, Local Government Board, Public Assistance Board.

Private letters/e.mails/telephone calls to the author.

Dr. A.A. Eckbert, *The Social Thought of the Christian Social Union*, 1990, (Bod. MS. M.Litt. c927)

Principal published sources:

anon	Hadleigh, the story of a great endeavour, c.1902 (London: SA)
anon	History of The Royal Philanthropic Society, 1988 (RPS)
anon	Some results achieved in the farm colonies and epileptic homes since 1900, 1905 (London: CSU/CUSS)
Thomas Beames	Rookeries of London, past, present & prospective, 1850 (London: Thomas Bosworth)
P Bean, J Melville	Lost Children of the Empire, 1989 (London: Hyman)
Ian Beckett	Home Front 1914-1918, 2006 (Kew: NA)
H Begbie	Life of William Booth, 1920 (London: Macmillan)
Caroline Benn	Keir Hardie, 1992 (London: Richard Cohen)
M Bondfield	A Life's Work, 1948 (London: NBA)
Charles Booth	Life And Labour of the People of London, 1902-03 (Brighton: Harvester)
William Booth	In Darkest England and the Way Out, 1890 (London: SA)
R Brabazon (Earl of Meath):	Memories of the 19th Century, 1923 (London: Murray)
R Brabazon	Memories of the 20th century, 1924 (London: John Murray)
M E Brasnett	Voluntary Social Action, 1969, (London: NCSS)
Michael Burn	Mr Lyward's Answer, 1956 (London: Hamish Hamilton) Board of Agriculture Land Settlement for Sailors and Soldiers, 1916 (London: HMSO)
J C Carlile	Christian Union in Social Service, 1913 (London: James Clarke)
S Constantine ed.	Emigrants and Empire, 1990 (Manchester: MUP)
W H B Court	Concise Economic History of Britain, 1967 (Cambridge: CUP)
Frederick Coutts	No Discharge in This War, 1975, (London: SA)
Walter Cranfield	John Bull's Surplus Children, 1915, (London: Horace Marshall)
M A Crowther	The Workhouse System 1834-1929, 1981(London: Batsford)
Judy Dewey	The Book of Wallingford, an historical portrait, 1977
E M R Ditmas	History of Benson [Oxon], 1983 (privately published)
Joseph Fletcher	The Farm School System of the Continent, 1852 (London)
Simon Fowler	Workhouse, 2007 (Kew: NA)
Alan Gill	Shocking Story of Child Migration to Australia, 1997 (Sydney, NSW: Millennium Books)
M Hancock, S Harvey	Hadleigh, an Essex village, 1986 (Chichester: Phillimore)
Roy Hattersley	Blood and Fire, William & Catherine Booth and their Salvation Army, 1999 (London: Little Brown)
Harry Hendrik	Child Welfare in England 1872-1989, 1994 (London: RKP)
David Hill	The Forgotten Children, 2007 (Sydney, NSW: Random House)
G K Horridge	The Salvation Army, 1993 (Godalming: Ammonite)
G Stedman Jones	Outcast London, 1971 (Oxford: Clarendon)
P d'A Jones	Christian Socialist Revival, 1968 (Princeton: Princeton UP)

Select Bibliography

R Kershaw, J Sacks	New Lives for Old, Britain's child migrants, 2008 (Kew: NA)
K Laybourn	Guild of Help and the Changing Face of Edwardian Philanthropy, 1994 (Lampeter: Edwin Mellen)
Jane Lewis	Voluntary Sector, State & Social Work in Britain, 1995 (Aldershot: Elgar)
Local Govt. Board	29th Report 1899-1900, 1901 (London: HMSO)
Norman Longmate	The Workhouse, 2003 (London: Pimlico)
James Marchant	J B Paton, 1909 (London: Jas. Clarke)
Dora McLellan	Brief History of the Christian Union for Social Service, c.1963 (CSU)
Andrew Mearns	Bitter Cry of Outcast London, [1883] 1970 (London: Cass)
R P Menday, J Wiles	Everlasting Childhood, 1959 (London: Gollancz)
R P Menday, J Hartley	To a Peak . . . and Beyond, 1995 (privately published)
R P Menday	The History of Turners Court, 1998 (privately published)
Allan Moore	Growing Up with Barnardo's, 1990 (Sydney, NSW: Hall & Iremonger).
Edward Norman	Victorian Christian Socialists, 1987 (Cambridge: CUP)
Joy Parr	Labouring Children, 1980 (London: Croom Helm)
John Lewis Paton	Life of John Brown Paton, 1914 (London: Hodder & Stoughton)
M T Pearman	History of the Manor of Bensington, 1896 (London: Elliot Stock)
William Peterson	Planned Migration, 1955 (Berkeley, Ca.: Univ California Press)
Harold W Pfautz ed.	Charles Booth on the City, 1967 (Chicago: Univ. of Chicago Press)
Pinchbeck & Hewitt	Children in English Society II, 1973 (London, RKP)
G F Plant	Overseas Settlement, 1951 (London: OUP)
G L Prestige	Life of Charles Gore, 1935 (London: Heinemann)
Frank Prochaska	Christianity & Social Service in Modern Britain, 2006 (Oxford: OUP)
Eric Richards	Britannia's Children, 2004 (London: Hambledon)
Alice Russell	Growth of Occupational Welfare in Britain, 1991 (Aldershot: Avebury)
Robert Sandall	History of the Salvation Army, 1955 (London: Nelson)
A G Scholes	Education for Empire Settlement, 1932 (London: Longman)
T E Sedgwick	Town Lads on Imperial Farms, 1914 (London: P S King)
G Sherington, C Jeffery	Fairbridge, Empire & Child Migration, 1998 (London: Woburn)
George R Sims ed.	Living London Vol. I, 1901-1902 (London: Cassell)
Gilbert Slater	Poverty and the State, 1930 (Cambridge: CUP)
Julie Sutter	Colony of Mercy, 1893 (London: Hodder & Stoughton)
B Taithe	The Essential Mayhew, 1996 (London: Rivers Oram)
F M L Thompson ed.	Cambridge Social History of Britain, 1990 (Cambridge: CUP)
G M Trevelyan	English Social History, 1944 (London: Longman)
Susan Turner	One Hundred Years of St. Piers, 1997 (Lingfield: St. Piers)
Victoria County History	Oxfordshire, Vol. 2
Gillian Wagner	Barnardo, 1979 (London: Weidenfeld & Nicolson)

Gillian Wagner	Children of the Empire, 1982 (London: Weidenfeld & Nicolson)
J Wiles	Leap to Life, an experiment in youth drama, 1957 (London: Chatto & Windus)
Alan Wilkinson	Christian Socialism, Scott Holland to T Blair, 1998 (London:SCM)
W D Wills	The Hawkspur Experiment, 1941 (London: Allen & Unwin)
W D Wills	The Barns Experiment, 1945 (London: Allen & Unwin)
P Wood	Poverty & the Workhouse, 1991 (Stroud: Alan Sutton)
S Yeo	Religion & Voluntary Organisations in Crisis, 1976 (London: Croom Helm)

Periodicals

Berks and Oxon Advertiser

Christian Social Service

[The] Friend

Home and School Journal

Oxford Illustrated Journal

Oxford Times

Social Service

The Times

APPENDIX I
Wallingford Farm Training Colony/School/Turners Court, 1911-1991

A. **CHAIRMEN** (of Wallingford Committee, or equivalent)[1*]

D.F. Basden MBE	1911-1936
Sir Herbert Read GCMG	1936-1945
G.A. Howitt	1945-1950
S.J. Farrant	1950-1953
Brig. Godley CBE	1953-1954
S.J. Farrant	1954-1956
Sir John Hedges CBE	1956-1975
M. Riley	1975-1992

B. **SUPERINTENDENTS, WARDENS and PRINCIPALS***

William Hunt	1912-1933
Lt. Col. Ronald Grant CBE	1933-1943
Capt. Tune[2+]	1943
Lt. Col. F.A.S. Hinton	1943-1951
G.N. Manley	1951-1954
Lt. Col. R.P. Menday MBE, MC	1955-1967
John Howells	1967-1989
Mike Cornfield	1989-1991

---

1 * taken from R.P. Menday, *The History of Turners Court*, 1998.
2 + not included in Menday's original list

Oxfordshire Colony

C. INSTRUCTORS, 'HOUSE' STAFF AND OTHERS, 1970s-1980s[3*]

This list is incomplete; it simply illustrates the range of posts during Turners Court's final two decades. Not all staff listed would have served at the same time.

Deputy Principal:	W E (Bill) Smewin (c.1970-1983); M. Cornfield (1983-85)
Principal's secretary:	Margaret Wilson
Principal's dog:	'Ianto'
Head of Instructors:	Peter Hayward

Instructors:

Bricklaying:	Mr Lock, Stan Batty
Carpentry:	Godfrey Payne, Mr Pomeroy
Catering:	Mr Greenslade
Engineering:	Peter Honeybone (1971-1991)
Farm:	Peter Laver
Horticulture:	Tony Harmer; R. P. Smith; Mr Brown (1980s)
Motor vehicles:	Ray Busby (1969-1989), John Glavey (c1973-1980)
Painting/decorating:	Basil Strange/Strong
Horticulture:	A.J. Smith

Teachers (English, Maths): John Glavey, Jo Elvin, David Edgar, Marion Shaw

House staff:

Albright:	Maurice Elvin (housemaster); John Fanshaw+ wife; Miss Thompson
Basden:	unknown
Cory:	Dennis Sewell, Dave Taylor,

3 * compiled with the help of Mrs J. Busby, John Glavey, Peter Honeybone, some former residents and 1987 issues of 'Turners Court Magazine'.

Appendix I

Ensor: unknown
Hedges: Roy + Heather Scott (1973-74); 'Mike', 'Alistair', Margaret Connolly
Hunt: Colin Bamford (housemaster)
Stapleton: Jim + Jill Palmer

Sports/social club: Mike Dornan

Canteen/shop: 'Pop' Hansen

Other staff: Anne Howard (Editor, Turners Court Mag, 1980s); Jenny [admin.,welfare, Cusack; Celia Andrews; Steve Fielding; Jackie Hazard; other training staff] Dave Thorpe; Marina Lister; Adrian Wheeler; Kerry Chiverton; Mr Salter; Mike Kidley; Marc Kerry; Danny Luke; Joe Warner; Allister Keating; Ged Andrews; Veronica Mowat; Mike Hedges

APPENDIX II
Other 'Christian' and/or 'Social' organisations

The 19th and early 20th centuries saw unprecedented proliferation of societies, associations, guilds and clubs of every kind; economic growth, the spread of education (especially after 1870), and improvements in communications – cheap printing and newspapers, public transport by train and tram – all encouraged men to join together for some common purpose: most associations were, of course, predominantly male. Against this background, the opening chapters of this book noted possible confusion between the **National Union for Christian Social Service** (NUCSS) - the organisation which ran the colonies at Turners Court, Lingfield and Starnthwaite - and other bodies with similar names and, in some cases, similar aims. Abbreviating NUCSS to **Christian Service Union** (CSU) hardly made matters better since those initials were shared with at least one other national organisation. The words 'Christian union' could also be used by churchmen and others to mean not an individual organisation but ecumenicism generally. So it is hardly surprising that both at the time and since, such confusion should arise.

In particular it was – and is – all too easy to confuse **Christian Service Union** - the subject of this book - with **Christian Social Union**, formed a few years earlier during

Oxfordshire Colony

the late Victorian revival of **Christian Socialism,** a political philosophy which first appeared in Britain around 1848 when its proponents had included the writers Charles Kingsley, Thomas Hughes and Frederick Denison Maurice; Maurice's book *The Kingdom of Christ* (1838) argued that politics and religion are inseparable and the established church should involve itself in social questions.[1*]

Those 1848 pioneers are said to have been both 'excited by [that year's] revolution in France' and 'fearful of the wrong priorities . . . of Chartism.' (E. Norman, *Victorian Christian Socialists*, 1987; p.2). They also gave fitful support to the ideas of Robert Owen and the creation of co-operative enterprises as a way of improving the situation of the working classes and producing a just society. Two short-lived journals appeared: *Politics of the People* (1848-1849) and *The Christian Socialist* (1850-1851). Both then and later, the Christian Socialist movement was marked by controversy and internal arguments between those mainly interested in educational work and pamphleteering, and those wanting to press ahead with overt political action and/or co-operative ventures. This pattern would persist, resulting, writes the same historian, in 'a discontinuous and fragmented history. .' so that it is misleading to speak of Christian Socialism as if it were any sort of cohesive 'movement'. (Norman, op cit, p.3).

By 1854, indeed, coherent Christian socialism seemed to have collapsed. The 1870s then saw the beginning of the revival, with the creation, by Anglican clergymen, of the **Guild of St. Matthew** (1877), described by its historian as a 'tiny, clerical-minded and exclusive pressure group', virtually a one-

1 * The hero of Shaw's play *Candida* is an Anglican minister, a Christian socialist and reader of Maurice.

man band, the one man being the Rev. Stewart Duckworth Headlam, a close colleague of Bernard Shaw on the executive of the Fabian Society and 'a stubbornly independent man.' (P. d'A Jones, *Christian Socialist Revival*, 1967, Princeton p. 99, 164).

Small as it was, the Guild seems to have punched above its weight, representing, that same historian continues, 'the shock troops of sacramental socialism' who in turn generated 'an army of occupation' of the Anglican church; one of this army's weapons was a new *Christian Socialist Journal*, first published in 1883. In June 1889, the **Christian Social Union** itself was launched – as would be the case five years later with the NUCSS - at a meeting packed with enthusiasts; on the platform were Henry Scott Holland, canon of St. Paul's, Bishop Charles Gore and other Anglican clergy (Scott Holland and Gore had Oxford connections; the former had been a don at Christ Church, and the CSU quickly opened a branch at Pusey House). Bishop Gore's biographer suggests that he and his companions wanted to dissociate themselves from the Guild of St. Matthew, because it had become identified with 'a rather flamboyant type of Christian Socialism.' (G.L.Prestige, *Life of Charles Gore*, 1935, London). Although Methodists played supporting roles, the established church predominated: 'the lack of ecumenical cooperation on social questions made this inevitable.' (A. Wilkinson, *Christian Socialism, Scott Holland to Tony Blair*, 1998, p. 65). The stated aim of the founders was to 'investigate areas in which moral truth and Christian principles could bring relief to the social and economic disorder of society.'

By 1911 the Christian Social Union, with nearly 70 local branches and a membership of around 6,000 (some seven times greater than that of the Guild of St. Matthew) was busy lobbying the Liberal administration and individual MPs on social issues and carrying out social surveys. Between 1889 and 1913, 16 out of 53 Church of England episcopal appointments went to supporters of the CSU, described as 'a highly distinguished and respectable institution.' (Jones, op cit, p. 164). Another new journal, *Commonwealth*, was launched. Part Fabian-style educational and research group, part pressure group, the emphasis was on education, research, lectures and sermons. Hundreds of small scale publications appeared on both local and national issues such as wages, town planning, working conditions and the **Guilds of Help** (which we have already met). A memorandum of 1909 supported the establishment of labour exchanges (part of the Lloyd George programme) and national unemployment benefit. Some branches funded activities such as settlement houses (on the lines of Toynbee Hall) or the purchase of workmen's cottages, which were repaired and let at affordable rents. Branch committees agitated for better working conditions in local factories and encouraged the public to buy what we would now call 'ethical' goods such as lead-free pottery and (in Oxford) bread from bakers who agreed to pay workers a minimum wage. A recent (unpublished) study comments that CSU members did not 'subscribe to a merely intellectual form of "leavening society"', but the activities quoted seem small scale compared with the tide of lobbying and pamphleteering.[2*]

Some, at least, of the mid-19th century Christian Socialists had been enthusiasts for planned emigration, which as we have seen, became a main plank in the Christian *Service Union* platform. Charles Kingsley's 1855 novel *Westward Ho!* added the benefit of peopling the globe with Protestants, and so helping defeat Popery, to the economic benefit of labour mobility. Another mid-Victorian pioneer, John Malcolm Ludlow, wrote in 1848 that emigration was both an interim solution to poverty in England and also 'positively and enduringly desirable as a means of extending British civilization.' ('Politics for the People' No. 14, quoted E. Norman, *Victorian Christian Socialists*, 1987, Cambridge, p.66). But by the 1890s opinion was divided: Hugh Price Hughes, a Welsh Methodist and fervent Christian Socialist, while lamenting that poverty was 'menacing social order and the stability of the state', rejected emigration as a solution: rather, he wrote in *The Philanthropy of God* (1890), we must look to the more fundamental transformation of society by state provision and moral regeneration. (Norman, op cit, p.150).

Other Christian Social publications commended more localised and immediate methods of social relief such as penny-banks, clothing and provident clubs, thrift societies, soup kitchens, dispensaries, crèches and the 'Poor Man's Lawyer' movement as well the importance of 'labour bureaux'.

---

2 * Apart from the works of Alan Wilkinson' (1998), E. Norman (1987) and P d'A Jones (1967), detail comes from Ashley Ann Eckbert's 1990 thesis *The Social Thought of the Christian Social Union 1889-1914*, (Bodleian library MS M.Litt. c.927).

Oxfordshire Colony

The 1909 CSU memorandum, 'The Treatment of the Able-Bodied', did include the establishment of 'training colonies' and 'detention colonies' for the 'unemployables', but without emphasising the link to emigration and imperialism.

In 1919 the **Christian Social Union** disappeared from sight: 'practically, the war stopped its functions' (A.A. Eckbert, *unpublished thesis*, 1990, p.158); the Lloyd George reforms, the experience of government intervention in wartime and the move towards professionalism in the social services, may all have contributed to its demise – or, rather, change of identity, since the CSU joined forces with the colourfully named **Navvy Mission** to form the **Industrial Christian Fellowship**, which continues into the 21st century as a broad-based ecumenical organisation for those who 'seek a better sense of purpose by relating their faith to everyday life.'

Unfortunately for the historian, the two Christian Unions, one *Service*, one *Social*, by no means exhaust the list of bodies to which socially conscious Christians might have subscribed in the late 19th and early 20th centuries. Other confusingly similar names include: **Christian Socialist League** (1894, almost entirely non-conformist); **Church Socialist League** (1906-1924, predominantly north of England Anglicans); the **Society of Socialist Christians**; **Society of Socialist Clergy and Ministers**; **Social Science Association** (linked to the co-operative movement and the trades unions). In individual towns and cities, local **Councils of Social Service** were effectively **Guilds of Help** by another name.[3*]

Nonconformist churches had their own societies; in 1910 the Congregationalists set up in 1910 a **Social Service Committee**, quite distinct from the Congregationally-founded NUCSS, to coordinate the preaching of the 'Social Gospel' among their own congregations. Other sectarian bodies included the **Baptist Social Union,** the **Wesleyan Union for Social Service** (1905), the **Catholic Social Guild** (1909), the (Roman) **Catholic Socialist Society** (1906), the **Socialist Quaker Society** (1898) and the **Friends' Social Union** (1904). Since several Quakers have featured in this book, it is perhaps permissible to note that in 1912 the last-named organisation, in commending the Seebohm Rowntree report on unemployment in York, touched on the efficacy of farm colonies; after 1919 it became the **Friends Service Committee**; still later the **Friends Service Council** concerned itself with overseas service in post-WWII Europe, Africa and Asia, while the **Social Order Council**, dealt with domestic questions.

Like the NUCSS/Christian Service Union, whose monthly *Social Service* has been liberally quoted from in this book, many other sectarian organisations also published journals, some of them short-lived. Apart from those already mentioned (like the identically-titled *Social Service*, organ of the National Association of Guilds of Help), the **Christian Social Union**'s

---

3 * In 1919, 'in that post-war period of released tension, when so many fine ideas of social reconstruction were finding expression', and perhaps mimicking the Guilds of Help/Councils of Social Service, an **Arts League of Service** was formed 'to bring Arts into everyday life'. Essentially a troupe of strolling players, it folded in 1937 (E. Elder, *Travelling Players; the story of the Arts League of Service*, 1939, London: Frederick Mueller p.1 & passim).

publications also included *The Economic Review*. Once more, the end of the First World War marks a water-shed: periodicals with similar titles, covering sociological theory and practice, then proliferate, but the newcomers are principally the work of secular bodies (like *Home and School,* which features in Chapter 7, along with its editor, G.A. Lyward). Between 1929 and 1939, for example, the NCSS published *Social Service Review*: the same title was used by the University of Chicago, and probably other academic publishers.

Neither the proliferation of 'social' organisations nor the disparate views of those within each of them went unnoticed at the time. Perennial differences of view (then, as now, often written of as 'a split') among what we might now call the 'broad left' of the **Christian Social Union** were sometimes reported in the press. On 3 May 1910, for example, a letter to *The Times* referred to the 'crisis' in the CSU which was, said the correspondent, divided between 'socialist' and 'non-socialist' factions, between those who wanted to concentrate on educational work and other who wished to take a more active political or propagandist role.[4*] New splinter groups constantly emerged, among them the **Progressive League**, formed in 1907 by the combative clergyman J.R. Campbell with its overtly socialist 'new theology'. One study claims that most members of *this* CSU were 'more anti-capitalist than pro-socialist' (Jones, op cit, p.197).

The possibility of confusion, duplication of effort and waste of funds by competing charitable bodies did not go unaddressed at the time. Improved efficiency in social service was the key aim of the **Charity Organisation Society** (COS),

4 * The 1910 letter reveals another familiar bone of contention – the proper place of the (paid) secretary on the CSU's executive committee.

whose antipathy to NUCSS and other farm colonies has been noted in earlier chapters. Founded in 1869 as The Society for Organising Charitable Relief and Repressing Mendicity, the COS first aimed to improve co-operation between the Poor Law administration and individual - primarily local – charities. In championing better research, organisation and record-keeping, the COS 'adopted a utilitarian philosophy and preoccupation with statistical investigation' as opposed to the overt Christian evangelism and 'saving' which informed Christian Socialism. (F. Prochaska, *Christianity & Social Service in Modern Britain,* 2006, Oxford: OUP, p. 75). Apart from regarding farm colonies as wasteful and inefficient, the COS devoted much time and effort to opposing the payment of Old Age Pensions from general taxation.

In 1910 the NUCSS – the organisation at the heart of this book – seems to have been instrumental in setting up an embryonic 'umbrella' organisation which might, among other things, coordinate the social work of Christian organisations; somewhat belatedly *The Times* of 20 January, 1911 carried a brief report on a conference at the Caxton Hall the previous November attended by many – perhaps most – of the bodies identified above. The January 1911 issue of *Social Service* goes a bit further, revealing there were at least two such Caxton Hall conferences, at the first of which (November 1910) there was 'a great deal of talk . . . but it looked as though there would be no practical outcome' until an intervention by the Dean of Norwich and the Earl of Meath (NUCSS President) secured general agreement that pressure should be brought on the Government to use 'national means for national ends' – in other words, state expertise and finance must supplement the 'training and discipline directed by religious enthusiasm'.

That first meeting produced a committee, to which Christian denominational social service and philanthropic organisations agreed to send delegates. Nicknamed 'Noah's Ark', this committee also included officials from Government agencies, including the Development Commission, and 'great [but unidentified] public services.' There followed a second conference in June 1911, on the 'Prevention of Destitution'. Delegates from religious and secular charities, local authorities, medical and caring professions were addressed by politicians (A.J. Balfour and Ramsay Macdonald); papers were presented on the future of Labour Colonies, Mobility of Labour, Detention of Defectives, Education of the Feeble Minded, Insanity & Destitution, Degeneracy, and Feeble Minded Prisoners. The main message to emerge was that voluntary agencies and the 'State' must work together: the committee would look into the better organisation of Christian church social services, the linking up of labour colonies and training schools for the unemployed, and the formation of a permanent body representing all branches of social work.

The records of this 'Noah's Ark' committee are not among NUCSS papers; once more there could be confusion between it and other bodies hoping to improve coordination between charities and government. Some founders of the NUCSS, including J.B. Paton, had also been involved in the 1904 founding of the **British Institute of Social Service** (BISS); the two bodies also shared the same President, the Earl of Meath. BISS's stated aim was to 'collect, register and disseminate information relating to all forms of social service

Appendix II

and industrial betterment'; it too published a journal, *Civic Progress*, from 1906 onwards. Apart from the NUCSS, BISS was supported by the Christian Social Union, Salvation Army, Church Army, Fabian Society, National Union of Women Workers and other religious and secular institutions.

At the end of the First World War officials of the Local Government Board published a memorandum urging better machinery to bridge the gap between the voluntary sector, local and central government with regard to social work. In 1919 this resulted in the foundation of the **National Council of Social Service** (NCSS), thanks partly to a substantial legacy from Edward Vivian Birchall.[5]* Initially with representatives of a dozen national voluntary organisations, central and local government bodies, the NCSS continues today, as the **National Council for Voluntary Organisations** (NCVO). Although many religiously-inspired charities such as the NUCSS continued through the 20th century, the national coordinating machinery was passing into the hands of the secular professionals.

---

5   * 1884-1916. The Birchalls were originally Quakers, but Edward was educated in the Church of England. He was a supporter of the Birmingham Guild of Help, interested in public health questions. Commissioned in the British army, he died of wounds in France in August 1916.

INDEX

A

absconsions (from Colony) 112, 126, 189, 254
Act of Settlement (1661) 24
Adoption Acts, 1920, 1926 82
'after-care' 132, 136, 173, 188, 262
'Age of Austerity' 158
agriculture xvi, 21, 23, 36, 39, 40, 75, 79, 90, 149, 159, 207, 242, 268
Agriculture, Ministry of 95, 100, 101, 133, 275
Air Training Corps 146
Albright House 103, 126, 140, 156, 173, 183, 186, 190, 207, 223, 284
Alexander the Great(1964) 199
Allen, Clifford (& conscription) xv
amateur dramatics 89, 109, 154
Approved School 21, 46, 180, 182, 203
Approved Schools 122, 186, 204, 205, 263, 266
'Arenascope', drama productions 191, 197, 198, 200, 257
Australia 21, 70, 71, 74, 75, 76, 78, 79, 80, 81, 82, 91, 111, 129, 187, 235, 261

B

Bacon, Alice (Home Office minister) 201
Barnardo, Dr (Society) 68, 187
Barns House, Edinburgh 248
Basden, Duncan 59, 60, 62, 123
Basden House 59, 103, 126, 156, 173, 183, 186, 192, 193, 207, 229, 231, 283, 284
Battle of Agincourt(1957) 197
Belfry Players (London) 154
Benson 55, 56, 57, 92, 93, 147, 192
Berkeley Homes (purchase Turner's Court site 230

Berks and Oxon Advertiser 87, 128
bible study 90
Bielefeld 2, 3, 5, 36, 48, 52, 66, 236
Bismarck, Otto von, German chancellor 6
Board of Trade 93
Bodelschwingh, Friedrich von 2, 3, 5, 9, 11, 22, 27, 30, 38, 48, 66, 90, 235, 242, 256
Bondfield, Margaret 81
Booth, Charles (author) 11, 29
Booth, William
  Salvation Army 1, 4, 12, 13, 14, 17, 27, 30, 238, 273, 275
boot mending 105
Borstals 61, 206, 265
Boys Club (at Colony) 191, 194, 201, 228, 240, 259, 264
boys' clubs (in general) 113, 168
Boy Scout(s) 59, 106, 138, 256
'Boysville' (USA) 9
Brabazon, Reginald. *See* Meath, Earl of
Brasher and Sons, builders 60
British Empire Exhibition, 1924 107
Brockway, Fenner MP (& conscription) xv
Brooks, Rev J L 41
Buckle, David ('Hostilities Only', 1999) 266
bullying, allegations of 222, 246, 248, 256
Burnett, Sir David 62
Burn, Michael (& 'Mr Lyward's Answer') 249
Burns, John (LGB) 35
Butt, Dame Clara 103

C

Cadbury Brothers, philanthropists 55
Cadbury, George 59

cadet forces (at Colony) 146
Campion, Sir William (Governor, W. Aust) 129
Canada 68, 70, 71, 74, 78, 79, 80, 81, 82, 187
Cape Colony 70
'care in the community' 226
carpentry 105
Carr, A T (farm manager) 101
Carr's Meadow 126, 184, 197, 212, 219, 230, 240, 275
Caughey, James 12
Chadwick, Edwin
  Poor Law Commission 25
charges (for residents) xvii, 97, 104, 107, 113, 125, 127, 133, 161, 177, 179, 186
Charity Commission 228
Charity Organisation Society (COS) 29, 236, 294
Chaucer, Thomas 55
Child Emigration Society 75
Children Act 1908 98
Children Act, 1948 162, 176, 182
Children Act, 1969 201
Children Act 1989 227, 276
Children and Young Persons' Act, 1933 122
Children and Young Persons Act 1969 204, 276
cholera 28
Christian Service Union. *See* National Union for Christian Service
Christian Socialism 10, 239, 288, 289, 291, 292
Christian *Social* Union 69, 288, 289, 290, 291, 292, 293, 294, 297
Christmas at Colony 90, 108, 153, 192, 193, 196, 218, 221, 229
Church Army 63
Church of England Men's Society 65
cinema 22, 107, 138, 139, 160, 178, 221
'City and Guilds' qualification 214
co-education 208, 210, 257

Colonization Society 68
community homes 203, 205, 206, 276
concentration camps 95
Congregationalist 1, 5, 17, 33
Congregational Union 10
conscientious objectors
  (COs) xiv, xvi, xvii, xix
conscription xiv, xv
Cornfield, Mike (Principal, 1989-91) 203, 204, 226, 232, 283, 284
Cory House 102, 126, 139, 156, 161, 163, 173, 179, 183, 184, 186, 191, 192, 207, 219, 222, 225, 259, 284
Cory, Sir Clifford MP 102
'Cranford' 23
Crowmarsh xiii, 57, 59, 87, 221
Crusaders, The (1961) 199
CSU (formerly NUCSS) 4, 5, 7, 17, 20, 34, 36, 37, 38, 39, 40, 41, 42, 43, 44, 45, 46, 47, 48, 49, 50, 52, 53, 55, 56, 58, 59, 60, 61, 62, 63, 65, 66, 67, 69, 70, 71, 72, 76, 77, 78, 80, 81, 82, 83, 84, 86, 87, 90, 91, 95, 97, 99, 100, 101, 102, 103, 106, 107, 110, 112, 123, 124, 125, 126, 127, 128, 132, 133, 134, 135, 136, 147, 157, 158, 159, 167, 170, 171, 172, 179, 180, 181, 183, 190, 234, 235, 236, 237, 238, 239, 241, 243, 245, 260, 262, 271, 273, 276, 287, 289, 290, 291, 292, 294
Curtis, Rupert (advertising agent) 176, 177, 195
Cyclists' Touring Club 143

D

Daily News 53
dancing at Colony 108, 152, 156, 190, 192, 195, 258
'defective' children 43
Development Commission 50, 133, 296

DHSS (Department of Health & Social Security) 201, 204, 206, 211, 212, 219, 227, 228, 230
Dornan, Mike, club leader 215, 285
drama, club etc at Colony 140, 154, 168, 195, 196, 197, 199, 245, 264, 270
Dramatic Society (Colony) 109, 152
Duke of Edinburgh's Award 193
Duty and Discipline Movement 66
Duxhurst (Surrey, farm colony) 19

E

Eccleshall (Board of Guardians) 18
Edgar, Dave, tutor 214
Education Act 1902 42
Education, Board of 46
Education & Science, Dept of 211
'Elberfeld' system 2, 53
Elton, Lord (CSU President) 132
Elvin, Jo, tutor 214
emigration 13, 21, 31, 36, 63, 67, 68, 69, 70, 71, 72, 73, 77, 78, 79, 80, 81, 82, 91, 123, 129, 150, 187, 227, 235, 239, 262, 291, 292
Empire Day 63, 66
Empire Settlement Act 1922 78
entertainment, at Colony 89, 107, 109, 139, 140, 141
epileptic
  epilepsy 35, 42, 43, 44, 46, 51, 58, 61, 66, 77, 159, 180
ethnicity, race, 'colour' 254
Everlasting Childhood, The (Menday & Wiles 1959) 121, 137, 167, 169, 170, 171, 181, 184, 189, 206, 262
ex-servicemen 36, 46, 95

F

Fable of Baghdad (1958) 198
Fairbridge, Kingsley 75, 76, 81, 82, 187
farm colonies 7, 15, 21, 29, 48, 52, 123, 293, 295
Farm Institutes 50

farm manager(s) 101, 150, 164, 171, 209, 213, 228
Fields, Gracie (visits Colony) 141
Figgis, T Phillips (architect) 60
finance and financial problems 129, 130, 131, 134, 158, 211, 212, 296
Finchden Manor, Kent 248
Fletcher, Joseph 7
Food, at Colony 93, 106, 136
Forward Movement xvii, 44, 48, 52, 102
Francis. Clare (and promotional video) 210
Free Church Union 34
Friends Ambulance Unit (FAU) (FAU) xv
Friends Reunited 266, 267
Friends' Social Union 86, 293
Froude, J A (historian) 72

G

Gascoyne-Cecil, Rev Lord William 8
George Williams College xviii, 109
Gloucester, Duke of 127
Glyn, Ralph MP 102
Grant, Col R (Warden 1933-43) 123, 283
gravel extraction 102, 105, 162, 213
Guardians, Boards of xvii, 18, 19, 77, 97, 111
Guild of Help 53, 54, 55, 297
Gulbenkian Foundation (grant from, 1966) 183

H

Hadleigh 15, 16, 17, 21, 40, 46, 47, 49, 56, 58, 61, 63, 232, 234, 243, 260, 273, 274, 275, 276
Hall, P, farm manager 213
Hansen, 'Pop' (tuck shop) 215, 229, 231, 285
harvest supper 208
Harvest Supper 62
Hawkspur Experiment, The (1941) 245

Health, Ministry of 97, 98, 134, 135, 137, 145, 159, 237
Hedges House 225
Hedges, Major John (committee chairman) 172, 173, 225, 283, 285
Hendrick, H
  'Child Welfare in England' (1994) 74, 76, 204, 227, 237, 238
Henley Technical College 209
Heuss, Theodor (President, W. Germany) 91
Hill, Octavia 10
Hinton, Col F A S (warden 1943-51) 124, 125, 127, 132, 136, 154, 155, 160, 161, 175, 283
Hollesley Bay (colonial college) 19, 50, 73
Home and School 249
Home Guard 147, 149
Home Office 46, 89, 95, 100, 122, 125, 159, 163, 171, 172, 174, 175, 177, 180, 182, 186, 195, 204, 211, 231, 275
Honeybone, Peter
  instructor 271
Horsfall, Frank xiv, xviii, 97
Hospital Saturday Fund, 65
house journals at Colony 155, 217
Housman, Laurence 245
Howells, John (Principal 1967-89) 203, 204, 205, 207, 208, 209, 210, 211, 213, 217, 219, 226, 257, 283
Hunt, Charles William ('Charlie'), Colony resident 164
Hunt House 185, 231
Hunt, Sir John 175, 184, 197
Hunt, William H (Hunt W H) xvii, 41, 58
Hunt, William (Hunt W H), Superintendent 1911-1934 xvii, xviii, 43, 44, 45, 46, 47, 49, 50, 61, 62, 63, 65, 79, 83, 84, 85, 86, 87, 90, 91, 92, 93, 98, 99, 100, 103, 105, 107, 108, 110, 112, 113, 114, 115, 121, 122, 123, 124, 125, 127, 129, 130, 131, 132, 133, 138, 141, 158, 159, 167, 170, 177, 183, 184, 186, 190, 191, 192, 193, 218, 226, 239, 241, 242, 243, 244, 246, 249, 253, 254, 256, 262, 272, 283, 285
Huxley, Julian 245

I

'Ianto', Principal's dog 218, 219, 244, 284
immorality (alleged at Colony) 12, 99, 238
In Darkest England 1, 4, 6, 11, 12, 13, 14, 16, 27, 31, 274
Industrial Welfare Society (Industrial Society) 131
International Voluntary Service for Peace (IVSP) 247

J

Jamboree (Scout) 107
John Burns (LGB) 50
Junior Detention Centres 206
Juvenile Courts 188

K

Kahan, Mrs V J (Oxfordshire CC) 176
King Arthur(1960) 199

L

labour colony 2, 4, 5, 18, 35
Labour Exchanges 50
Lads' Drill Association 66
Lads for the Empire 74
Laindon (Poplar colony) 19
Lansbury, George 27
Laud, William 23
laundry 60, 84, 85, 86, 105, 126, 184
'Learning to Listen' experiment, 2006 272
Letchworth 86, 87
Libury Hall (colony) 20
Lighthouse Group, Bradford 272

Lingfield xvii, 39, 40, 41, 42, 43, 44, 45, 46, 47, 48, 49, 51, 56, 57, 58, 59, 60, 61, 63, 66, 77, 78, 84, 87, 104, 105, 124, 130, 142, 147, 155, 159, 180, 234, 236, 239, 246, 256, 260, 287
Lloyd-George, David 78
Local Government Act 1930 100
Local Government Act 1934 122
Local Government Board (1871) 26, 35, 50, 71, 97, 260, 297
Loch, Sir Charles (COS) 39
London County Council (LCC) 43, 66, 91, 101, 144, 177
Lyward, G A (and Finchden Manor) 249

M

Macdonald, Ramsay xv
Manley, G N (warden 1951-54) 125, 161, 283
Manley, G N (Warden 1951-54) 162, 163, 164, 165, 167, 171, 173, 203, 215, 257
Market gardening 48
Marlborough, Duchess of 127, 162
Marple Dale (colony) 19, 45, 46, 47
Mayhew, Henry (author) 11
Mays Farm 57, 102, 126, 158, 182, 185
Mearns, Andrew ('Bitter Cry of Outcast London' 44
Meath, Earl of 5, 55, 63, 65, 132, 235, 238, 295, 296
medical care at Colony 6, 84, 100, 127, 129, 131, 135, 225, 226, 296
Menday, Col R P (Warden 1955-67) 58, 59, 60, 80, 91, 95, 97, 100, 104, 108, 121, 122, 123, 124, 125, 126, 137, 138, 141, 155, 158, 160, 162, 163, 165, 167, 168, 169, 170, 171, 172, 173, 174, 175, 176, 177, 178, 179, 180, 181, 182, 183, 184, 185, 186, 187, 188, 189, 190, 191, 192, 193, 194, 195, 196, 197, 198, 199, 201, 203, 206, 207, 209, 210, 211, 212, 213, 215, 220, 221, 222, 225, 226, 228, 231, 232, 233, 234, 240, 241, 242, 243, 244, 246, 252, 253, 254, 256, 257, 258, 259, 262, 263, 264, 272, 273, 275, 283
Menday, Inga 168, 169, 176, 182, 190, 198, 200, 201, 257
Merxplas, Belgium colony 7
Methodism 12, 44, 291
Mettray, France, colony 9
Meyer, Dr F B 2
Military College (Cowley) 61
Mills, Herbert V 45
Mixed Clubs, National Association of 169

N

National Childrens Home 82, 187
National Council for Voluntary Organisations 55, 297
National Service 66, 160, 161, 271
National Union for Christian Social Service, see CSU xiv, 1, 33
Newnham Murren 57
New Zealand 71, 74, 76, 78, 80, 187, 235, 261
No Conscription Fellowship xv
Nuffield, Lord (William Morris) 101

O

'Oakley Court' 231
Ogilvie Hall 103, 126, 140, 149, 154, 194, 198, 199, 231, 240
Ogilvie, W M 103
opening ceremony (Turners Court) 62
outdoor relief 24, 26
Oxford Colonial Club 75
Oxfordshire County Council 133, 160, 162, 176, 182, 243
Oxford Trades and Labour Council 142

P

Paton (House) 5, 6, 35, 36, 37, 38, 40, 41, 42, 44, 55, 62, 84, 85, 88, 122, 126, 140, 155, 156, 173, 183, 184, 186
Paton, J B 2, 34, 62, 296
Paton, Rev J B 5
Peace Society xv
penal colony 8
Pittuck, W E (journalist) 87, 88, 89, 90, 96, 104, 105, 111, 128, 139
pocket money at Colony 27, 74, 113, 136, 160, 186, 247
Poor Law Amendment Act, 1834 25
Poor Law Commissioners 25
Poor Relief 24, 30
'Poplarism' 27
Potters Farm 182
Prevention of Cruelty to Children Act, 1894 71
Public Assistance Board 129
Public Assistance Committee 145
public houses 16, 20, 45, 49, 57, 139
punishment (at Colony) 98, 174, 242, 253
Purves, Thomas 56

Q

Q Camps 113, 244, 247
Quaker 46, 55, 86, 89, 103, 113, 142, 238, 248, 268, 293

R

RAF (at Colony) 139, 149, 152, 192
Ragged School 22, 70
rationing 94
Reading 57, 59, 62, 77, 105, 109, 149, 153, 189, 225
Reading, Lady 149
Read, Sir Herbert 123
refugees, at Colony 95, 96, 147, 148, 149, 273
Remand Homes 206

Rhodes, Cecil 15
Rhodesia 15
Richards, Eric 262
Rookeries of London 72
Rowton House 85
Royal Commission on Housing 28
Royal Philanthropic Society 21, 40, 68, 70
Royal Victoria Asylum 7
Royston, Col (Deputy Warden) 164, 169, 170, 172, 173, 179, 200
rural depopulation 37
Ruston, Joseph 42
Ruthwell (colony) 20

S

Sail training for 'colonists' 216
salaries, (at Colony) 97, 131, 150, 159, 163, 179, 186, 209, 211, 213
Salvation Army 2, 4, 13, 14, 15, 17, 30, 37, 40, 46, 56, 58, 61, 63, 68, 93, 110, 232, 234, 243, 260, 273, 274, 275, 276, 297
sanatorium 42, 103, 126, 135, 184
Scorrer, Miss A M (Home Office) 175, 182
Sedgwick, Thomas ('Lads for the Empire') 74
Seebohm report 205
Self-help Emigration Society 63
Selfridge, Gordon 106
'settlement'(s) 58
'settlements' 45
Simpson, A W 46
Sladen, Edward xiv, xviii, 90, 109, 140, 195
Small Colonies Holding Act 1916 95
Smewin, 'Bill' (boys club leader) 194, 204, 284
Smewin, Bill (Boys Club leader) 203
Smith, Peter, instructor 214
Social Club, at Turners Court 218
'social imperialist' 31, 76, 235

Social Service xv, xvii, 7, 8, 9, 17, 18, 20, 30, 33, 44, 45, 46, 47, 49, 50, 54, 55, 56, 57, 58, 61, 63, 65, 77, 82, 83, 85, 87, 90, 97, 104, 106, 107, 108, 109, 112, 123, 132, 133, 138, 140, 141, 144, 149, 152, 153, 155, 165, 205, 218, 239, 242, 244, 249, 253, 254, 256, 287, 293, 295, 296, 297
Social Service, National Council of 55
Social Workers 207
Speenhamland 25
Sports and Social Club 215
Starnthwaite 45, 46, 47, 58, 63, 124, 180, 239, 287
Steinmhle (colony) 97
St. Mary's Bay, Kent (camping at) 144
Sturge, Edward 59, 123, 142, 154, 162, 238
Sturge House 155, 184, 185, 208, 211
summer camps 106, 191
Sunday Pictorial 181, 198
Sutter, Julie
  Colony of Mercy 2, 4, 11, 27, 37, 39, 42, 52, 235, 238, 242, 256
swimming pool 103, 126, 183, 215, 231, 265

T

The Labour Colony 5
Tinling, Rev J F B 1
Tioli, 'George' (and 'communists') 142, 144, 145, 146, 239
Trevelyan, Charles xv
Trevelyan, G M 23, 24, 25
Trojan Horse, The (1959) 198
Tuck Shop 140, 160, 195
Tune, Capt (warden 1943) 124
Turners Court 55, 56, 57, 58, 59, 61, 65, 70, 77, 79, 80, 82, 83, 84, 85, 87, 89, 91, 94, 95, 96, 97, 98, 99, 100, 101, 102, 104, 105, 106, 108, 109, 111, 112, 113, 114, 121, 123, 124, 125, 126, 128, 129, 133, 134, 135, 137, 138, 139, 141, 144, 145, 146, 147, 149, 150, 152, 154, 155, 156, 159, 160, 161, 162, 163, 164, 167, 168, 169, 170, 171, 172, 173, 174, 175, 176, 177, 178, 180, 181, 182, 183, 185, 187, 188, 189, 190, 191, 192, 193, 194, 195, 200, 201, 203, 204, 205, 206, 207, 208, 209, 210, 212, 213, 215, 217, 219, 221, 224, 225, 228, 229, 231, 232, 233, 237, 257, 259, 267, 274, 283, 284, 285, 287
Turners Court Youth Trust 232, 277

U

'underclass.' 28
'unemployables' 22, 37, 39, 40, 41, 43, 63, 100, 233, 236, 292
Unemployment Assistance Board (UAB) 122, 134
Union of Democratic Control (UDC) (UDC) xv
Unions (Poor Law, parish) 18, 25, 26, 292

V

video, promotional (1986) 207
vocational training 207

W

wages (at Colony) 5, 13, 25, 26, 85, 94, 96, 131, 290
Wagner, Gillian 262
Wallingford 56, 58, 113, 123, 129, 142, 209, 224, 247
Warren Hill 102, 126
welfare officers at Colony 131
Wentzel, Cyril (actor) 197
Wiles, John (author/director) 121, 169, 196, 199, 206, 240
William Baker, technical school (Hertford) 187
Wills, David (author) 113, 114, 137, 244, 245, 246, 247, 248, 249, 252, 259, 260
Wingfield, Mr & Mrs 96

wireless/radio 108, 141
Witzwil, penal colony 8
'Woodlands' (sub-colony) 99, 122, 126
workhouse xvii, 7, 26, 42, 46, 48, 51, 71, 78, 96, 122, 138, 165, 260
World War I xviii, 54, 68, 71, 78, 87, 105, 106, 131, 132, 147, 185, 235, 237, 294, 297
World War II 14, 77, 92, 94, 106, 115, 123, 124, 129, 133, 159, 196, 235, 237, 250

Y

YMCA xviii, 79, 92, 109, 110, 145
Young Farmers' Club 156, 192
Youth Hostels Association (YHA) 143